First We Ate

Your Wife

by adeena gerding

ISBN 978-1-77628-033-9 (Paperback)
ISBN 978-1-77628-034-6 (eBook)

www.bearfootgypsy.com

A catalogue record for this book is available from the *National Library of South Africa*.
228 Johannes Ramokhoase Street, Pretoria, 0001, South Africa

Typeset in Linux Libertine and Open Sans
First Print Edition: May, 2021

Sorry Mom.

A Quick Note

Y**ou** have no idea how difficult it is to write a book until a few years in, when you still haven't perfected it.

In many ways, I wish that I had written a fictional account of my travels, but this journey threw so many unprecedented twists at me that I felt compelled to tell it as it unfolded.

I'm still trying to fathom the gravity of some of the hardships that I endured on the road. It may seem odd that the story simply continues after near death experiences; but survival is not a destination, it is a way of life.

I've tried to keep this tale as true to life as possible, with a light-hearted outlook. Humour is a great painkiller. (And also essential in developing a six-pack.)

Assuming that this isn't a pirated copy, you should find a glossary and some other useful tools at the end.

Travel diary excerpts and thoughts have been *italised* and blog posts have been centred so that they can be differentiated from the main text.

While pictures are said to be worth a thousand words, I wrote 110 000 of them and have decided to leave visuals on my blog, www.bearfootgypsy.com and other social media pages.

Forward

IF giving up is not a choice, there is no point in looking back. As the basis of existence was shrinking on board, the collaboration between two souls became essential for survival.

The journey I shared with Adeena was by far the most humbling and astonishing trip of my life. It was a crossfire of impediments and catastrophes but also magical wonders and love. I could not have wished to share it with anyone else than her.

// Karl-Oskar Wicksell

THIS girl! She knew me only a day but when I got lost somewhere in Kuala Lumpur in the middle of the night, instead of leaving me behind and partying like everyone else, she had been walking around the streets showing my pictures to strangers and asking them, "Have you seen my blonde friend?". This moment I knew I could rely on her and I wasn't wrong! Later on, during our many adventures, she made me the best life vest ever seen and proved herself to be a great entertainer as she kept me going while we were swimming for our life and I almost gave up. Sleeping in a totally random places was a daily routine with her, whether it was a cinema, a bar or a deserted island, she never lost her smile and always made it a funny and memorable experience (as long as there was enough beer). Nine years later I still feel like it was yesterday when I sang my last karaoke with her, wrote a list of 100 weirdest things we have done together and left her for my regular adult life. Luckily I am still promised to be invited to her wedding (if and when it happens), so I can secretly look forward to some extra legendary stories for next generations.

// Helena Kubátová

WHEN I first met Adeena, she was walking around barefoot in a Hanoi nightclub and trying to convince fellow backpackers to hitchhike with her… If anyone was crazy enough to walk around Hanoi without footwear, they must also be crazy enough to attempt to ride a bicycle over the Annamese Mountains into Laos. Sure enough the next day, after recovering from our Bia Hanoi hangovers, we took a trip out to the 'bicycle' street and got Adeena sorted out with a 'mountain bike' complete with a set of panniers and handlebar streamers. Adeena neglected to mention that she would also be travelling with a giant teddy bear and had no idea how to use the gears she had on the bike. To her credit, we did eventually make it across the border into Laos a few days later, but not without having to spend a night sheltering from a tropical deluge in a bamboo hut beside the road… having to repair a flat tyre with some help from a friendly Vietnamese truck driver who happened to have the right size wrench for removing the non-quick-release bolts on her bike. Since that fateful first bicycle trip across the top of South East Asia, Adeena has gone on so many more two-wheeled adventures and misadventures. As I sit at my cushy, well-paid 9-to-5 office job and read about her latest barefoot endeavours, I can't help but feel slightly responsible for teaching her how to use bicycle gears on those back streets of Hanoi.

// Rohan Ahmad

'A **DEENA** is here! Here in Guadalupe," I announced to the crew! It had been nine months since we'd last seen Adeena, leaving her behind in her homeland as we set sail from Cape Town. She'd been good crew and wonderful company on our trek from Borneo to South Africa, but she'd been away from home traveling for three years, and we couldn't convince her to leave so soon after arrival. Six months later the allure of the sea had overcome circumstances on land and she found herself a spot crewing another boat from Cape Town to Spain via Brazil. But pirates had greeted them in Brazil and they had limped up with what little had been left them to the Caribbean where the captain was laying up his vessel and discharging his crew while dealing with the insurance claim. Adeena was about to be homeless ... and available! So we slipped anchor and sailed around from the other side of the island, planning to meet her for breakfast. Her captain had expected her to help him sail on to the boatyard, but he had additional crew, and after tense negotiations we managed to buy her off him for a box of cookies. Some debate followed as to who got the better part of that deal -- those were premium cookies! But most importantly, Adeena was back! And back with more tales with which to regale us. Yet in so many ways her greatest adventures still lay ahead. And the grand total of her tales (to date!) await you between the covers of this book!

// Kirk Hilliard

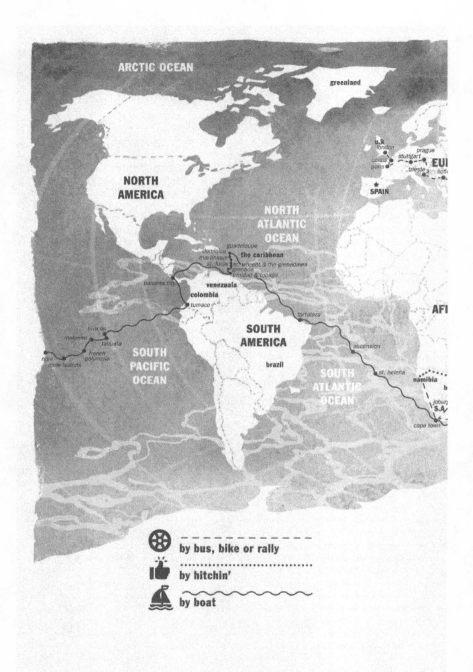

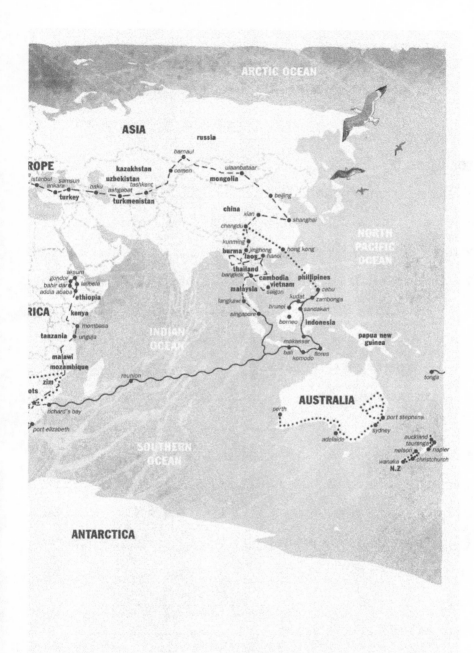

THE JOURNEY

As a basic rule, whilst travelling
-whether to the moon or simply reconnoitering the back garden-
a journal of sorts must be kept.
There is something about putting pen to paper that not only
comforts a lonely traveller,
but acts as an eternal record of mysteries, absurdities,
and random encounters.
It's a mirror that reflects the traveller's soul.
(If they have one.)

This is my story.
It's full of epic adventure,
and many in-between every-day mundane things and human
happenstances,
for no tale can be told in exploits alone.

It's about extraordinary places and exceptional people,
Love, and other perilous endeavours.
A testament to how much abuse the liver can withstand,
And how a little faith in God goes a very long way.

More importantly, this is an insight to what can happen when you step
out of your front door and leave your known world behind you.

1.

I dangled from a thorn tree some hundred feet above the smoking crater. The pain was excruciating. The devil thorns pierced deep into my sorry excuse for a bicep, keeping me levitated. The blood pulsed through my veins and down my arm, dripping onto my bare feet. My heart beat too quickly. A billion thoughts raced through my jumbled mind. I was petrified of heights and didn't want to look down, so I turned and saw the faces peering worriedly from above. As I waited to be rescued, I carefully scanned my surrounds; I somehow managed to secure myself onto the only vegetation on the entire rim of the volcano.

There were two things I realized on that fateful Kenyan day:

- You can't die when you have travel insurance[1].
- I was going to live the rest of my life to the fullest.

---

[1] This is solely the belief of the author! Please do not in any way attempt to prove/ disprove this fact-theory!

I was twenty-two, pudgy, with no sense of direction and a complete lack of knowledge on all things History and Geography [and common sense too for that matter]. I owned a hairbrush, but I didn't use it often. The same went for shoes – I had claustrophobic feet. I pretended to be brave but I bore a nightmare-inducing fear of tomatoes and failure. My good-natured Christian school girl, well-mannered and overly-polite halo sparkled in the African sunlight. My smile was my only real asset.

I had left South Africa before, but this time was different. This time I was setting off on an adventure. I'd spent months working to save every cent (because even a lot of South African Rand don't take you very far), planning and finding people to cover my work contracts. I bought a brand new blue-black 75-litre backpack that was far too big for my body but was needed to carry all my shiny-new state-of-the-art camping gear. Deepest darkest Africa was a dangerous place. Three months was going to be a long time.

JOHANNESBURG, South Africa. 5 July 2007

Ten of us hugged our friends and family goodbye. All new to the world of exploration, we pretended to look confident by awkwardly swinging our oversized luggage onto the Intercity Bus that loomed in front of us. We were buzzing with excitement and eager to experience the world. The boys sat behind us, religiously studying the *Lonely Planet* whilst the other girls chit-chatted away. I was glad my monstrous sunglasses concealed my tears. I didn't let people see me cry. We hadn't even reached the border and I was missing South Africa already. We were finally beginning the adventure we'd spent so long fantasizing about, but I wasn't sure I was quite ready for it.

We took buses, ferries and even hitch-hiked our way through the tropical beauties of Mozambique, over the mountains of Zimbabwe and on to Lake Malawi. The group had shrunk to six as we reached Tanzania. And four of us remained to climb Mount Kenya, venture the Masai Mara and continue on to Ethiopia.

Having ADHD and being a workaholic meant that I always juggled way too many contracts, school and university subjects, and managed to have a busy social life. This trip was a bit of an adjustment for me. It took me two months to relax and just be. I learned to simply enjoy whatever grassy knoll, palm tree beach or chicken and goat laden bus I found myself on. It was an incredible experience that I shall refer to as "hammock time," for there was a lot of that hanging around.

We lived in tents and slow-cooked meals on our not-so-trusty multi-fuel burners. We allowed ourselves beers and chocolates on only special or especially trying days. But the beauty of life, nature and foreign cultures more than made up for what we lacked in our comforts. Every day was a surprise and held new interactions with bizarre and fascinating people. Each day taught us something new about the world, and more importantly, about ourselves. Every day was a new adventure.

We couldn't get visas for Sudan, so we decided to fly to Egypt instead. The cheapest way was via Johannesburg. We opted to do a ten-day stopover to see friends and family and flush toilets. But the others quite missed the comforts of the homelands and decided to cancel their tickets and stay. I was distraught. I had only just begun to savour the flavours of the world and wasn't ready to stop sampling them. I had a terrible case of wanderlust and I wasn't quite sure how to cure it.

꙳

I found myself on a one-way flight to **London**. I had no idea what I was going to do when I got there, but it was as good a spot as any to start to seek a cure for my disease. And with almost empty pockets, I needed to replenish the bank account!

I moved into a dilapidated house with 14 boys and even more rodents. The shamble was a welter of dirt and strange people. For £34 a week (including bills, internet [stolen from the neighbours], tea, coffee, and milk), it would do.

In desperation I began job hunting, seeking employment in the entertainment industry (where I'd spent my whole working life). Unfortunately, even if I walked for an hour and a half to the interview (to avoid the 90p bus fare) I got turned down because they only wanted people with experience within the UK. Or there were too many rounds of interviews. I couldn't wait, my funds were running dry. I had no choice but to broaden my search.

"Swimming Instructor needed…" I could swim! Not that they asked me this during the interview. Two days later my phone rang, "Can you be here in an hour?"

I stopped at the nearest supermarket and bought a £4 swimsuit. An hour later, I was in a pool with eight smiling six-year-olds staring at me, expecting me to teach them something life-changing. I literally got thrown in the deep end!

I spent a little over a year hopping around Western Europe from my Londonly bases, immersing myself in culture, music and tomatoes[2]. I grew up quite quickly as I learned about exercising the liver and how little sleep one really needed to accommodate a party lifestyle. I discovered a lot about myself and tarnished both my liver and my halo sufficiently. I took on some random jobs to fill my pool-free life (an occupation I came to

---

[2] I really needed to overcome the fear of the fruit, and the Spanish *La Tomatina* provided the best way to face my fears head on. Or at least I thought it did. 145 000 kg of tomatoes get pulverised on tens of thousands of people who pack so tightly in a little street that most of them hover in the air above the teeming masses. Beer and urine and tomato puree flow until every bodily orifice is filled with gooey liquids. I retained both the fear, and the remnants.

adore, even if it consumed 48 hours of my week and the chlorine dissolved my toenails). Despite pushing my socialising and random country visits to the maximum, my wanderlust grew. Life was livid, but man was it good!

On my last day as a Londoner, I woke up in the garden. I knew it was time to leave!

But Europe did teach me quite a lot:

- Always check the weather to avoid walking home barefoot in the snow.
- You can use superglue [twice daily] to salvage your toe when a small cut [that doesn't heal because it is in chlorine all day] becomes a gashing wound threatening to amputate itself.
- If you plead long enough, you can talk your [pink] limousine driver through a McDonalds drive-through.
- Hamburg is not the capital of Austria (and never was).
- If you keep drinking alcohol, you stop getting hangovers.
- Meat prices may be high, but to avoid becoming anaemic, you need to find alternative sources of iron and protein. Even if UK doctors are free.
- Solo travel is not only for weird societal misfits and loners. You meet so many more people when you adventure alone, you're free to change plans whimsically, and you constantly get pushed out of your comfort zone. It's a life-changer and one of the best ways to discover the world.

Travel diary entry, **Georgia - Azerbaijan Border**. 3 July 2009

It all happened so quickly. After glancing at our passports, four armed guards marched the car to a park, grabbed me, and walked me past the visa office into another building – through two sets of doors and into the back room. Guns poised, they stood in silence. No one offered any explanation of what was going on. I waited.

"What you were doing in Armenia?" asked the poor man that was shoved in the room with me a few minutes later. He tried very hard to be a translator.

"I'm just a tourist," I pleaded whilst they grabbed my bag, emptied it, and contemplated its contents. "You prove you are tourist," they said pointing to my camera. I only had three pictures of Armenia (and these were just before the pictures of the world's coolest beard).

"Who is this man?" they asked pointing at the beard (beard envy, I'm certain of it).

"Why you have picture?... Is he militant?"

"Three photo, no tourist... what you were doing Armenia?"

I fetched the laptop from the car – all our photos had been dumped on there. A sudden shudder crept through my vertebra as I recalled all the military pictures we'd taken in the last four days: troops marching, barracks, tanks being loaded onto trains...

I wondered what they would think about us transporting an Armenian hitch-hiker across borders...

...I tried to show them a few of our early leopard-print-dress-in-drag costumed pictures to warm their hearts...

"Armenia!" roared the chief.

I found the right pictures, swallowed hard, and started scrolling.

Not one picture of tanks, of the military, or of the hitchhiking Devil woman (her name was deceivingly just "Anna") showed up[3].

"Ok. You tourist. But you have visited Nagorno-Karabakh?"

I looked at them blankly. Then I realised that I was just staring, which isn't very polite (even less so when there are guns involved), and they were getting angry...

---

[3] When the same folder was re-consulted later, they were all accounted for, in order.

"Yes, no, maybe… I don't know, I never know, my brother navigates."
The translator wasn't sure what I was trying to say, so I switched to
an Oscar-winning performance and asked if they had a map.
They did not.
I asked them what I would have seen there, in "Na-gor-no Kar-a…"
- that way maybe I'd be able to answer properly.
"Armenia troops have moved and claimed more of our land," the
translator filled me in. "Fresh war now! Happen this week. War in
Nagorno-Karabakh."
I gasped! "No, no, I definitely didn't see any war."
It was their turn to stare at me, so I tried to smile.
"If you are telling truth, we run background check."
This basically involved me drawing them a family tree – I was tempted
to put some inspirational celebrities into the tree (like Rowan
Atkinson and Tina and the Hoff) but I thought better of it; besides, my
family is actually exceptionally awesome as is!

While I might be the eldest [and wisest], my brothers got all the brains and
the responsible genes. Brendon (the youngest) only ever wanted maths
books for gifts and company. His hobbies included cleaning out the fridge,
being the head student, and captaining every sports team. He's always
been worshipped by women: every girl loved him, every teacher adored
him, and every mum used him as an example for their offspring.

Jeandré started exploiting the world at a young age; devising ways to
effortlessly earn cash and win competitions. He sometimes won without
even entering. He DJed every house party. He filmed videos for corporates
and schools. He always got an *A* (unless, of course, it was an *A+*, which
was more often the case). He went through a brief metro phase of matching
his underpants to his shoes. Apart from that, he was always far too good
at life.

Both brothers towered over me in both brains and stature. Both carried my dad's Dutch genes with shoe sizes that weren't listed on the human scale.

My parents were on some sort of procreation mission and popped the three of us out in as many years. Had dad not died when I was three, there may be countless tribes spreading across the lands. He had been a surgeon, and a somewhat legendary human being (obviously, he co-created the three of us), but I never had the chance to get to know him properly.

Which brings me to mum. I still can't quite work out how she single-handedly raised the three of us and crafted the fine masterpieces you see today. She took on a strange assortment of jobs just to be close to us. She was a bit like Mother Theresa on a pogo stick (to say "steroids" would be wrong on so many different accounts). Someone would just mention a slight lack in their life, and we'd come home to find she'd donated the microwave, the lounge suite or the car to "those people who really needed it." She'd always had a strange love for Asia and at any given time our house would be filled with Chinese, Taiwanese, Korean, Singaporean, or Japanese guests she'd somehow adopted... When the phone rang, we never quite knew which language to answer it in.

If you turned down a cup of tea or coffee, she would go through the entire house inventory and then offer to run to the shops; just to make sure you had everything [and more] that you could possibly need. It didn't matter if you were her offspring or a complete stranger, mum cared about your well-being!

They photocopied all my papers and made a lot! of phone calls. And then handed two passports back. I looked inside: Jeandré – where was he?

They showed me the door and said: "Go."

I figured I was done and we were legally Azerbaijanis, but apparently, I hadn't even reached immigration yet.

I found a very worried brother standing on the other side of the

building. I'd been in there for hours, and men kept coming in and out
of the room – he'd assumed the worst.
We [force] parted ways again.
"See you in five on the other side," I said.
I didn't mean five hours.

Cemen, Khazakstan. 1 August 2009

It's in the name of charity and adventure that Jeandré and I find
ourselves on this quest. Four months ago, I wasn't sure where
Mongolia was. Now I'm busy driving there in something closely
resembling a tin can. A mere eleven-thousandish miles from London
(if we navigate correctly), it's a pleasant little joy ride making for
incredibly good sibling bonding times.
Our trip has been phenomenal so far. Europe was remarkable, but
since we've left it, the epicness has risen to new levels of absurdity.
Men keep wooing me with melons. And, because we have no maps or
GPS, every time we stop to ask for directions, we wind up in a different
home sipping coffee or tea, smoking shisha, and eating more food
than our bodies can handle!

We accidentally picked up hitchhikers. We were trapped between borders
where they threatened to keep us for months with only trucks and a crazed
horny doctor for company. We had an assortment of food poisoning that
spread stools of art across Central Asia. Jeandré threw up in other people's
gardens; I threw up on national monuments. It was an adventure into the
absurd.

30 countries, 11 827 miles (18 923.2 KM), and only seven showers
between us, we weren't the most hygienic pair when we pulled into
Ulaanbaatar, Mongolia at 23:57 on August 25th, 2009.

Believe it or not, our little Suzuki Alto survived to the end despite
being stuck in a ditch, then a canyon, on a pile of rocks, in a river, and in

the desert (or dessert - I always forget which is the sandier one). Our car was unscathable until the road-less Mongolian wilderness took over. We sustained 21 flat tyres (which is not great when you have only one spare wheel), lost our rear suspension, then the shocks. We severed our brake cable on a rock, and the last 710km were done with no brakes at all. Only 800m from arrival, we hit a pothole that slew our steed completely. Nonetheless, we pushed him over the finish line where he Rests in Pieces.

Jeandré returned to work and I was left mulling in lonely confusion. There were only two flightless options, so I let the coin pick my destiny. Heads and I'd head to China or tails and I'd tail back through Russia to Europe.

I packed up my [still too-many] belongings and set off to find cheaper accommodation. With no idea where to relocate to, I wandered the streets with teary eyes and bumped into a troop of friendly Englishmen. They promised that Betsy would take care of me, and guided me to The Cheapest Guest House.

In the safe confines of her hostel-home, they convinced me to acquire a horse. And then I'd head to China. Probably.

I messaged mum to ask if she wanted to join me.

MEET MUM[4]:

> **me**: Hello mummy!!!
>
> You got Skype at work????
>
> 9:17 AM hello??
>
> ring ring
>
> ring ring
>
> 9:18 AM **Mum**: Hi honey...sorry...no ring!
>
> 9:19 AM So glad you are alive... have sent your message out for prayer cover... and will send an SMS to others just now!

---

[4] This is an actual Skype conversation. Copied and pasted and spelling corrected.

14

9:20 AM You going to mission in China! YAY!

9:21 AM But so wish you went with Jeandré! ...ALL things work together to them that love the Lord...!

9:23 AM Maybe you come home with a Chinese guy! ...giggle...

9:28 AM SOOO wish I was with you!

9:29 AM **me**: come join me???

[...Timepass... Delay...]

10:12 AM **Mum**: You horsing with guys like "men" or mixed?

I worry about you...not everyone can be trusted!

me: I trust them!

Seven guys

Mum: gulp!

Is one of them THE one? Please be careful... especially when they are drinking!

10:25 AM May He protect you & cover you with His blood that HAS been shed for you!

10:26 AM **me**: Yes mum

and no

10:27 AM **Mum**: no...?

oh..."The One>>? God IS working. He will meet with you. He must love Jesus with ALL his heart! Wait for him...he is worth it!

(The conversation resumed a week[ish] later when unable to walk from the pain in our knees, or sit thanks to the wooden saddles, we traded in our horses and returned to Ulaanbaatar).

8:44 AM Don't you want to fly from Beijing to South Africa?? It's on special!

me: No!

I'm not ready.

8:45 AM **Mum**: Don't let your mind be messed with... you have to settle down some time!

8:46 AM You Ok? Besides horse sore... were guys OK... not give you trouble??

me: No, they are very nice.

Mum: You Sure?? They didn't try anything with you?

Praise the Lord... am so glad & thankful!

[I didn't bother replying]

9:56 AM **Mum**: So great you got shoes! In Tajikistan & Muslim places you can't go barefoot, it must be closed-toe & closed front & skirt, not too much leg showing...

9:59 AM I really hope & pray that you don't get swine flu too! Apparently, it is still rife in China!

10:00 AM **me**: DON'T WORRY!!

Mum: Keep washing your hands... you get special soap to wash salads with...

me: I'll be fine!!

Mum: You sleeping OK? Eating OK?

me: YES MOM!!

10:03 AM and having the time of my life

10:04 AM **Mum**: you got deodorant?? They don't use it??!

Having a good time!? > Wow, am so glad! Thought you're lonely and all at loose ends!

So, you go by train on Sunday? From Ulaanbaatar?

10:05 AM **me**: I leave on the train tonight. Arrive in China Sunday morning.

10:23 AM **Mum**: Have a great trip! Keep passport & valuables IN FRONT of you...! Enjoy the land of millions of peoples & tons of smoke!!

Three months had somehow spanned over the two-year mark. My wanderlust was now a terminal disease. It had taken over all my major organs, including a good portion of my brain. All I could think, do, or eat was adventure; especially the eating - I never knew what was on my plate.

My brother had returned to work. I returned to a life of trouble.

Although, not quite the trouble mum was anticipating. Clearly very worried about me, and having always wanted to visit China, I arrived in **Beijing** to find in my inbox an email (which I shall paraphrase for your sakes):

"Hi, honey. I just quit my job; I'll see you on Thursday."

Mum enjoyed her time in China so much that she decided to move there and returned to South Africa to pack up her life.

I pushed on to Laos, which led to Cambodia, and then Thailand, and Malaysia, and Burma. And then in 2010, back in Bangkok, I could not handle the bustle anymore, or the tourists. I needed to escape. Immediately! I tried to book a flight to India and, after the internet would not accept my debit card, some very strange miscommunication led me down a different path:

"What's your cheapest flight to India today?" – Me.

"Where in Africa do you wish to fly to?" - The INDIAN travel agent.

"No, not Africa, In... Wait... what is your cheapest flight to Africa today?" I was feeling a little homesick and...

"You can fly to **Johannesburg** for [less than] $300" - Paraphrase of the Indian guy.

f

Mum[5] stood at the airport gates boldly displaying a beautifully hand-written "MARIJUANA" sign to everyone coming through the airport doors. She scanned the crowds carefully sizing up people to detect the

---

[5] Who had yet to immigrate.

Romanian she was expecting (I may have lied to her about who exactly it was that she was collecting). The tears flooded down my face as I laughed in hysterics at the beauty of mum (and the group of security officers carefully observing her).

I continued to arrive with hugs for unsuspecting family all around the country before surprising Brendon with a one-way ticket to **Namibia.** He was on study leave and smart enough to not actually have to study. Unsure what exactly we needed to do once we got there, we proceeded to hitchhike through Botswana, Zambia, Zimbabwe and Mozambique. Coast to coast across Southern Africa and back to Johannesburg. For the first time in years, we had the whole family under one ceiling.

With ten days till kick-off, I somehow landed a Soccer World Cup contract. This was great for my budget but slightly detrimental to my soul. I'm not the biggest soccer fan and having to watch 64 games of football in a few weeks was hellish. I opted to up my interest levels and swore I'd move to whichever country won.

I needed a goal. I needed direction. I needed another journey.

Because I'd already agreed to visit Australia (and because there was no way that they were going to win at anything involving soccer), I declared that I'd start there – on the far side of the world - and flightlessly travel over land and sea to my new home... wherever that may be.

Contenders:

Algeria, Argentina, Australia, Brazil, Cameroon, Chile, Denmark, England, France, Germany, Ghana, Greece, Honduras, Italy, Ivory Coast, Japan, Mexico, Netherlands, New Zealand, Nigeria, North Korea, Paraguay, Portugal, Serbia, Slovakia, Slovenia, South Africa, South Korea, Spain, Switzerland, Uruguay, USA.

THERE'S A GYPSY IN MY GARDEN.

2.

P **ERTH**. A fairly cosmopolitan little city with a park the size of a small country. It has no kangaroos and a pretty river that smells quite sewerly. But the thing that impressed me the most by far was the *Exeloo*.

Yes, they have normal toilets too (and the paper one likes to find accompanying them) but the *Exeloo* is special. With one button the iron door slides open, music starts playing and a God-like voice welcomes you and informs you that you have a maximum of ten minutes to do whatever it was you came in for. It also makes you wonder if there might be someone watching you.

The classical tunes continue, either distracting you or making your 'stay' more pleasant, possibly lulling you to sleep. And, in aid of personal hygiene, the toilet does not flush until you have washed your hands.

Obviously, there are other things to see and do in Perth: buy expensive beers, eat an array of [over-priced] oriental foods, visit the zoo, visit the plethora of [speedo cladded] beautiful beaches, go gambling, explore the roofs of hotels, ride the free buses... But a visit is incomplete without a trip to the *Exeloo* - Try it - You'd never know that public toilets could be so *Star Warsy*!

❢

While the toilets were amazing, **Australia** was not quite what I had anticipated. So many South Africans had moved there calling it "the land of the free," "the land of the brave;" "the land where all your hopes and dreams come true…!" Fearing their homelands would be raped, pillaged, and destroyed, they'd fled in their masses in 1994 when Mandela had become inaugurated. They set up [refugee] camps around the world and labelled them "Paradise'. From a safety and security perspective they were – In Johannesburg it's the citizens that live behind bars, not the criminals – but…

…Imagine a land full of colour and even more colourful people. A land teeming with lions, leopards, wildebeest and oceans full of fascinating creatures and real sharks. A land rich with mountains and forests and beaches and deserts; a feast for the eyes. And the soul. And food and scents and aromas to tantalise your taste buds. We believe in flavour. We call it a "*braai*" because the word "barbeque" does not come close to doing it justice. There is no arguing that we make the best wine in the universe, never mind the world. It's a land rich in culture, music and beats; and afternoon thunderstorms. We call things like they are: if it's "really awesome" it's "*lekker*" or "*kiff*." If it's not, it's "*kak*." We don't complicate things: A "traffic light" is simply a "*robot*," a "shopping bag" is a "*packet*." We're tough people: we grow up barefoot, we play rugby and we work hard. There is no place for *wusses*.

Now imagine leaving that behind? And imagine leaving family and friends behind with it! Of course you're going to sing the praises of your new home; you want people to come to visit! But mostly, YOU want to believe that YOU love it. And you probably do, but there is no place quite like South Africa. There never will be.

And, Australia? Well... it's big! Make that HUGE! There's beaches, deserts and forests. Yes, it's beautiful but...

"Put some shoes on mate" – I constantly had the authorities tell me. "Health and safety" they called it. And, to make matters worse, "thongs"[6] aren't good enough for bars and restaurants. As a staunch anti-shoeist, it's hell!

I later discovered that to give a child a band-aid, three pieces of paperwork were needed: the child's report, mine, and a witness'. If something almost went wrong ("a near miss") it was four – A4 and double-sided. A teacher needed to verify all the accounts.

And when it came to licking strangers, they didn't make it very easy. It is a practice that has entertained me through so many awful clubbing experiences, tedious museum visits and "cultural enlightenments" around the world. It's normally best to discreetly lick the clothing, but in Australia, they barely wear any clothes. It's mostly '*wife-beaters*' and skirts that once functioned as belts. I'm not even all that keen on licking strangers, it's just nice to have the option!

A cup of luke-warm coffee costs you R60, and a flat-flavourless beer costs you R100. If you have friends who smoke, they need to hang out three blocks away, around a corner so that you can't possibly converse with them.

The police are always wandering over to tell you to put some shoes on or to stop licking strangers; or trying to stop you from yelling at your friends who are having a casual drag on the other side of the country.

But at least they're a friendly people!

---

[6] "Slops" for the Africans, "jandals" for the kiwis, or "flip flops" for the rest of the world.

❦

In an attempt to line my pockets and stay on the right side of the law, I set off into the countryside: **Tincurrin**. A population of seven and a half (which had been more than doubled by just the members of my staff house). I spent 38 hours a week hanging out with trees, dirt and sheep; and the rest of my time trying to get clean (which was not so bad really, because there was nothing else to do out there). After planting 196,506[7] trees, doing my part for future tree huggers everywhere, it was time to keep moving.

SURVIVAL OF A HITCHHIKER

Blog Posted in **Adelaide.** 3 February 2011

Ever wonder what sort of person picks up hitch-hikers?
Ever wonder why they leave their passengers dilapidated-dead in the desert?
Ever wonder if you could survive a hitch-hike... if you had to?

I had no option. I had to hitch.
I had to be in Adelaide by Friday, February 4th.
Yes, music festivals are important.
The train was full. The bus took too long.
Flying was not an option (principal not price).
I had no car. No bicycle. Only feet. Feet and two thumbs.

Sally told me that hitching was a great idea, as I sat in her sunny Bunbury home.

---

[7] Exactly.

She must be the only mother in the world who believes that hitching is
potentially the best way to travel; despite all the *Wolf Creek* nonsense
everyone else had tried to deter me with.
She and her lovely daughter Jess, even gave me my first ride – all the
way to the Albany highway - on their way to work.
I won't pretend I wasn't petrified as I watched them drive away leaving
me stranded with my "Toward Albany Please" cereal box sign.
It was to be my first ever lonely hitch.

In only a few minutes I was on my way again with Vince, who was
carrying with him radio-active material (he repeated this information
twice).
He'd agreed to take me to Kirup.
I had no idea where that was, but I was keen to get moving.
He'd successfully lived on the dole for six years by fabricating his own
rejection letters from imaginary companies; but eventually he got tired of
skating his life away and got himself a real job (something to do with soil
and, of course, "radio-active" material).

Not long afterwards, Sid picked me up.
It was quite a scenery change climbing in with the suited-up sales rep.
He was on his way to the Chain Saw Shop in Manjimup.
[Obviously, images from the Texas Chain Saw Massacre flooded my
brain.]

Herbie took me as far as the turnoff to Northcliffe.
("Nowhere," 45-minutes down the road.)
It began to rain.

There was no traffic at the intersection.
But at least I was getting a bit of a shower.

By chance, a car drove out from the campsite down the road.

They waved, shrugged a "we're full" and disappeared;

and then they came back.

"We forgot we have a fold-up chair in the back," said Simon, "Couldn't leave a girl stranded on the side of the road. Especially not in the rain!"

Sammy (aged 3 and a half), was so intrigued by *Dora the Explorer* that she didn't realise I'd climbed on board; and the Grandparents were just glad to see that the years of hitchhiking were not dead and buried.

And that's how I crashed a family holiday and got to see Fernhook Falls and climb Mt Franklin.

From Walpole I hopped in with Katrina, a mother of three on her way to see the principal at her daughter's school in Denmark (The town, not the country).

Seconds later Jack pulled up. The 73-year old's mullet suggested he may have been a psycho killer; but the two toddlers in the back seat seemed to suggest that he was more the human trafficking kind.

Jack had just left his 24-year-old [third] wife in Thailand and was evidently living out of the car whilst getting settled back into 'the real world.'

I'm unsure if he remembered that the tarred road was where most of the driving was meant to occur – but fortunately, the road's shoulder didn't kill us.

He gave me a tour of Albany before dropping me at a hostel where they gave you free luminous green cake for breakfast.

Saturday greeted me with rain – lots of it.

Fortunately, I stopped to ask the direction to the highway because Rob offered me a ride.

It was a good 8km out of town.

As I prepared my "Towards Esperance" sign, a car had pulled up.
I should have noticed the alcohol straight away and probably should have
waved them off; but I hopped in with Mick and Chuck who had just
finished an all-nighter and were still drinking.
They took me as far as the fork in the road and offered me a cash "job..."
I opted out and walked a bit, for obvious reasons.

Fredrick, a university student, was on his way to his parent's farm and
dropped me off at Manypeaks where I did not see many peaks or
anything much.
Several local farmers pulled in for a friendly chat – but rides were
looking scarce.

Some boys pulled in to ask for directions to a campsite.
They returned 20 minutes later to tell me they'd given up on finding it,
and may as well just go all the way to Esperance. Now to only find some
space in their car...
While they rearranged an insane amount of luggage, a bus pulled up
where Larry and his son smiled kindly and said "Esperance? Why not?"
So, I waved the boys farewell and clambered aboard.
The six-hour drive flew past as the Scotsman told me life tales of his 18
years in Australia, and the future rock-star son debated music.
And if the ride wasn't enough, they let me sleep in their school bus for
the night and proceeded to feed me bacon and eggs in the morning.
I think I may well have been God's favourite!

Larry's good friend Sarah, who had the most charming smile and
incredible life story, gave me the tour of the picturesque town on Sunday
before driving me to the Norseman road turn-off and giving me the
massivest hug goodbye.

I needed the hug!

The whole of the Esperance Golf Course looked on and laughed as I
patiently thumbed on the side of the road.
Dave pulled up. When he found out I was headed for Adelaide he made
it very clear that under no circumstances was I to attempt to walk across
the Nullarbor.
I laughed – but he was serious.
He didn't let me out of the car until he was certain I understood that
trying to walk the 2000-odd km desert would be foolish.

I grabbed an iced coffee in Gibson as I waited for the next ride.
It was a long wait.
Kylie was on her weekly Kalgoorlie commute and made excellent
conversation about breast cancer survival, kids, marriage and forensics
all the way to the turn-off to Adelaide.
Another hug.

I started by talking to the truckies.
They were all headed for Perth.
They all ran on the same schedule – but they offered to pick me up on
Wednesday if I was still around.
With the flies and the heat and the dust, I could imagine nothing worse
than being in Norseman till Wednesday.
A massive storm hit. I ran for the pub.
Trash cans flew around, and the wind whipped whirlwinds of dust all
over the place.
The power went out.

My heart sank as the cashier told me that the last hitcher had been stuck
there for five days before he got a ride.

I decided to stay positive.

The storm died down, but daylight was fast disappearing.

One more try for today, I figured.

I walked up to the "Wright Truck" pretty sure that this would be the "wrong" one.

Chase said he could take me as far as Port Augusta.

Once again, I had no idea where that was – but I agreed anyway.

I started celebrating when I found out that it was only 302 km from Adelaide.

A word on long-distance truck riding: Choose carefully!

Even if you have limited options...

Hitching in Australia is nothing like Africa. There is only one passenger seat and health and safety prohibits the 168 other passengers you would find cramped into the truck bunk.

Many of the trucks only come with one bed.

You don't want to have to share that bed with the truckie...

My luck was impeccable. Not only did I get a wonderful, kind-hearted trucker; but I got a whole container to spread myself out in and make into my bedroom.

The 54-degree temperatures that the next day brought with it, stretched our trip over two nights.

I almost blew away as I tried to hold my now-crumply cardboard on the side of the road in Port Augusta on Tuesday.

I knew that someone would pull up eventually; and thankfully Jay did.

His only concession was that we needed to stop and feed his pets on the way.

What he didn't tell me was that his pets included a herd of cattle, a horse, 100 birds that he was breeding, three dogs, and an iguana.

He gave me the tour of his property and showed me his family pictures.

He grinned massively as he told me all about his favourite grandchild –
Spork.
At 70 he was still trucking every day and single-handedly running a
farm.

My phone had committed suicide a few days prior and all my numbers
had been lost.
But luckily enough I had typed out a "To Visit" list for Australian
immigration just in case they didn't want to let me in.
I found the number and sent a text from Jay's phone:
"Adeena will be at the Gold Fields Highway and Port Waverly Road Pub
in 25 minutes."
I willed it to send. It was nearly 21:00.
And that's where Jay sat and very courteously waited with me for my
final ride.

Shane arrived and drove me to his "Homette."

And that's how I made it the 3116 km from Bunbury to **Adelaide**, where
tomorrow's music festival had better be worth it.

Oh, and if you're waiting to hear more about desert murderings, thievery
and sellings into slavery… then I'm sorry to disappoint...
Those days may well be over.

ｆ

My phone rang.

"Are you still looking for a ride to Melbourne?" The elderly American
couple asked.

I panicked. Hyperventilated. Said I'd call back.

I was looking for a ride. Or at least I thought I was.

But I didn't know where I wanted to go to from the lovely Adelaide. Or when. Or how…

I returned the call. I accepted.

It was set to be a five-day trip in a rental car.

By the description, it sounded like five days of fine dining and luxury hotels.

It sounded terrifying!

But there they were – Nils and Hannah. And our Hyundai Getz.

It turns out they weren't American at all. They were German. I should have seen it coming: the whole world seems to be turning German these days. Also, instead of the 60-somethings I'd anticipated, they were my age. I wasn't alone either, they'd conned Dutch Max into coming too. The four of us squished into the teeny two-doored car with our massive backpacks – instantaneous closet companions!

We drove. We drove. And drove a little further. Almost half an hour down the road we reached the McLaren Vale wineries and the tastings began.

I can't possibly imagine a better road trip to **Melbourne** – Great food, great wine, great company, great experiences… The Great Ocean Road, the Grampians, white kangaroos, dead kangaroos, a billion beautiful beaches, and lots of llamas. How do you beat llamas?

I was a school nurse for a couple of days (I administered four band-aids and one ice-pack) before a friend forced me and an unsuspecting Frenchie into his camper van. We spent weeks foraging for food as we slowly crept up toward **Sydney.**

I really planned to find a job there – honest!

But there were far too many unavoidable distractions: The beach… the mountains… the folk festival… another camper van…

A night in the park.

Nights on the beach.

I woke up outside Domino's Pizza.

I woke up in a weed plantation.

I woke up on a farm.

I woke up at Bush Camp.

ONE TIME, AT BUSH CAMP

Port Stephens. 29 September 2011

I was quite impressed by my hitchhiking efforts as I pulled up for
induction at 07:00 that Monday morning.
I'd been on the road for a while and had nothing that resembled clean
clothes let alone interview attire; but they let me in anyway...
I wasn't quite prepared for what I stumbled into.

There were 17 of us altogether.
Two Kiwis, an elderly woman and a random mix of young Aussies.

After a brief introduction, it was challenge time:
Some strategizing. Some heights. Some harness activity... It was all new
to me!
(I even had to ask if it mattered that I'd put the harness on inside out.)
By the time we got on to knot knowledge, I was just about ready to do a
runner.

We lost two inductees that Monday night.
Neither of them gave an explanation. One left in tears.
I spent most of the first-night job hunting...

I survived the Tuesday *Leap of Faith* and 20+ meter climb for pulley threading.

I survived Wednesday's canoe and heights rescues. By Thursday, I was amazed that I was one of the nine that remained.

I moved into more permanent accommodation. It was only a shipping container, but it was a massive step up from the tent I'd lived in for the preceding months.

Week one as a newbie was rough.

I climbed the abseil tower and stared blankly at the ropes for 20 minutes while one of the managers painstakingly assessed me on my set-up.

I failed rock climbing tie-offs. Twice.

I failed pretty much every hard-skill there was, but somehow, I made it through the week.

And the next one.

Eventually, I overcame my fears and inabilities and passed all my assessments.

I was handed a dark blue "Outdoor Activities Instructor" shirt and a contract.

I only planned to stay a little while - Spain awaited!

(As did the 200 odd countries I had yet to visit…)

But I lasted the whole school term and even came back from New Zealand for a second.

My bank account gained weight.

My life grew in richness.

My feet began to itch.

ϛ

Australia taught me:

- A whole new language: *dunny, goon, bogan, fair dinkum, chockers, sook*, and that a *piece-of-piss hard-yakka* gets you some *frothy* with your *cobbers*.
- That if you want anything bad enough you can make it happen. Even if you're afraid of heights, knots, failure and all the odds are against you.
- How to tie my shoelaces; as well as bowlines, figure eights, alpine butterflies, and a whole lot of other knots even more complicated than shoe-laces.
- That there are more complicated knots than shoelaces!
- Never to put petrol into your diesel camper van.
- To always have premium roadside assistance so that when your Kiwi friend, Steph, uses the wrong fuel, you can get a free night in a hotel and a bus ticket back to work while your camper van gets a free tow the 557 km back home where Radar, your resident diesel mechanic, will fix it for a crate of beer.

3.

YOUR FUTURE HOLDS WET PANTS

ANGKAWI, Malaysia. Sunday, 15 January 2012

L We spent eight days collecting scraps of whatever we could scavenge to build *The Illegal Immigrant*. Our skills were vast. Our nationalities vaster: One Yank, a Dutchie, an Estonian, a Czech, a Teddy and an African.

We split into task groups and used scooters to gather sturdy shrapnel. Six massive blue water drums (of varying sizes) formed the hull. The airport was doing a revamp and provided aluminium to build a frame. Freight companies supplied old pallets for our base. An umbrella stand was used to hold "the mast". Some Brazilians donated us an old sail which we altered to form a *main* and *jib*; not that any of us knew what those were. We negotiated with [and arm-wrestled for even further reductions] kayak companies for broken paddles, just in case there was no wind. We sought flares and life jackets, but they exceeded our budget.

Construction took longer than expected, but mostly due to the friendliness of curious passersby and the price of the [duty-free] alcohol. Every night, swarms of intrepid souls would party on board. Every morning new strangers were found sleeping on her deck. Even on days where we swore to avoid those liquids entirely, people would wander over and gift us [too many] tasty beverages. We needed to get off Langkawi! - Our livers depended on it!

We island hopped the nearby archipelago and fell in love with our little vessel. So many friendly sailors warned us about our cockiness, but she was "invincible"! And so it was that we loaded her up, and set sail for Thailand.

Dawn; and the world was perfection. Tired of our lengthy goodbyes, the boys set off without us. We chased them down the beach and plunged into the sapphire sea, catching them just before they reached the ocean depths. We paddled into the abyss and as the day progressed scores of friendly backpackers came out to well-wish us: on kayaks and speed boats and wakeboards and a series of inflatable tow-toys. We weren't going anywhere quickly.

We stopped on an island for lunch, and continued in sun hats and sarongs that sheltered us from the barbeque-sun. We found the wind.

We hadn't considered what conditions would be like out of the *lee* of the islands. We didn't realise there'd be waves. We hadn't considered the strength of the wind. We didn't know that rope stretches when it gets wet.

"What was that noise?" asked the Czech. We told her she was imagining things. And then she heard it again. We all did. A barrel floated away. I tried to play hero and dived in to chase it. I tried to fling myself over it like they effortlessly do in all the movies. But even when I eventually had it in my control, there was no way that I was going to swim it back against the current. I had to let it go. As I returned, we lost another one.

None of us took the situation too seriously! Instead, we laughed and had a quick rice picnic on the half-submerged remains of the vessel. We scanned the horizon and agreed on a distant island beach to evacuate to. The boys were overboard in seconds, racing to land. We had to yell at them to come back and take supplies. One carried the cooler box. One took water. One transformed a sail into a bag and stuffed what he could into it. And then they were off again.

"I'm not a very good swimmer," said the Czech with eyes that screamed terror. It was a bit late to be gifted this piece of information, but seeing as there was now no way out of the predicament, we did what we needed to. We strung empty water bottles together to build a small raft. We stuffed what we could into the bottles, everything else we had shoved into plastic bags and my sleeping bag cover which I tied to my back. We latched a rope to the raft, Helena to the raft, and the raft to me.

Nothing is ever as close as it seems. To boost our morale, we sang as we swam. We sang the whole way. Made up songs about sailing and shipwrecking and survival. We liked to sing about survival. We were too scared to look in the water, as we didn't want to know what lurked below. We kept our eyes pointed at the destination. It took hours to swim to the island. As the sun began to sink, we eventually made it to the shallows. But we had new problems: the "sandy sanctuary" was surrounded by a coral garden and it was a challenging maze of urchins and other hazardous beauties for our shaky legs.

We collapsed on the beach where we found the boys similarly exhausted. The Dutchman was in bad shape: he'd had too much sun, had been stung by jellyfish and urchins had made themselves at home by festering in his feet. To make matters worse, light had almost vanished and a storm was brewing. We set off to find shelter and failed. Instead, we dragged bamboo along the beach and laced them together to make a frame to rest our sail upon. We gathered wood and started a fire to warm our bodies and dry our belongings. As the heavens opened up, we huddled together and laughed at the ridiculousness of life: we had shipwrecked and were stranded on a deserted island.

After dinner, we tried to get some rest, taking it in turns to look after Dutchy. He'd begun hallucinating and was running circles around our camp, screaming at "the tarantulas" and further-damaging his feet. Despite exhaustion, rest was not easy. The mosquitoes swarmed and the crabs attacked our toes.

As "romantic" [without any actual romance] as it was to be stranded on that beautiful island, we knew we needed to get off. Only seven litres of water had made it ashore, and medical attention was incumbent! We knew the basics of shipwreck survival and started the day etching "S.O.S." into the sand. Air traffic could see it, but there was nowhere to land a plane. The passing fishing boat completely ignored our cries and pleas, no matter how bright the garments we waved in their general direction. We set off to explore the island properly but didn't find much. No water. No shelter. Then, a frantic search broke out as we realized we had lost the American.

The day was about to end when we saw a speed boat nearing over the horizon. We waved and yelled and then noticed a familiar face. While we were thrilled that our Yank was alive, we were ready to punch him for the anguish he'd caused us. We'd imagined that he either drifted out to sea or passed out unconscious. Instead, he'd swam to the next island. When he'd found nothing there, he rounded to the far side and swam to the next where he eventually found a private resort; and a boat.

We gathered the remains of our belongings, leaving behind a small bamboo monument to commemorate *The Illegal Immigrant* and our survival.

As I sat waiting for the Dutchman to be released from the hospital, excitement had built. I couldn't explain it, but despite all the complications the seed was sown. I needed to learn how to sail. There was something about being a sea gypsy that screamed my name.

ƭ

"Jesus Christ, I wish you the best of luck. And I hope that in time of need you can channel your inner Chuck Norris and defend yourself and that no one robs you or any other horrible stuff that can happen when you're travelling! Stay Aliveeee!!" — Travis

*"**Rape kit***

Adeena, Sorry, when I read about your plans, I immediately became worried for you.

Do not do this hitching, please. Even if you are the fattest ugliest horniest woman in the world you are asking, knee begging for trouble. You plan to hitch-hike through a couple of countries where Asian women are kidnapped and sold into sexual slavery. You're a white woman. Do you WANT to be trafficked like a piece of meat? Beaten and starved into submission repeatedly raped? Used like a rag?

I don't think you want that kind of adventure.

A rape kit is some equipment that a western police department uses to gather evidence after a rape.

Good luck!" -James

"My bum is blue!"

-Diary excerpt, **Vietnam**. Friday, 16 March 2012

Let me rewind a little so that you don't mistake me for a weirdo...

It was over lunch the previous Tuesday that his friends led me to contemplate the mission. No mention of course that Rohan had actually done long-distance cycling before or that his fitness levels resembled that of a Kenyan Olympic marathon sprinter. On the Wednesday, I awoke sold

41

on the idea and roamed the streets in search of a worthy steed, some luggage carriers, and a bell. $25 later, I was set.

It had recently been brought to my attention that I had a wedding in three weeks. Not mine. No, that would have been more worrying! But despite her functioning as my moral reasoning on a frequent basis over the previous 14 years, I need to express my annoyance at both Debbie's choice of location and especially the timing for her wedding - Koh Samui, Thailand - April 3rd. *Seriously? Koh Samui?* – I had been in the area back in January. Now I was 2163km away (as the cow flies) in Hanoi, Vietnam. I had sold my motorbike. And I didn't fly. Flying isn't good for you! I'd sworn off the bus and just discovered that there was no train. I reckoned that hitchhiking was my best bet, but something about Northern Vietnam made me not want to do it on my own…

Flashback to **New South Wales**, Australia. 10 April 2011

I was in high spirits as I finally bid Bellingen farewell. Even though it was raining, I was okay - it's generally easier to hitchhike in the rain. I didn't even make it to the suggested hitching spot, 100m down the road when a friendly trucker pulled up and told me to hop in. Bruce even pulled over for me to see the waterfalls and the scenery as he drove me to Dorrigo.

I was headed to a farm job, packing apples in Orange - a town 500 or 800 km to the South West. I was finally going to mark off the remaining 46 days of rural work that I needed for my second-year working holiday visa (just in case I ever decided to brave Australia again)! I was glad that I'd secured a job, and was even more excited that all my timings were going to work out perfectly!

Bruce apologised profusely for not being able to take me any further, and apologised even more for not being able to stop the rain. I liked him. But as he drove away and the rain bucketed down and the mist descended, so did my high-spirits. I got drenched as half a handful of cars sped past, splashing me. I was wet. I was miserable.

I had stood there for hours (or perhaps 15 minutes) when Rocco pulled up in his ute. His cap pulled low, sunnies on. But he smiled.

"Where you goin?" I asked. My accent had basically Australianised.

"Armidale," he replied.

He gave me the creeps, but I brushed it off. Australia had only given me goodness!

"Mind if I jump in?"

He seemed surprised that I did and carried on rolling his joint.

We were only a little way down the road when he told me he'd had a tip-off and was on the run from the cops as we sped at 140km/h down the windy road. He wouldn't tell me why he was running - just that he'd packed up house that morning and was going to hide out in Armidale for a while. I tried to ease my way out of the vehicle, but he didn't want to stop; so I plastered a fear-concealing smile across my face and chanced a new topic...

"Kangaroos..."

He steered off the main road and down a dirt road. I started to get really worried. He sensed my panic. "Don't want to go through any of those police checks," he muttered.

But I'd watched Wolf Creek and I knew how these things worked. I could already feel my corpse dangling from a tree. I glanced at my phone – still no reception.

"If you like kangaroos, you really ought to come and see my hide-out house."

I thanked him for the kind offer but declined.

"There are koalas too," he threw in, as if it were an infomercial.

As we continued towards "somewhere" passing "Armidale" after "Armidale" signs pointing in the opposite direction, Roc told me about his days as a biker and how he was now a kangaroo whisperer. He can talk to them - it's the language of the clicking tongue. I nodded believingly but was more focused on watching for oncoming traffic to wave down and shout "help!"

"Let me just drive you to Orange," he said.

Why did I tell him where I was headed? Why?

"I need to meet up with a friend this evening," I lied. But I think lying is okay when you're doing it to stay alive.

"Ahhh, but I need to go to Orange anyway," he continued, "We'll swing past mine and pick up my swag.*"*

I saw another car and asked him to pull over - he refused.

"I swore to drive you to Armidale and that's where I'll take you. Besides, you never know what kind of weirdo might pick you up."

He was on his third joint when the new plan evolved: he wanted me to deliver the "package" he had taped under the car to a friend - I was to pose as his girlfriend while doing it.

The clouds erupted with more rain. I was spared.

"I don't want you to get wet my sweet sweet darling."

Why on earth was he calling me "darling?!"

"How lucky am I to pick up someone like you?"

What did he mean by that?

!!!!!!!!!!!!PANIC!!!!!!!!!!!!!!

We sat in silence for a while before I noticed signs of civilisation on the horizon.

"I haven't eaten anything all day," I lied again, suggesting lunch.

I've never been happier to arrive in a small town. Even if we were down a quiet back-alley so that no one would recognise him. The hours of tension that had seeped into my bones were still crippling, but the important thing was that I was still alive!

Rocco wandered off to get some beers and I scribbled a quick note on a napkin and handed it to a waitress. "Call the police," I whispered pretending to glance at the menu.

Roc took his time, eyeing me carefully from the bar as I took a seat. I watched him play with the drink, it looked like he was mixing something in there.

"Here you go my darling."

I reached for the other glass, but of course he got himself a 'light beer.'

Our food arrived as we sat discussing his collection of Papua New Guinea Voodoo art. I pretended to sip the beer twice - but even through the sunnies that he had yet to remove, I could see him eyeing my drink. I waited till halfway through my meal when I 'accidentally' knocked it over.

"Let me just take you to Orange," he said one last time.

"No! Thank you." I said - "I'll walk back to the highway from here."

"Get in the ute."

"No. I'm not going with you. Give me my stuff."

"Get in."

"No! Give me my stuff!"

"Get in the f*#king ute!" He said forcefully, grabbing me on the arm. His face went pale.

The waitress and the entourage she had assembled on the pavement watched intently, arms crossed and unyielding, as he finally let me take my bags. I felt like crying and throwing up at the same time, I was that shook up.

f

I now knew well enough to always follow my gut instincts.

There would be no compromise.

This time I wouldn't disobey, I wouldn't be hitching alone!

I spent two days seeking companions.

I plastered posters on every hostel board and made posts online. I became that annoying person that joins your table and disturbs your meal to pester you about things you couldn't possibly want.

All I received was people trying to talk me out of it.

The first week of cycle-touring taught me:

ƒ Don't start cycling in a mountain range.

ƒ Gears are not just for decoration.

ƒ Keep your luggage light. A 75-litre backpack might not look like much, but it throws your bike a little off balance. I also strongly dis-advise the carrying of oversized stuffed toys. No matter how cool they are.

ƒ Don't buy a [cheap] Chinese bicycle. The wheels are inclined to solidify with the body of the bicycle, making riding a lot harder than it should be, if not impossible.

ƒ On occasion, the handlebars tend to follow their own minds and duck and dive, making braking and gear changing a nightmare. This will conveniently happen while you're racing downhill.

ƒ Don't tell your cycle buddy that you'll meet up in the next town when he has all the local currency on him. It's rather unpleasant when you ride the last 30 km of the day without a drop of water in a country where you sweat a litre a minute and can't drink the tap water.

ƒ Don't cycle at night. Even if it is only 21 km in the dark. You won't realise that you have a flat tyre, especially when you don't have any lights (or you forgot to bring batteries). Eventually a sporadic thunderstorm breaks out and you get drenched, become miserable and end up sleeping under a fruit stand on the side of the street where mosquitoes molestorise you and frogs don't shut up.

ƒ Take some tools with you. Even when you have a puncture repair kit and a spare tube and pump, you might just realise at that inopportune moment, 14 km from the next town, that your wheels don't have quick-release. 14 km is a long way to push.

ﬔ Buy gloves or grow a pair of man hands - blisters suck, and you get to the point where you can't even change gears any more. Gears are important. I know this now.

ﬔ ENJOY IT! While it might be hard and painful; it's worth every second! Your body will thank you. Your soul will be refreshed. And ultimately you will be the happiest you've ever been!

I survived the cycle.

I survived the strange disease that swelled my throat shut and threatened to kill me.

I survived a robbery.

I survived a luxury hotel with air-con.

I survived the wedding.

But....

YOUR FUTURE HOLDS WET PANTS

Bangkok, Thailand. 18 April 2012

Monks are chasing you with guns, toddlers are plastering you with toxic chemicals.

Around every corner lies a vicious terrorist just waiting to attack.

There is nowhere safe... Nobody you can trust.

It's just you and at least a million of them! 72 hours of 'kill or be killed'.

This is the year 2555. This is your future.

After cycling down Thailand, we decided to short-cut [cheat] back. But our train arrived four hours late, so instead of sneaking into Bangkok in the wee hours of the morning [as planned], we arrived in the thick of it.

The thick of Songkran.

Whilst most of the world celebrated New Years with fireworks and parties; all of Thailand shut down for a three-day water fight that spans streets, alleys, hotels, bathrooms and restaurants.
It's ruthless - they don't care if you're unarmed, carrying electronics, or a giant teddy bear... The more you look like you don't want to be wet, the more troops swarm in to attack!
This made my newest cycle buddy, Katie and I prime targets as we cycled the 4kms from the station to our dodgy brothel-ish hotel.

Checked in, guns loaded, we headed back to the streets armed with less-than-ideal weapons.
We were greeted by a gang of Thai alcoholics who welcomed us with shots of strange liquor and bucket loads of ice water.

In search of new victims, we rounded the corner to Khao San Road where we hit a wall of people dancing to the best of Thailand's hip hop DJs. Foam floated around us while water fell from the skies.

As the sun faded away, the streets got busier and the water got icier. The celebrations turned more hardcore and the ladyboys came out to play.
Madness, that's all I could say.
MADNESS!
And this "madness" increased by the day, maybe even the hour.

After slipping for the umpteenth time and breaking my toy gun, I invested in some hardcore artillery and spent day three seeking down those who'd targeted me before.
It's so much better with a real gun!
It's even better when you've accumulated an army of Thai freedom fighters who supply only you with the iciest water.

18 hours of solid revenge.

Three days of hitting it hard had Bangkok quieter than I'd imagined
possible.
Apart from the remnants of talcum powder that plastered vehicles and
dripped from skyscrapers, it was the cleanest too.

Anyway, it's now the year 2555 in Thailand and time for a fresh start...
It's time for me to rekindle my hatred for my bicycle.
Next stop Chiang Mai... 850ish km away... and this time it's just me and
the Teddy Bear.

Swasdi Pi Mai Thailand!!
Happy New Year!

Being my longest travel companion to date, I suppose I really should
introduce Teddy. No, he's not a real bear [But don't tell him that.]
Weighing in at just over 2kg, and composed mostly of polyester fluff, he
may be an incredibly useless dead weight, but he does make an excellent
pillow! And you'd be surprised at how he attracts smiles [and dirt]!

With the spur of the moment decision to flee Australia, my send-off
doubled as a birthday party. Apart from being forced to drink a colourful
array of alcoholic concoctions, some Aussie friends bestowed upon me
"Goat," a giant unicorn with a skewiff horn that looked a bit like a gay
polar bear[8]. And, without any knowledge of the former, some Kiwi friends
"gifted" me an even bigger teddy bear. To keep things fair, I was forced

---

[8] The unicorn's life was later sacrificed for the greater good as a "Goat" was
required to qualm a volcano on Java.

to sign a contract agreeing to carry both creatures for a minimum of a month before opting out. I'd staggered to Sydney International Airport very heavily laden.

❦

Chiang Saen, Thailand. Monday, 21 May 2012

Bang Bang Bang! Bang Bang Bang! [there was definite urgency in the bangage]. I flung the door open in my PJs to find an exasperated Mat standing there: "Let's go!" "What? Where?..." I jumped in his car with disgraceful hair and abysmal morning breath and sped off to immigration.

There was a chance I'd be hopping on a boat sometime on Monday, but it was more likely happening in the afternoon. The reality of all the "maybes" made me half suspect it would never happen. But there I was at 08:04, stamped out of Thailand with about half an hour to make it to the port where I would board some sort of boat that would allegedly take me somewhere in China for a yet to be discussed cost. There was no turning back now!

I threw my belongings into my saddlebags, did a Facebook update so people would know where my bodily remains would be located [if it came to that], got on my bike, and pedalled like the wind [on a particularly breezy day].

I made three wrong stops en route, but there before me lay my glorious timber boat – *Fengshun IV.* Mat and May-ee met me on board. I'd met them on Saturday while trying to organise the "non-existent", allegedly-impossible vessel.

Mat spoke some English and Thai.

May-ee spoke Thai and Mandarin.

The crew spoke ONLY Mandarin.

Through the various interpretation channels, we negotiated my fee.

The rules were laid down:

- Under no circumstances was I allowed to go to the front, the roof, or the captain's sector of the ship.
- If they pointed to my room, I needed to get there as quickly as possible and close the curtains.
- I was not allowed to disembark in Laos or Myanmar.

And that was it – not a lot of rules considering it was currently illegal to take passengers up The Mekong River. My mere presence on board made them far more likely to be targeted by Mekong pirates, of which there had been a lot lately!

I bid my translation duo farewell and settled into life as a semi-stowaway.

There was no need to have hurried though – it took hours before we eventually departed.

With the Golden Triangle drifting further and further away, the scenery became increasingly breathtaking! I met the crew in staggered introductions; but with only charades to communicate with, I didn't even get their names.

Mealtimes brought with them table-fulls of delicious foods and plenty awkward conversation [I assume] about the stranger in their midst! At dinner, I was overloaded with rice wine as they "Gambei"-ed me in rounds trying to out-drink me. They did. I was honoured to share a room with the cook – she won the love and appreciation of both my heart and my stomach!

The rest of the seven-person crew included one man manning the wheel, two men who sat at the front of the boat with bamboo sticks to check the depth of the water, one man in the boiler room, one man keeping watch, and - at any given time, for no apparent reason - there was always one person doing laundry.

Geraldine was the only one who had any time to spare, so I spent a lot of time babbling to her. I tried not to get too attached. Being a turkey, I feared she too may be joining the dinner table.

Monday evening had me chased to my room for the first time, where I sat for a couple of hours with the curtains drawn shut while the world went by outside.

Tuesday morning it happened again.

On Tuesday afternoon, after I'd finished washing my bike (I had to at least pretend to look busy), we had the military board our ship with guns… but the excitement was short-lived. They too departed.

Being the dry season and heading upstream was no easy task. Every time we hit rapids or a sandbank (all too frequently), two of the crew would swim ashore with ropes and tie us to the closest country. Here an intricate uber-pulley-rig would slowly lug us forward to calmer waters. The crew didn't mess around.

The engines fired up by 05:30 each morning, and we docked at the very last light – around 20:00. By 22:00 (latest), the generators were off and a world of moonless darkness engulfed us. The others, having worked a 14.5-hour day, would all drift straight to sleep while I would lie awake feeling the bugs crawl on me and having a few unwarranted encounters with 'the rat'.

I'd heard that the trip could take anything from 2 days to a week. From the second afternoon, any time I saw any sign of civilization my heart would start beating. "Is that China?" I lost track of how many times I asked that question. Not that it would have made much of a difference I suppose, but I did have to ration my coffee.

Eventually, by the third afternoon, we definitely crossed into Chinese waters. There was no mistaking the flashing lights and massive "Border Police" sign. I packed up all my belongings in anticipation, but it would still be hours before we reached the port.

I climbed down the stairs to find Geraldine tied up and bamboo-stick-man-number-two holding her by the neck with something shiny in his hands. I ran upstairs. I couldn't watch. She'd come so close to surviving…but...

Minutes later I watched her be hidden on the roof in the safety of her cage, and covered with a blanket. Stick man motioned a "shhh!" to me and I smiled a massive sigh of relief!

When we eventually did arrive, the border police were very surprised to find me there. After they excessively searched some of my luggage, my crew helped me lug my bike across the four cargo ships we'd tied up to.

I touched dry land for the first time in three days.

It took me five attempts to fill in my Chinese immigration card. Apart from that, it was problem-free. Far too easy even. I had arrived in China at last and my Chinese bicycle [and probably most of my other belongings too] were home!

4.

THE POWER OF THUMB

"May your child be born with a perforated anus…"
This is China (I'm sure of it!) and even the profanities are arbitrary.

I cycled to the capital of the province I'd never heard of and found a cheap hotel. I skyped mum to let her know that I was finally in the same country as her. With tears of joy she cried **"Jinghong**? I have friends there." They just happened to be driving past and stopped and picked me up on their way to the hospital.

Minutes later I found myself holding the two-hour-old daughter of a complete stranger. It was the family's fourth child, but they'd decided to have this one at a hospital because they wanted her to have a birth certificate. The mother and baby were not allowed to wash for a month.

Every day of that month, the mother had to eat a whole chicken. If they couldn't afford that, they'd eat a dog.

It had been much harder than I'd anticipated to say goodbye to my trusty bicycle, but I knew I'd made the right decision. The phenomenal South African missionary family needed it a lot more than I did; and I needed a change.

The transition to hitchhiking wasn't particularly smooth either. It took an hour to explain [via Google Translate] to the poor receptionist at my hostel what I intended to do. Eventually I walked away with a Hanzi sign and a point in the right direction.

It had been a while since my last hitch and it took time to suss out the perfect spot and figure out the correct hand actions. I took a deep breath, held my sign up valiantly and began the 2500+ km journey to mum.

An hour in, I'd created a few minor traffic jams and had caring civilians point me to the nearest bus station at least five times. One of them even drove me to the ticket office. The heavens opened up, and I took shelter in a stranger's garden.

Another hour of failure bestowed itself upon me. It rained again. I questioned my mission. I looked longingly toward the bus terminal.

Some cyclists brought with them hope and smiles. While we conversed in *Chinglish*, a whole string of cars pulled up to find out what was going on. My luck was about to change.

Cyclist number 1 ran off to find cardboard for a new sign, while cyclist number 2 educated the masses in the ways of alternative transport. Then the police pulled up and I got my first ride.

My second ride came from a bus driver who read my new sign and welcomed me aboard (for free). He talked another bus driver into giving me a free ride too. 162 km from Jinghong, I called it a day and checked myself into a middle of nowhere hotel.

It's confusing enough just traipsing through this country without throwing [the yet to be invented in these parts] hitchhiking into the equation – but if a life of bewilderment surrounds you, you may as well immerse yourself in it!

I got an earlier start with an altered sign, but my backpack broke as I stepped out of the hotel. I stitched the shoulder strap back on and walked up a mountain, heading back to the highway. I prayed that I'd have better luck than the previous day.

Two businessmen pulled up in a brand-new Audi and off we zoomed at speeds faster than some planes fly. The scenery got better by each turn through the mountainous roads. I clung on so tight that my knuckles turned white. My heart was racing so fast that I hardly had an appetite when they treated me to an immaculate lunch.

Dali was so incredible that I didn't believe I actually survived the 562 km of winding road. I may have died and made it to Heaven instead. There was so much good food, so many quaint intricacies; an old town abuzz with wild music and the perfect amount of craziness.

Two days later, I lugged myself to **Li Jiang** with two friendly twenty-somethings in a VW Polo. The town was a cultural experience of note, constantly humming with local tourists adorned in rainbows of clothing. People stumbled from one 'Yak Meat of the Naxi Sister' shop to the next, stopping to buy pashminas and colourful leggings [and an array of other strange purchases] before bar-hopping between gangster rap, rock, acoustic sets, pole dancing and… It was the kind of town you could get lost in for days. I did just that – but mostly because I have no sense of direction.

I left with a Mandarin-English dictionary and a shirt that read "I don't understand" (in Chinese). And because nobody understood me either, I ended up walking more than 12 km to get out of town before accidentally hopping in a taxi.

I car hopped between families all the way to Shangri-la (or, as they say, "Shan-go-li-la"), while the 7-year-old beside me more than doubled my Mandarin skills. I chanted, "Open the window, close the window" while my instructor giggled in obedience.

I was quite looking forward to some good company as seven of us ended up hitching out of Shangri-la. Two were headed South and the rest of us North. But it was only when I was checking out that I consulted a map and found that my planned route cut straight through the Tibetan Autonomous Region. Foreign tourists weren't allowed to enter Tibet, unless they had a guide, a permit and four other people of the same nationality. It's harder than you'd think to find five South Africans in China, let alone ones who planned to go to Tibet.

Although the streets were littered with hitchers, it was another lonely walk for me while the Chinese roamed freely. The road to Litang had me off the highway, heading down the dirtiest path yet.

There was a lot going through my mind as local construction trucks sprayed mud all over me and Teddy. Litang was still out of bounds for us touristy types. Two monks had burned themselves and over 600 people had been arrested there just a few days earlier. I walked onwards half fearing that I'd spend a whole day hitching and walking just to be sent back again. I don't like doubling back.

Whilst far away in worry land, a car pulled up and offered me a ride. My first Tibetan hitch. They only drove me about 30 kilometres, but it was far enough to be committed to the path.

Two trucks, a tractor, and several herds of wild horses later, a car flew by so fast that I fell off the road. It was either the elegance of my fall or a sense of deep-rooted guilt that made them double back and pick me up. Either way, I was in. They had mumbled something about not going to Litang, so I assumed I was only going a couple of villages up the road. I kept my pack on my lap, not wanting to get too comfortable.

Four hours later, once we were far from anything that even resembled a road, I eased into the ride. The driver steered with a GPS [and a beer]. It was a wild ride as we drove through rocky dirt roads, passing mountains, rivers, herds of yak, sheep and frightened villagers. A quest to prove the capabilities of the four-by-four. Once I showed them my altimeter, we began racing toward the biggest mountains just to conquer the 5000m elevation mark.

Darkness was rapidly descending, and by 21:00, we were still in the middle of somewhere. We climbed another mountain; and on the other side there was a road. A tarred road.

By 23:00, I had thanked them with hugs and plodded off to find an affordable hotel. It's amazing how you can negotiate down from ¥580 to ¥90 for a room.

The morning brought with it even more confusion. Very picturesque confusion. I had no idea where I was. Nobody spoke English, or Mandarin either for that matter. Everything was written in Tibetan, which meant nobody could even understand my hitching sign. Although the village was beautifully paved, it didn't appear that there were any roads out.

One thing is certain, I have illegally crossed into Tibet.
I wonder what the implications will be?
Today's going to be a very interesting day indeed!

I walked and walked, found a road, and walked some more. A couple of hours later, a car finally passed and I got a ride to Daocheng. **Daocheng** is on the map.

I sat on the edge of town debating staying in the picturesque prefecture. Then I watched a man kick a dog off of a bridge and immediately changed my mind. Right then and there a minibus driver offered me a "mianfei" (free) ride to **Litang.**

Despite it being on the tourist trail – it was a hole of a city – it had no soul, no vibe, and no nice hostels. Being the only foreigner in town (thanks

59

to the tourist ban), I was greeted by a mob of cowboy-hatted Tibetans that attempted to chase me into mouldy guest houses.

I spent one night observing the esteemed caterpillar larva trade on the street. I ate the worst Chinese food yet. And then failed to sleep while listening to the dogs howl at the full moon.

At first light, I left. In the rain.

I was feeling quite sorry for myself as I walked up yet another mountainous hill adorned in a poncho while balancing an umbrella under my arm. I held a soggy sign in one hand and stuffed teddy bear in the other. Eventually I looked up and saw the snow-capped mountains that surrounded me. I instantly felt a whole lot happier about life. Sometimes I get so distracted by mild discomforts that I forget to look up.

Fifteen minutes later Jeshu pulled over, and I was off again. His snazzy car thermometer measured one degree. We chatted about everything from the weather to work to "Do you think that China's present rural reform is making progress?[9]" When we ran out of conversation topics, he played bad club anthems and flashed the lights. As we danced in his car disco, we sped past hundreds of cyclists on a terribly muddy road. 200 km took an entire day.

Tagong on the other hand, was incredible. The hills were alive with prayer flags and monks. It felt like being in some sort of western movie scene – One dusty road in, one dustier road out. Only there were fluffy yaks and short people instead of life-sized cowboys and herds of cattle.

A beautiful Tibetan lady pointed me to a hostel. It greeted me with a dead horse and a vicious dog. I'd been bitten twice that week already and was starting to develop a phobia of rabid-looking dogs. I had to run away from the owner who was trying to force me in. I'm quite glad I did because only down the road, under a beautiful rainbow, I found a haven of comfort.

---

[9] I came to love the 'friends' section of my new phrasebook.

The Chinese tourists in my dormitory had never seen a rainbow before.

My shortest distance yet (111 km) took 4 1/2 hours and 3 rides. It was slow, but I had company – one Irishman and a Swiwi (Swiss-Kiwi). When in good company, little can go amiss[10]!

Danba hosted more [living] animals than I'd seen in the rest of China combined. It was a great stop that consisted of sipping on yak butter tea, singing karaoke, and drinking way too much coffee. I tried to buy razors to avoid being mistaken for a hippy, but Chinese women don't shave their legs and the men struggle to grow beards.

I joined forces with an Israeli. We lucked out with the lovely people from China Mobile who drove us the last 387 km into **Chengdu**. We stopped along the way so that they could feed us, shower us with gifts and show us ALL the tourist attractions of the Sichuan Province. This included a 6500m mountain range, the destroyed schools of the earthquake zone, far too many community signs, monuments, and even pandas. I struggled to see clearly from all the camera flashes: every stop [including the toilet breaks] came with a photoshoot!

And that was that!
2687ish km. 18 rides.
18 Chinese and 9 Western converts to the power of the thumb.
And finally, after two years apart, there was mum!

We hit China so hard that Mao had almost risen from his mausoleum! Together we climbed 3706m for a mountain sunrise (which happened to be at 04:00 – that whole one time-zone thing). We endured many bus and train rides, as well as undergrounds (Normally in the wrong direction). We

---

[10] Apart from your mind. Especially when you play those childhood car games. Do you have any idea how frustrating it is trying to think of a song with the word "motorbike" in it?

cycled the dark alleys, valleys and highways of the South. We visited mud baths, caves, hot springs and countless beautiful landscapes. We were caught in the rain more times than we stayed dry. Even when we did stay dry, we sweated so much that we were drenched anyway. We ate so much chilli that we both cried[11]! We savoured so many strange dishes that we are positive our faeces would come out looking better! We met good people as well as bad people (many more of the former). We spoke far too much Chinglish. I felt more confused than ever!

Sadly, my two weeks of motherhood are over. We are about to catch a bus to catch a train to catch a bus to catch a plane. Mum is off to South Africa for the next two months.

Normally I'd start looking for new adventures on my quest. Not this time. This time I knew exactly where I am headed: I'm off to Borneo (flightlessly, I hope), to become a vegetarian!

Chinese lessons that might change your life:

- Trying to understand what is going on around you is a frivolous action that will simply make you more confused.
- It is better not to know what's on your plate. Ignorance is tasty bliss.
- A woman with chopsticks might find eating challenging, but a woman with one chopstick goes hungry.
- Don't judge an ice-cream by its wrapper. It might not even be an ice-cream!
- Always stop to read the signs. They will never give you any actual information, but their translations are the funniest

---

[11] And I eat chili for breakfast.

thing you may ever read.

- ❡ Read up on hostels before you stay at them. It may look like a normal hostel on the outside, but you don't want to go checking your mother into a party hostel where it's standard procedure to copulate in the dorm.

- ❡ Always carry toilet paper. ALWAYS!

❡

LOSING MY ASIANITY

Camiguin, The Philippines. 17 July 2012

It's normally easy to slide in and live amongst the natives;
Having dark skin and even darker hair makes me practically Asian.
By default.
And sometimes I can even use chopsticks...
But in **The Philippines**, all that has changed.
I now stick out like a sore thumb- but it's mostly a sore foot that's done the damage!

I've been 'disabled' for two weeks today. I take my hat off to people with real disabilities because it's not easy having people constantly asking,
"What happened to your foot?" and feeling sorry for you.
It especially sucks when you carry a big backpack and an even bigger teddy bear.
To put it all into perspective: I walk so weirdly that most people don't even notice Teddy.
But if there's one place where you can rest and enjoy some beauty, it's the Philippines.
[Apart from all the walking, adventuring and exploring that lures you

away from recovery.]

There are the magical waters and corals and clams.
And a plethora of waterfalls.
The people are overly nice and excessively friendly.
The transport is ALL colourful [and only a little uncomfortable].
Karaoke bars can be found in almost anyone's backyard.
The landscape is absolutely perfect.
Apart from the spiders, most of the animals are cute and cuddly!
The food's interesting. Even when it's not particularly tasty, there's always fresh chilli about to help.
You can get a massage just about anywhere for under $5.
They have real beer [unlike China's 2.5 – 3.3%].
It's cheaper to buy two beers than a painkiller.
So, I've been medicating myself on the liquid.
The beaches look like postcards.
There are hot springs, cold springs and volcanoes.
Every day the sun sets more perfectly than the last!

It's the kind of place you can get lost in forever!
At this rate, I just might!

𝄑

*"If you travel by bus in the **Zamboanga** peninsula, you may not get kidnapped. But if you keep doing it, eventually you will."*

"The only reason I am alive today is because my family fled Zamboanga when I was young."

"It is too dangerous for you, do not go there…"

"You don't like your life then?"

I do like my life, I like it quite a lot; but there's only one ferry that runs between Borneo and The Philippines, and that ferry leaves from Zamboanga!

So, after an epic day of white water rafting in Cagayan Da Oro, I headed to the bus station and endured more warnings. "But mum it is so very dangerous for you," "I will pray for you mum", "Are you sure mum?" I will admit to being a quite concerned when strangers were asking: "And what is your currency in Africa? The Euro?" "You travel alone?" "Will you be meeting anyone there?" "Mum, do you carry a weapon?" It was more worrying when people asked if I spoke Basilica and then proceeded to talk about me on countless cellphones spotted across the bus. But, as we all know, when it is your time to go, it is your time to go. Fortunately, that 14-hour bus ride was not my time to exit the planet.

As I wandered the streets looking for cheap accommodation, a lady dragged me into her home and handed me a headscarf. She welcomed me into her family and called me her cousin from Pakistan. They walked with me in the middle of them. I felt like I had personalised bodyguards for the first time in my life. Only once did I have a gun pointed at me. Right at my forehead to be exact. In that moment my heart stopped, until the man smiled and said, "It's just plastic mum!"

This city is truly amazing - full of smiling people, churches and a 'musically gyrating dancing fountain!' I am proud to remain un-dead and un-kidnapped (hoorah!). After an evening karaoke session, I will set sail for Borneo. If all goes according to plan, I'll be converting to vegetarianism by the end of the week! Which is exactly why I am ending this here and going to join my temporary family for Sunday roast

THE BOTTOM OF THE FOOD CHAIN

5.

HE was a level of luxury my gypsy soul struggled to comprehend. I wasn't quite certain my reality wasn't a dream. I was eight months out of Australia, constantly on the road. Always moving toward some thing or place. Never certain where exactly I was headed. It was a constant mystery as to where I'd sleep and who I would meet in the day. After far too many imprudent adventures, I needed something different: a change of set. I'd planned to turn West from China, going through Tajikistan and Iran, but I'd received an offer that was too good to refuse.

Somewhere on the way to **Kudat**, Malaysian Borneo. 3 August 2012.

The day greeted me with good news and bad breakfast. At last, V-day[12] has arrived! After 5 and a half weeks of emails back and forth,

---

[12] In preparation for vegetarianism, every meal consumed was of a meaty nature! I didn't expect delays to continue as they did, and found myself overdosing on the substance. I was more than ready to take on this new phase of life!

I'm finally on my way to meet my crew. My heart's a little butterfly! Carrying a bulk delivery of marine electronics with me, I've been forced to break my travel religion and take a share-taxi. Asian time has run consistently; my 11:00 departure happened at 16:16. An hour later, the taxi broke down on the side of the road. And seeing that it's Ramadan, and the sun has just set, the new driver has just stopped the replacement vehicle for dinner...

It was 22:20 when I finally arrived to a beardly man smiling on the side of the road. After crossing the boatyard, 13 steps up a wobbly ladder remained to **Fiddler**: a 60-foot steel *sloop* that was about to become my home.

It was after midnight when we finally sat down for dinner. As I feasted on non-carnivorous-goodness, I looked across the table at my crew and knew that this next chapter was going to be epic!

Captain Kirk is wise beyond his years and, being extremely well-read, he is an expert on almost any topic. Apart from being our skipper, he is also our in-boat chef extraordinaire - without him, a diet of peanut butter and chilli-coated starches would prevail.

James, Kirk's nephew-brother, is our engineer, plumber, electrician and resident DJ - he likes to subject us to the wholesome lyrics of murderous gangster rock. Fortunately, he also fixes our toilets and fans when they break.

BOATYARD

My very first task was to build a wrench so we could install the *Fish Finder* (whatever that was). As interesting as the project sounded, I decided that time could be better spent borrowing said spanner. I ventured off to familiarise myself with the neighbours.

Tim and Sarah were in front of us on a *ketch*. Next to us was Jim (who later became known as "Battery Acid" when one exploded in his face). Henry, who had forgotten to lash his ladder to his boat, sat across from us with a broken femur. The "Spirulinas" who come from "Earth" and are known by "whatever name we wish to call them" were two boats across. They were busy completing a manifesto on how [wo]man can live on seaweed alone. The office held friendly Frank and pregnant Li. Between them, I managed to attain what was necessary to procure the *sonar* and returned victoriously.

After a sundowner on the deck I was ready for the Borneo LuckyFun Fair. It wasn't particularly "lucky" or "fun," but in all fairness, it was in Borneo. We gave up and joined the [under-age] boys who'd been *sand-blasting Fiddler* at the Golf Club for karaoke and a couple-too-many jugs of beer instead. The warped English and shoddier singing more than made up for the disappointment of the fair.

Day two had a rough start as I wobbled out of bed, braved the ladder and stumbled my way to "the spider"; as the toilet was affectionately known as (on behalf of its residents). After some chores, an afternoon swim across the bay had me forget that just that morning I had sworn to "never drink again!" The Spirulinas came for dinner and seemed surprisingly happy to eat food that wasn't plankton. Their facial expressions upon savouring real food again, revealed how much goodness they had been depriving themselves of, even if they professed otherwise while trying to convert us.

When I needed a break from the preaching (and to break the seal), I clambered down the ladder and ventured to the spider. I had just passed the café and was blissfully enjoying the stars when a pair of glowing eyes ran at me and caught me on the calf. IT bit hard and clung on until I kicked it off. I willed it to be a simple flesh wound (as my Chinese attacks had been), and stumbled into the light of the office. Still hopeful, I slowly lifted my flowy Thai hippy pants and stared as the blood began to pulsate through the chasms and cascade down my leg.

Kirk assured me he didn't mind my blood oozing onto the deck as he cleaned and dressed my wounds. He body-guarded me back and we found the bitch wallowing in guilt. We also found her new litter of puppies. Due to their cuteness, forgiveness was granted.

I had been a vegetarian for less than 48 hours and already I was at the bottom of the food chain. What used to be food[13] now wanted to eat me!

The office was very apologetic and claimed full responsibility, despite it being a stray dog. Li even drove me to the hospital. In my five years as a gypsy, this was my very first admission[14]. We managed to reconnoitre all the local clinics since they all just happened to be out of rabies shots. Eventually, we gave up the search. I braced myself for a tetanus vaccination and then opted to skip the six injections that formed an anaesthetic and simply got stitched up. The pain was far worse than the dog bite had been, and Li screamed as the doctor thrust his fat needle deep into my bloody flesh. He was kind enough to offer to make soup of the mutt, but seeing as I had become a vegetarian, I had to refrain.

Painting. Sanding. Learning to use power tools. Pretending like I knew what I was doing (although it was blatantly obvious that I didn't have a clue). As the days ticked by, I got sucked deeper into the community. Everyone had something to offer and teach. The yachties had each other's back.

Finally, after two weeks of dust, sweat, and [painted] tiers, the day arrived for us to put *Fiddler* where she belonged - back in the water - a

---

[13] Perhaps I'd been in Asia too long?

[14] Where I was the victim, and I wasn't checking anyone else in.

boatyard was no place for a sailing vessel of her distinction. We did the final touch-ups and evacuated the cat (and some of the spiders) that had taken up residence on board. We disconnected the water drainage systems we'd constructed, and eventually, our *travel-lift* arrived, and it became a mad dash to prop cardboard between the straps and the freshly painted *hull*. All set, we clambered aboard and started edging toward the slip-way. The Americans began shouting commands I couldn't understand – What was a *fender*? Which side was *Port*? What the flip does *lazarette* mean?

We christened the anchoring with the fitting *Lonely Island* song *I'm On a Boat*. Being the new recruit, I then dropped to my knees and scrubbed the deck. With a hard day's manual labour out of the way, and with a couple of pairs of scissors [and beers], I removed my stitches and settled into my new surroundings.

I was potty trained:

First, you flick the lever and do ten to twenty pumps to flush in the seawater to fill up the bowl (but not too full, that's asking for trouble).

When you're finished, you flush the bowl with another ten to twenty.

You then turn the lever and pump in more [sea] water to clean and clear the pipes.

Urination requires about 30 pumps. For any other "business," calculated discretion must be utilised.

Nothing goes in the bowl unless you eat it first. James made sure that I understood that if I block it, I was fixing it.

I had to learn how to walk again, as the ground constantly shifted beneath my feet. The first, and most valuable, rule of boating is:

"One hand for you, one hand for the boat."

No exceptions!

Everything on a boat has a very different, slightly more complicated or peculiar name:

The kitchen is the *galley*.

The dining room is the *saloon*.

My room was a *cabin*; my bed a *bunk*.

The toilet is the *head*.

Ropes are *lines* and some are *sheets*. Others are *halliards*[15] or *halyards*.

Buoys ("boys," which they called "boo-weys") are actually *fenders* unless they are lying in the water and you are using them as markers or *mooring balls*.

... And all this had to be learned in a whole new language: American!

The boys had all-but become permanent residents of Kudat, which made an embarking party all the more necessary. So, with a boat-load of vegetarian dishes and fellow boatyard dwellers, painters and friends, we celebrated our last night as boat people in style before waking up sailors.

DETOX

We fired up the engine and pulled up the anchor before we turned into the wind to raise the *mainsail*. We'd been a bit of a mess that morning, so the early departure had been closer to 16:00.

It was great to finally feel that cool ocean breeze and see the sails in all their splendour. It was good to be on the move again. The boat started tilting to the side. "What's wrong?!" I cried, clinging on for dear life. I soon learned that that angled way of life was something that I had to get accustomed to. That was *heeling*. That is sailing. That was... *blagggggggghhhh!* – Port side and I became well acquainted! It took only 4 hours and 24 minutes for my first vomit to spew forth, and I repeated it

---

[15] Not to be confused with "Hilliards" – they were the crew.

another 18 times before first light.

The second law of boating is, and this is an important one: "Always puke to lee;" or, in layman's terms:

Don't vomit into the wind (the same goes for peeing)!

I questioned whether sailing was for me. I didn't think my body could handle much more abuse, even if it was an effortless detox. Fortunately, James helped distract me through the night with life tales and deep and meaningful conversation. Distraction was paramount!

And then morning came with a perfect sunrise over Mt Kinabalu accompanied by calm seas. Life was all as it should be - beauty and hope returned to my being. The previous night felt as if it were simply a bad dream!

I sent the Americans to bed and took the first *watch* of my life. I was feeling quite smug about it too – this was a new sort of epic on my scales! But their rest and my reign were short-lived. In the not-too-distant waters lurked something mysterious: poles shooting out of the water. "Kirk Kirk!" I screamed. He abandoned the conditioning of his beard and ran up to the deck just in time to teach me how to disable the *autopilot* and steer the boat around the bamboo fishing poles that stretched across our path.

Brunei arrived all too quickly! But I'd done it. I'd finally sailed across countries. I knew the boys didn't think much of our two-day adventure, but for me, it was a milestone. It made the involuntary detox completely worthwhile and opened my eyes to a whole new world of possibilities!

RUNNING FROM RAISINS

Immigration was straight forward, and would have been easy, had they possessed a photocopy machine. They needed five typed copies of the crew list, but they couldn't offer us the services and they wouldn't let us into the country to find them either.

The 189 mile [in the wrong direction] voyage to Brunei served two purposes. Firstly, it was one of those strangely bizarre countries that few people visited and even fewer recommended; but it had an American embassy and James needed pages added to his passport. Secondly, it had ridiculously cheap fuel. The former was only a struggle to find and enter in working hours. The latter was a full-blown mission.

We arrived at the same time as Hari Raya[16], which was great for chanting mosques and fireworks, but bad for fuel. Nobody was doing any work. Fuel had to wait.

We used the time to sail up the Brunei River; an excellent voyage, apart from the countless near-death experiences we provided encroaching fishermen. We found a perfect anchorage about 17 miles up, just across from the palace.

Ashore, I set off on a forgiveness mission to attempt to atone for the soundtrack James had been subjected to in my poor performance as a seaman. I was going to buy him a pack of smokes. At the time, under the leadership of Sultan Haji Hassanal Bolkiah, there was a peculiar tobacco and alcohol ban. People could smoke, but they were not allowed to buy or sell cigarettes. The only place that people (only foreigners) were permitted to drink, was at the Royal Brunei Yacht Club. Even then, you had to bring your own drinks ashore with you.

The afternoon proved to be more of a mission than I'd anticipated. I scanned Bandar Seri Begawan (the capital), for smokers. There weren't many, and they themselves were quite hidden about their foul habits. It was a long-winded mission that contained far too many red herrings. I found a dealer who expertly under the tabled me a pack of Marlboro Reds for the ridiculous price of $37 (the asking price in duty-free Malaysia was just $2). I bought but one and returned triumphantly, proud of my day's

---

[16] Muslim New Year, the holiday that comes after a whole month of Ramadan fasting.

accomplishments.

With tobacco in his system, revitalised James joined us for an extravagant pizzeria dinner. We returned to our beautifully calm, city-lit anchorage where I stared out into the reflective abyss for far too long. The setting was so stunning that I couldn't possibly leave it and opted to sleep on the deck.

It's not the first time I've been awakened by the police. But this time was different - this time the Sultan himself ordered them to get rid of us...

And when the Sultan's personal police representatives kindly requested our rapid relocation that Sunday morning, we probably should have been expecting them sooner. It was hard not to stifle a giggle as they informed us, "The Sultana has asked that you leave immediately." Technically we were running from a raisin...

We sailed back down river and found ourselves in a prime location for the height of Hari Raya. The fireworks were spectacular, but my heart was far away. I was homesick. Worse than that, I was people sick. As much as I liked Kirk and James, I longed to be enjoying this with life-long friends [and a gorgeous Frenchman I'd met back in Kuala Lumpur].

I lounged around the yacht club all morning replying to emails and plotting a cycle route from Northernmost Norway to Southernmost South Africa, when James returned in a flurry. He'd not been as successful on the cigarette front and was in a critical state of nicotine withdrawal. It may have been illegal, but we fled to the less stringent islands of Malaysia for supplies.

47 slabs of cheese, 36 crates of beer, and 15 cartons of cigarettes later, we returned to Brunei victorious and had the anchor down by 04:00. We dug deep into our supplies to celebrate our success and then tried to get a

bit of sleep. The fuel run began at nine.

Royal Brunei Yacht Club, Thursday 23 August 2012

Today I used a washing machine for the first time in three and a half months. It's a huge accomplishment that makes this world a happier place! I also finally got that dirty travel companion of mine a passport. And so it is that Teddy Teddison, from the Untied States of Teddistan, has become an official being.

I was feeling particularly good about life; until Kirk returned to the anchorage.

Fuel cost 55c a litre off the floating station, whereas in town it was only 26c. It was first suggested that we save money and fill *Fiddler* by bicycle, but logistically that was going to take us weeks. *Fiddler*'s tanks held just over 2000 litres. We needed a car.

With Kirk came the first 575 litres of diesel. With a 25-litre jerry can in each hand, we scuttled from the car, down to the water, over the dock, and into the dinghy. When the dinghy was full, we returned her to *Fiddler*, where we syphoned the fuel into her tanks and returned the empty canisters.

The second trip ran smoother, but our arms ached. That night I broke the rules and celebrated what would possibly be the last movement of my arms by ordering fish and chips (Shhhh!! - Being on *Fiddler*, I had to pretend to be a vegetarian!)

Day two was tough. We loathed the smell of the liquid. Our bodies ached. We did a third fuel run and then a fourth. We'd passed the 2000-litre-mark, but Kirk wanted more. We scrummaged a few 55-gallon (208 litres) rainwater barrels so that we could have a third day of fun. All the quality time spent with the driver had Kirk actually considering taking the man aboard [as a "stowaway"]. He'd imagined crossing the Indian and the Atlantic Oceans so that he could fulfil his life-dream by swimming ashore to Canada, and starting a new life there.

FAIRY-TALE CREATURES AND FEROCIOUS MEN.

We island hopped through Labuan for supplies and Tiga to climb a volcano and set fire to muddy methane bubbles. On Snake Island, land-sickness had me falling all over the dangerous endemic grey-striped sea-snakes that slithered through the rocks. We called in at Kota Kinabalu for an afternoon, and then returned to **Kudat** to pick up another parts order. That "bitch" was still alive; so I was probably rabies-free!

Henry had used his disability time wisely and built a fibreglass washing machine that worked magic by simply dragging behind the boat. I was so impressed by it, that when I leaned over to get a closer look, I dropped my brand new $4 sunglasses in the water. Tim and Sarah had unfortunately hit a submerged container and had returned to fix their propeller and their hull. The Spirulinas had started sneaking real food on the sly. *Fascination*, a South African boat, not only invited me in for a beer but for *biltong* and *boerewors* too! I was actually glad to be back.

At low tide, I swam over to Henry's to retrieve my sunnies. About three-quarters of the way there he started screaming: "Get out of the water!" I thought he was joking, but he persisted in his Aussie accent: "Get out the water! Climb on board!" The yelling had attracted the curiosity of the neighbouring boats who'd all come out to see what the racket was about. Some say that it was a giant sea-snake that had been chasing me. Others claimed that it was a salt-water crocodile. Someone else proposed that it was an enormous goanna. Whatever it was, it only left my trail, when I left the water.

The rain arrived while I tried to find the bravery required to swim back (I gave up on the glasses) so I escaped inside for a beer. I was very much enjoying touring other people's boats, and found myself particularly amazed by Henry's. He'd managed to store a Royal Enfield under his saloon table.

A red moon rose as Kudat finally drifted out of sight forever.

At first light, the captain commanded that we stop in the name of a snorkel! We followed orders and took it in turns keeping *Fiddler* at a hover while we swam in to explore Pilau Lihiman. The water was so beautiful that I did a second lap of the island. On the furthermost side, I wandered my way straight into three sharks and had a rather unsettled return. I'd definitely become a little more fearful in my older age.

Sat in **Sandakan**, where I had first stepped foot on Borneo, had me feeling like I was there for the first time. Time seemed to be multiplying. Days held so many adventures that they felt like years.

The clock struck midnight and we were off again. Kirk really enjoyed late-night departures. I took the first watch and enjoyed the infinite sky of stars. I tried to awaken the captain to take over, but there was no luck. Instead, I watched the sunrise and the morning dolphins and the rainbow. Eventually I fell off the helm seat sound asleep. I should've known better, for no [wo]man's an island; but Bum Bum is - we sailed straight past it!

Mabul was a rainbow of fish, turtles and coral. I'd never seen anything quite as spectacular. But I accidentally knocked myself out while trying to clean the *cockpit*, and the massive lump on my head prevented my mask from sealing. I had to give up the unbelievable underwater for a while. Instead, I explored by kayak and foot.

I stared out at that distant oil rig for days before I finally recovered and found the courage to swim over to it. I surveyed the waters below and clambered up, casually greeting any and everybody I passed as I ascended the many stairwells to the top. It was much higher than it had looked. The bystander's faces seemed to suggest that it was a bad idea. Kirk was certain it was and had the dinghy ready for rescue. I hoisted myself skyward and found myself in free-fall to the tropical waters below. The crowd of onlookers cheered as I dropped. They "oohed." They "ahhed." But nobody followed. I felt free. I felt liberated. I felt slime as I splashed into a school of unsuspecting fish.

James' birthday was the first to be celebrated on board. It was quite the party. It's amazing how much happiness comes from a day spent on, in, and under the water.

Happiness is but a fleeting emotion. It comes as it pleases and leaves without saying goodbye. The world rocked as I climbed out of bed the following day. Despite going through the motions and two cups of coffee, there was something horribly erroneous about the day. We sailed onwards to **Tawau**, but nothing amazed me. Everything was blah. I even skipped my daily sundowners and hid so that I didn't have to introduce myself to the neighbourhood when we arrived. I looked over at the yachty Kirk was conversing with and felt my stomach churn. Then I burst. Tears came streaming down my face and I had to make a run for it. James was working near my bunk so the only feasible hiding place was the head where I hid for the greater part of an hour before wiping off the evidence and exiting with a feigned togetherness.

Tawau was an interesting little town with its New Strange Enterprise and Fook Hing Loong Enterprise and Pizza Hut. James's birthday celebrations would not have been complete without pizza. We headed back for an early night. "So, this is where the party is?" Jim asked a pretty group of gaggling Chinese Malay girls sitting near our dinghy at the Royal Tawau Yacht Club. Next thing we knew we had beers shoved into our hands (Kirk, a teetotaller, included) and it was 02:00.

I woke up drunk. By the time we'd reached immigration, the hangover was arriving. By the time we'd been cleared out of Malaysia, it hit. Hard! We changed the last of our Ringgit to Rupiah. We were about to hop in the dinghy and depart Malaysia when we bumped into the neighbour. It took only a couple of minutes to realise why I hadn't liked him. "I'm not a paedophile," he said ".... but Indonesian children – nom nom nom!" ... "My fourth wife, who I married when I was 40, she was still 17 – sexiest woman alive!" He continued to tell Kirk how tight his current wife's pussy was. When Kirk gave him that look, he shot a smile over to his wife who was waiting patiently in their dinghy. "It's okay, she's deaf." My blood pressure boiled. James put a hand on my shoulder to calm me down and hold me back. There's far too many of his calibre on this planet!

Flashback to **JAVA**, Indonesia. December 2011

I returned to a locked guesthouse to hear her screams. The Frenchman was drunk again. He beat her again. "Why don't you leave him?" I begged as I helped clean up the mess.

"When he gets drunk, he gets very angry. And when he is angry, he beats me. And when he beats me, he normally locks up the house so that nobody can hear my screams. I can't leave because I have nowhere else to go," she exclaimed.

It was her guesthouse, in her name. Foreigners weren't allowed to own businesses. As a woman, she didn't have any rights. He had all the money. He even locked up her jewellery. He made sure that if she ever left him, she'd do it in only the clothes she was wearing on her back.

"What about the police?" I asked looking at her bruised face and broken spirit. "Twice he was so drunk that he tried to kill me. The first time he tried to strangle me with the iron cord and the second time he tried to suffocate me with a pillow. He was arrested, but he paid off the police and was released after only three days."

It was "normal." Simply a "domestic dispute." Husbands owned their wives. Husbands were allowed to beat their wives. Her family had thrown her out because she slept with a man before marriage. In desperation, she'd sought out another foreigner to take her in. She had two boyfriends at the same time. The English man was kind but the Frenchman wanted to stay in Indonesia...

Her situation was far from unique. There were a half-dozen other women who had been thrown out of their communities down at the beach bars alone. They all dreamed of finding the right foreigner to "save" and cherish them. But their desperation didn't afford time for choice.

Her words stuck with me:

"Women have no rights and local women even less."

I jumped in the ocean to try and wash the sailor's filth and the hangover from my being. By 13:15, we were on our way. I took the 20:00-00:00 watch and life was pretty good until the final hour. I was just about to summon the captain when he came running to the deck. We'd hit a storm. Waves crashed over the *bow* as I steered and scanned for fishing boats and shallows while the boys fought to bring in the sails. It felt like it would never end. But eventually, with three sets of hands, the sails came in, the route resumed, and the rains got harder.

The others had the magical ability to fall back to sleep, so I resumed the watch. But after I'd run inside to find wet weather gear, things started churning in my stomach. At 00:16 Kirk's exceptional aloo-gobi dinner came gushing back out. Kirk took over and I escaped inside to hibernate. Overcoming seasickness is all about timing. You need to lie down and fall asleep straight after you puke, otherwise, you're just going to get sick again. I missed my fifth sleep window. And the sixth. Eventually, the winds started dying down and I found rest on the couch in the *pilothouse*. I woke up every hour and in some of them I didn't puke.

As I sat staring into the new land of adventure that lay ahead - with an empty stomach, and an aching head - I couldn't help but smile.

Saturday, 15 September 2012. 07:29.

It's weird how you start on a simple mission that becomes something mammoth. A three-month trip stretches past five years. A simple quest for Spain becomes cross-continental cycling, hitching, biking, stow away-ing and far too many [right] turns in the wrong direction. Life has thrown so many incredible people, beautiful places, and crazy twists at me that I wouldn't change a thing. Life is flipping awesome (not so much while sick at sea though). I think I must be one of the luckiest people alive - maybe even God's favourite.

6.

FROLICKING IN THE WAKE

AFTER visiting immigration twice, customs thrice, the airport, the coastguard and the ferry port, we were told to wait until Monday to clear immigration.

Scores of children followed us as we *Pied Pipered* our way through the maze of markets, hunting the dingy docks for our new recruit. One jetty. Two jetties. Three. Eventually, we gave up and took to the water to get a clearer view. In the distance, we saw the blond hair and fair skin of the Fin glistening in the tropical sunlight.

Memo is a real sailor. And an even more real human being. She is free-spirited, wild and strong. Proud to be an anarchist. It's great having another female on board! The only downside are the ages: Kirk's 47. James 37. I'm 27. She really ought to be 17...

THE LIFE OF A DEAD KITTEN

Tarakan, Indonesia. 20 September 2012

On our second day as illegal Indonesian immigrants, we found a kitten.
A kitten so small its eyes hadn't opened yet. Mewing helplessly under a
tree. Squirming at the pain caused by the puncture wounds in its neck, as
the ants bit their way into its flesh.
Next to it lay its dead brother.

We just stood and stared. Eventually, James bent down, picked it up and
stroked the ants off its trembling body.
The silence was deafening. There were big decisions to make here.
We could put it back down and walk away as if nothing had happened.
We could try to find someone else to take it in.
We could help it find rest faster.
Or we could get completely involved and do what we could to nurse it
into catfulness.

The silence shattered as our footsteps wandered off in search of milk.
"Can we call her Ninja?" I asked, "because Ninjas never die."
And that's how "Ninja Taracat" came into our lives.

ƒ

Sat on the deck, I started jotting down a list of random life memories.
I tried to swat a mosquito and accidentally threw my pen overboard; and
went to get a new one.

Down below, Ninja TC had stopped crying and started taking in milk.
At last!

Coated in deet-infused mosquito repellent, holding a brand-new pen, I
continued with my list.
I thought long and hard about what I'd be doing with my life if I'd taken a
career seriously, or if I'd never caught the travel bug, or if I'd settled
down and bought a goat or...
I suddenly remembered what we all know but seldom consider:
It doesn't matter what we do or where we do it. It doesn't matter what our
past has held - it's up to us to make sure we make the most of every
second of the now for however long we have to live it.

Solomon, allegedly the wisest man to have ever lived, once said:
*"Young man, it's wonderful to be young! Enjoy every minute of it. Do
everything you want to do. Take it all in. But remember you must give an
account to God for everything that you do."* - Ecclesiastes 11:9

And whether you're religious or not, I think it's an important thing to
grab onto.
The only person you can blame for a life filled with regrets is yourself.

James stayed up all night nursing Ninja. In the early hours of the
morning, she died.
At least we knew that everything that could be done for her was.
She may not have lived very long and I was too scared to get to know her
well. I didn't want to have to say goodbye. But she made an impact on
my life all the same.

You only die once. Make sure your life ends doing something you love.
Make sure you die happy.
But please don't die any time soon!

❢

11:14, and the anchor was up. Wild seas converted to crystal clear waters. Floating debris transformed into flying fish. The smog evaporated into clear skies, and by nightfall there were billions of stars where the mosquitoes used to be.

I woke up in **Kakaban**. We swam through a most exceptional coral display and clambered onto the shore. The island was a treacherous rainforest: wild and overgrown. In the middle lay Jelly Fish Lake where the four species are said to have evolved to become stingless due to lack of predators[17]. The teeming jellies floated in abundant aimlessness. When you somersaulted around them, they got spun about and confused senseless. Head-on collisions bounced them backwards, and when you twirled them around, they spun-top away. I spent hours playing with the critters. I'd found paradise!

We needed to arrive in **Derawan** in the daylight, so we did a slow sail over. So slowly, that we let the 0.0 knots of wind do its work and allow the current to drag us backwards. The 17.5 miles stretched to over 20 before the wind finally filled the sails. I sat on the deck leisurely sipping a beer and sampling cloves, discussing life as a stormy night passed overhead, transforming into a very impressive electrical storm.

Fish of every shape, form, and school abounded; as did turtles. We went on a shore excursion to watch them haul themselves onto the beach to lay their eggs. In the still of the night, I heard a rustle and turned to see the cause. Horror filled my eyes as Deja-vu struck; a mutt was running in for the attack. James leapt in front of me to scare the dog off. It fled, but my heart continued to pound.

Unable to sleep, I lay on the deck watching the shooting stars be

---

[17] However, I'm not sure if that is entirely true, the first one I licked stung my tongue.

swallowed by storm clouds. When the rains started, I crept downstairs and hauled myself into my bunk listening to the pitter-patter drench the steel deck above me. What an exceptional world I was losing myself in.

Sangalaki: The island's only flaw was that it was too beautiful. We'd just left the boat when the manta rays approached. I dove straight in and the mantas swarmed around me in a loop; and then vanished.

We landed ashore and I squinted into the distance. "It couldn't be, could it?" I ventured closer. The only other people on the tiny blip of an island were Luke (who I'd been seeing when I lived in London) and his wife. And they were on their honeymoon! Of all the places in the world to run into someone... God really does have a sense of humour!

Maratua welcomed us with Noordin, a friendly character who helped himself on board, and then just sat staring. "Don't worry," said James, "In ten years' time you'll be a pervert too."

I finally started getting the hang of being the boy's rescue driver as they drift-dived. But I kept losing them as I was captivated by underwater anomalies that seemed to be placed there purely for my distraction. The plethora of tropical fish sparkled brightly against the rubbled coral. Everywhere I looked, beauty abounded around me. Even "One Tree Island," in its barrenness held a certain sense of wonder.

I am in a constant need of crying in amazement, of drooling in dumbfoundedness, and leaping in happiness! But still, something is missing. Even with my new-found boat family to share this with, I miss people all over the world. Little fragments of my heart are floating scattered about on distant oceans waiting to be captured so that one day I can be complete again.

It's a terrible thing, being surrounded by too much beauty. It makes your mind wander. I've thought long and hard about the things I am missing out on. That could have been me on my honeymoon...

Mantas, hammerheads, the bluest waters swarming with unicorn and "down syndrome" fish, eels and fluorescent coral. Life is mellifluous. I'm happy to be exactly where I am! (But flip, do I need a hug!)

❡

We were Southern Hemisphere bound! James summoned me to take over at 06:00. And by 06:21 the *lumba lumba* (dolphins) that were meant to be all over Maratua, finally decided to show their face. One pod. Two. Three. I was trying to count them so that I could update my diary tallies when I realised that they weren't dolphins at all. We'd finally found whales!

The second and third hour of my watch trailed by too slowly. I was in an almost-sleep when *WHAM,* two of the four pulleys that held the dinghy broke and a mad retrieval operation ensued. The winds and waters calmed enough to allow me the luxury of a rehumanizing shower when Mo took over. I walked into the galley and was just about to make lunch when she called from the cockpit: "Um guys... the sail just broke." We ran up to the deck to find the main ripped in half.

The day's dramas weren't done yet. First, the toilet paper landed up in the sink. Then in a similar feat, the "loo roll" engine filter decided to completely break itself.

Beer o'clock was well-deserved! So was the foot massage that James delivered in the evening. For the first time in three days, I finally slept.

I woke up to the sweet smell of equatorial pancakes, which are like normal pancakes but green and in equatorial shapes. We were still four minutes North, which gave me time for a couple of cups of coffee as well as time to check the drainage theory. If you were wondering: water flows clockwise down a sink at a minute North.

The purple seas swarmed rigorously around me as I tried in desperation to locate South and more importantly, the captain. Clearly, the breathing of fresh Southern hemisphere air was too much for him to handle. Only a few feet before the equator, he'd hurled himself mercilessly over the railings and into the ocean depths. In an attempt to save the sharks from indigestion, I'd leapt overboard too.

00.00.000 N, 119.37.773 E. The swells were bigger than they'd looked from the deck; but there in the distance, glistened what could only be his beardfullness (or, I suppose, a very large hairy fish). Eventually, *Fiddler* returned to rescue us; but Kirk's craziness had contaminated the crew and now everyone wanted to swim the equator. We about-shipped and crossed the line again, doing it in the same attire with which we came into the world.

Teddy revealed that he was really King Neptune. James was cursed for not wearing his underpants on the outside [as is allegedly common practice for the back-to-front upside-downness of the South]. After nine months in the North, I was finally back in the home hemisphere. The beer was cooler. The air was sweeter. The popcorn was crispier. But water still went down the drain the same way. When the moon finally made an appearance, we bust another equatorial legend. We still saw the same side.

"We're heading for rain," came the cry from the cockpit as I abandoned the kettle to batten down the hatches. It rained hard. When the blue skies returned, so did the dolphins that were so plentiful that I'd mistaken them for a tidal stream of driftwood.

We ran out of bread - we learned to make our own. We ran out of fruit – we resorted to taking vitamin C tablets and munching on popcorn[18]. We ran out of contact with the outside world – we learned to survive without

---

[18] It's got seeds, it's kind of a fruit.

Wikipedia and *Facebook*, and instead connected deeply with the humans onboard.

It was just another day in the grand expansive world of the ocean. The seas were calm and the winds were about as functional as we could have hoped. All of a sudden, without warning, *Fiddler* went berserk. I sat at the helm watching her shudder and flicker and refuse to cooperate. All hands were on deck as we tried to get to the bottom of it. "What the hell is that?" asked Mo pointing at a dark mass spewing forth from *Fiddler*'s ass. A submarine. *Fiddler* had given birth to a submarine! None of us had even suspected that she was pregnant. In fact, none of us had even known that boats could get pregnant. But seeing is believing. I suppose we may never find out who the father was though.

Staring in disbelief, I offered to take the offspring for a test drive. James cut the umbilical cord and I delved into the ocean depths. So that's where all the whales were hiding! I brought her in for closer inspection. They seemed to be having a secret gathering. I glanced down at the control panel and pushed the *translate whale* button. "And that's how we'll sink them," said the ring leader, "and take their ship." "And what of the crew?" asked a youngster. "What of them?" Sneered the elder. "Fish food, jewellery and dental floss."

The meeting was adjourned.

I needed to warn the others, but telecommunications were not yet linked with the mother ship. I needed help! I recruited an army of dolphins who led *Fiddler* back to Langkawi while Ninja-dolphins distracted the whales. We needed to get them to unfamiliar territory. We stood no chance against the warring whales on their own turf.

We found Water World, and it was perfect. As the whales followed us up ginormous water slides into shallow splash pools, they beached themselves left, right and centre. They turned the watery playground into a truly "Whale of a Time" kind of place.

I woke up very confused but found we were still heading for Makassar. With coffee in hand, I headed to the cockpit where I found a worried Kirk still buzzing from the cup he'd drunk 19 hours earlier. The autopilot had died, so he quickly schooled me on hand-steering under sail, before he abandoned me to brave the intricacies of the engine room in order to try and find out what was going on. While he did this, I lost the *charts*, I lost the *bearings*, I lost the *radar*. It was just me trying to read the wind while attempting to sip coffee. A full hour passed and I was still only halfway through the cup. Kirk solved the problem eventually but still we kept a manual helm, I needed the practice. And good practice it was. Life became a computer game of dodging the wooden fishing boats that swarmed us.

The evening cracked in with a beautiful sunset and an even more impressive rising moon. A shooting star illuminated the whole sky before we played a little game I termed "Survival," as we dodged and darted tankers and container ships. Finally, at 12:46 – 615 Nautical miles (113 hours) away from Maratua, we dropped anchor.

Makassar was an interesting place filled with Chinese shops and strange people doing tai chi, yoga, and other exercises in the parks. It was the first commercial civilisation we'd visited in weeks, and we were overjoyed to be able to spend money again. The boys almost traded me for 2000 litres of fuel, but fortunately, we didn't quite have space yet after the Brunei refill.

It was a big day! *Ted*, the movie, was making its debut appearance on the cinema screen. As a 27-year-old lugging around a giant stuffed toy, I felt compelled to see what it was about. We turned it into a family outing, dragging Teddy along for a giggle. After the show, people swarmed me for photos and autographs. With the language barrier, all I could do was laugh and sign. We enjoyed a pizza dinner and, in true Kirkly custom, we did a midnight departure.

After drowning my iPod, I crawled into bed at 04:47 feeling relieved to be done with the day. The evils had only just begun. When I opened the fridge for breakfast inspiration, Kirk's three-bean noodle-soup salad (packed to the brim) slammed onto my foot before exploding onto the floor. The milk I poured in my coffee was sour. When I tried to go back to bed that night, we *tacked* and I got thrown off my bunk across to the *starboard* side. I collided with the desk, before bouncing back onto the stairs and eventually falling to the floor.

I was excited that yet another new day was upon us, but as I arrived in the cockpit to take up watch, Kirk beamed at me, "Would you like to discuss differential equations?" "No, I would not. Not at 04:00. Not before coffee." I think I broke his heart!

Flores arrived just in time. I was shocked to find it held tourists, a breed of human I'd long thought went extinct. With the strong scent of meat present in the air, I abandoned the others as they ventured off on their pizza quest, doing the dirty. Evil never tasted so good!

Rindja[19], Indonesia. Sunday, 7 October 2012

I've spent a good portion of my grown-up life chasing mythical creatures: mermen, unicorns, leprechauns, "the one", and now a new sort of quest has evoked me – THE DRAGON HUNT!

And for this quest, I had GOALS:

- Light a cigarette with dragon fire.
- Ride a Komodo dragon.
- Lick a Komodo dragon.
- Actually see a dragon.

---

[19] Or Rinca or Rincha. In fact, there were almost a dozen varied spellings for the island.

They may have been optimistic, but they were goals.

Safi met us at the dinghy dock and before we could argue, he became our guide. We took on the friendly guide for two reasons. A) We had to. B) A man with a big stick to fight off dragons is better than no man with a big stick to fight off dragons.

The island was as mysterious as we'd hoped: a desolate mass teeming with deer, wild horses and macaque. It only took a few meters before we were met by a valor of dragons. They were as big as I'd envisioned, but the docility made it hard to imagine them ever running at 18km/hour. Suddenly one rose majestically, took a dump, lashed its forked tongue, and lay back down again.

We ventured deeper into the island and learned that almost all humans who had ever been bitten, had died. Our guide continued to explain that you're much more likely to be bitten when you're having your period because dragons can smell blood five kilometres away. "Another downside of being a woman," James mocked. After they bite, they follow the victim for up to two weeks until death by infection. What a horrible way to go!

Fortunately, we all survived. We enjoyed the experience so much that we arranged to meet Safi again in the morning. 07:00 sharp.

Safi abandoned us. But we found another guide and followed him into the abyss (after negotiating the abysmal fee). Solitary dragons lay hidden in bushes [and the young in trees] guarding their nests and digesting their bellies. They ate but once a month. When they did eat [monkeys/ buffalo/ horses/ humans] they ate everything – fur and bones included. It probably explained their hairy poo. The guide nearly had a heart attack as he watched me lick it.

It was exceptionally hot, but the day was beautiful. We seemed to walk forever before we finally made it to the top of a hill where exceptional views awaited us. We sat down to gaze upon the prettiness. Unfortunately, less-exceptional views were seen too… I wandered over to a nearby cluster of trees; and sure enough, my worst fears were realised. I'd started my period. The second of the month. Fortunately, women are always prepared for these things; but I tried to use my drinking water to wash the marks off my baby blue shorts. Only there wasn't very much water left. I ended up just smudging it and making my femininity issues far worse. I had nothing to change into and nothing to tie around my waste. I had two options. I could return to the others, explain and apologise for being a woman and putting their lives at risk. Or, I could chicken out and hope nobody (including the dragons) noticed. I opted for the latter.

Our "guide" got us lost again. So we sat down under a tree and waited for him to work out his bearings. We had just resumed walking, when he glanced in my direction and his whole face went white (which is quite a feat for an Indonesian). "The dragon. It will come!" He cried. In what was undoubtedly life's most embarrassing moment; the boys grabbed sticks for protection and the guide exercised extreme caution. His face looked like that of a man who knew his end was nigh. So much for me wanting to ride one of those beautiful beasts!

Overjoyed to still be alive, I lay on the deck watching the stars fling fiery balls across the sky. Jim came out to join me and I wasn't entirely sure I was glad about it. He shattered my fallacies by informing me that shooting stars were not dying stars, but tiny meteorite dust particles. So many false beliefs had been pointed out that I was going to leave *Fiddler* far too intelligent. And what hope was there for an intelligent woman?

Komodo treated us to violent landscapes: pink sandy beaches and dry mountainous rolling hills. We reckoned that there may have been a fire ban in place with it being the dry season. There was still hope that the dragons may actually breathe fire. As we explored alone, our hearts raced as we expected the giant creatures to approach from every direction. A second day exploring brought us to caves, cliffs, jagged rocks and beehives. When night fell, we were greeted with phosphorescence that glowed so violently that we could finish writing our names in the water before it dissipated. The stars sparkled brightly in the forgotten dragon world. It was a truly magical place!

As we sailed off into the abyss (destination unknown) insomnia struck hard and I managed to sit and chat through all four watches. On James's morning, I sat in the cockpit with my feet up sipping a chilli coffee shake. He christened a nearby island "The Kingdom Jimland" and spun *Fiddler* off to explore it. On the way back to course, we *gybed* and ripped through yet another *reef* of sail, leaving our main with only one.

Even though we were dishing out every joke we had ever heard and the puns were flowing, the days drifted by incredibly slowly.

Fun fact: Relative to body size; barnacles have the biggest penis.

We tried to *heave to* and head for the **Gili Islands**, but got pulled off course by the current and went to Lombok instead. The place teemed overwhelmingly with tourists. In desperation, we fired up the engines and *beat* back.

While I was far from a self-sufficient sailor, I found solace in the fact that I was an excellent anchor location scout. I perfected the art of jumping off the boat to find sandy anchorages amidst the bountiful corals. In the Gilis it was more of a case of checking the moorings. You didn't want to tie 18 tons of steel to something that couldn't support a surfboard! Gili T was our first failed attempt at mooring. Gili Meno the second. But at Gili Air, we finally came right and were treated to a gorgeous island with experiences to match.

The islands were about as simple as boat life, but they came with a vast assortment of colourful people to talk to. We spent days exploring the lands by foot and their watery expanses by dinghy.

I woke up in **Bali.** It took me 11 months and six days to do the full loop of East Asia. I was back to where I'd escaped Australia from. We had a lot to do, but the priority was the mainsail. Getting it off and packed into its little bag took the whole morning. Shopping took the afternoon; and the sunset stole the evening, making the day more or less bearable.

The following day was less so. The boat needed a wash and a polish. For the first time, I wished to be on a smaller boat. *Fiddler* shined; but my hands were peeling and blotching from the chemicals and I had a headache from all the ammonium. Waxing the boat was a far better experience, even if it took James and I the whole day to do just the deck! The following day was the windows and I.

I took a much-needed break and wandered ashore. I sat eating *Nasi Campur*[20] at a *warung*[21] before a friendly face arrived and gave me the hug I'd been craving for months! I hadn't seen Brad since I had hitchhiked in his van in Australia. We had a lot to catch up on. We enjoyed a Bintang before we hopped on his bike and headed to Uluwatu, where he'd based himself for the month. After the Saturday night beach party, I crawled into a real bed [on land] for the first time in 79 days. I awoke with a jolt, quite certain that I'd fallen asleep on watch and crashed us into land.

Again I'm tempted to change my plans… Maybe I should just hang around Indonesia a little longer? Buy a board, rent a flat, and write a book? I mean what does South Africa really hold for me? Do I need to head back? If we are even going there… If we delay any more we will be too late to cross the Indian Ocean and perhaps…

---

[20] A delicious rice dish you really should try!

[21] A little restaurant or food stall.

I gave Kirk a call to see when I was expected back. "Noonish tomorrow" it was. This gave me another day to explore, get a massage, replace my iPod, hit the beach to surf and party. It was all fun and games until I had a look at the shopping list he'd sent through.

When I could carry no more and had over-abused my new friend, the security guard, to watch the bountiful surplus of purchasings I had acquired, I called it a day. He was kind enough to call me a legitimate meter taxi. I loaded up, jumped in the shotgun seat for a better view of Bali, and off we sped.

The friendly Cabbie introduced himself as Made ("Maa-day"). Like the rest of Bali's population, it means "second born" and comes after "Whyan" ("firstborn"). "You want to stop for massage?" he asked. "Only cost you 70,000." I declined. The next time I looked in his general direction, I caught his hand down between his legs. *Guys scratch themselves all the time*, I tried to justify my thoughts. As it continued, there was no denying that he was jerking off.

What do you do when you are the only passenger in a taxi and your driver's jerking off?

I leapt out of the cab the second we arrived. But then the stray dogs started to swarm. I wasn't sure if I was safer with the bitches or being Made's bitch. Kirk arrived like a knight to whisk me (and my many many shoppings) away. It was good to be reunited with the family, even if they wouldn't let me hear the end of their hysterical cabbie jokes.

I wasn't used to having a passenger, but I was glad to be back in the driver's seat. Memo had tried her hand at a second scooter but given up in the name of crazy Balinese traffic. The rental guys had suggested Sanur as a decent supplies destination. We wondered if it was a good idea after reading the article James had found about the [Hard-Cock Wonderful] "Men of Sanur."

We stopped only for the evil of *Makaan Ayum* (food chicken) before shopping got a little out of hand. Although we were very successful on the account of items I'd failed to purchase the previous day, I think we may have underestimated certain practicalities! When Mo tried to clamber on the back of the bike, she fell over with my colossal backpack pinning her down like an inverted tortoise. People swarmed to laugh and help. That was but the start of the problems. Kirk's pack was meant to wedge between my legs and still give me the freedom to drive... We got pulled over by the cops. But I had decided two things already:

1) There was no possible way either of us were getting off that bike until we arrived at the anchorage.

2) We were not going to pay any bribes.

The officer tried every line in the book and didn't buy any of my excuses until I pulled the fake tears, at which point he gave up and waved us on.

The final shopping spree was fresh produce. It was a tough one because we only had one fridge and we weren't sure how long things would last. Onions, garlic, potatoes, cabbage, peppers, carrots, fruit... I settled on five kilograms of chilli[22]. Everything was washed, brought aboard, and stowed away. Our sails were repaired and the boat was prepped for sea.

It's our last day in Bali. We've checked out. This is my last chance to get anything that I've forgotten. It's a scary thing with all that ocean looming before me! What will I miss? What will I want to make hard days better? What do I need?

---

[22] And still was not certain that this was enough.

After a long walk, I finally licked land goodbye and tried to get an early night.

THE END OF MY WORLD

Serangang, Bali; 22 October 2012

TEN.... NINE.... EIGHT... Thoughts are racing around my head like a giant disorganized herd of pregnant water buffalo playing ice hockey with sharpened samurai swords.

Are we really ready? What have we forgotten? Will we have enough food, water and basic supplies? Will the back-alley stitching on our three reefs of broken sail hold for the entire 5800 miles home?

SEVEN.... SIX... Asia is incredible.... I miss land already... and there are so many epic people about, so much good food to eat and too many good surfs to be had...

So many places I haven't yet been.... So much more to see... So much more to lick... Australia's so close I could almost swim there... it's not too late to abandon ship and turn in the wrong direction... Again...

FIVE... FOUR...I haven't been home for two years. What happens if people have changed too much? Or worse: what if they haven't changed at all? Will people even recognize me? Apart from my Nigerian skin tan, am I even still an African?

THREE... TWO... There are so many people I meant to talk to, so much I had to say...

How many more birthdays will I miss? How many more people will get married? And engaged? And born? And intoxicated? And knighted?

What major events will be happening around the world in the next month? Maybe the world ends, and we get left behind...

ONE: It's the very end. Six months of direction change, hitching, boat work and island hopping have finally brought us to the ocean crossing. In the next 24 hours, we'll be raising anchor and launching into the unknowns of The Indian Ocean.
Our world is about to shrink to the confines of the ship and the marine life that surfaces. And the stars.
That's all we'll have until Reunion.
There'll be no popping in to grab some fresh bread and chilli.
No skyping mum a quick "I love you". No Facebook (oh! The horrors!). No doctors (hopefully we won't need them). No sneaking in a non-vegetarian meal on the sly. No human interaction apart from the crew (luckily they're a nice bunch).

And while I'm so terrified that I couldn't bring myself to sleep last night, I'm pretty sure this is exactly what I'm meant to be doing with my life right now. I know we'll be okay.
And I know that for the rest of the world life will go on as normal as we blip up and down on the vortexy abyss of ocean blues.
But know that you'll be severely missed, dear human!
If you get a chance, spare us a thought, a wish, and a prayer.
I'll post out the infrequent message in a bottle... See you on the other side. See you in Africa.

ZERO...

7.

THE GREAT VORTEX OF BLUE

SO much for first light, it was 10:00 sharp when we finally raised the anchor. By 12:04 we'd passed the first five *waypoints* and the next one lay 3512 miles (which is 6504.224 kilometres, for nautical miles are not like regular ones) away.

Stocked up with canned vegetables, a freezer full of chillies, enough tofu and tempeh to circumnavigate the globe [and the rest of the planets] at least 27 times, we watched land shrink into the distance as we've ventured deeper into the great vortex of blue.

As land vanished from sight, the dolphins arrived from every direction. The sun set magnificently and we rocked gently off to sleep in the lulling sway of *the trade winds*.

The 04:00 to 08:00 watch was a good one. The moon sank before the sun rose with a bow full of dolphins, starting a perfect day.

They told me that we'd set the sails and then sit back and relax. They weren't lying! The whole sailing thing was literally a breeze!

Life was pretty much perfect, until I tried to put music on my new mp3 player. The boat rocked, leaving the remnants of my morning coffee to be drunk by my computer. Computers don't like coffee.

Days were broken up into watches:

00:00 – 04:00 The Mid Watch (The worst one).

04:00 – 08:00 Sunrise Watch (By far the best).

08:00 – 12:00 Morning Watch.

12:00 – 16:00 Noon Watch.

16:00 – 18:00 First Dog.

18:00 – 20:00 Last Dog (So that we rotated shifts).

20:00 – 24:00 Evening Watch.

The winds had whisked us out of Bali just in time to celebrate Captain Kirk's birthday. Mo was already hard at baking when I started ballooning and decorating the saloon. Party hats went on and the celebrations began. The festive season was upon us. Whisky. Cake. Presents!

The next day was Halloween and we busied ourselves carving watermelons and assembling outfits. This was conveniently located the day before Christmas [Island] - creating a trio of convenient celebrations to mark the start of our crossing.

"What do you do on an ocean crossing?" You ask. "How do you keep yourself entertained?" This was a very good question. I was petrified of boredom. There can be nothing worse in all the world. I was so petrified of it that I once, all the way back in 2006, sent this email to every interesting-sounding company I could find on the internet:

BOREDOM KILLS

If octopus could talk... Attempting to keep herself amused, Sussie Jacobusson Van de Merwe attached a 7 legged specimen to ceiling fans in several adjacent rooms. Whilst taking a nap in the strangely created hammock, the fans began to spin and tragically she was never to awaken again.

Kobus Smitherie encounted a similar termination. Whilst brushing his teeth he attempted to toast his foot as all the spare time on his hands had resulted in him spending far to much time pondering the fate of bread. All would have been alright had the laws of science permitted water and electricity to safely concur...

Finally, Johnny Edwardson. To most it appeared his life was perfect- retired, with all the money and time in the world... He tried knitting, bowls, all the usual activities for the aged, but non bought him any satisfaction. Before giving up on life completely, he decided to give song composition a try... dear Johnny did find his true calling and passion... but it resulted in the lives of millions being tormented as the majority of the songs he composed were the Christmas carols which have long bought agony to all those dragged by their parents to 'carols by candle light', those who have to endure them whilst browsing the shops, and to those who have them take control of even their car radios.

Upon reading the above, you will no doubt agree with me that boredom kills!!!!! So I ask you today to be brave- become a hero and save a life! So much emphasis is put on helping the poor, the homeless, and the orphaned- what about the bored¿¿¿

It has been a whole day of doing nothing (well, general house work doesn't count)- and already I'm bored! It's two weeks until my next known job and I think that time frame may kill me. So, with a desire to live, I ask- 'does anybody out there have [almost] ANYTHING for me to do¿ Creative consulting¿ Writing¿ Reading¿ Filming¿ General office work¿ Polishing your shoes¿ Rearranging your office furniture so nobody can find their anything¿

Freelancing is fun- but the gaps are deadlier than being in a room with not only six or seven sharks, but a mutant hamster, a seriel killer and a nuclear bomb simultaneously... So if you need anything give me a call (CV attatched).

Save a life today!!!
Call Adeena- 072

Blah blah blah...

Despite my terrible grammar and many spelling mistakes, it landed me a job at a branding company doing short-term contracts and recruitment; and another at a record label.

For the Indian Ocean's vastness, I was prepared. I had bookshelves of reading available. I had pencils, crayons, paint and a sketchpad. I had many notebooks to write in. Jewellery to make. A book to write. I was going to learn Spanish, how to cook and how to splice rope... But the miles flew by all too quickly. I didn't have the time to be bored. Not once.

We had bi-weekly movie nights on the deck and our cuisine improved by the day. The dolphins made regular visits; as did the birds, sometimes even coming in to land on the deck. We perfected swimming off the *transom* ladder (although I gave up wearing bikinis while doing it - the current ripped them straight off.)

And then, quite suddenly, the wind died. Our 8.7-knot average reduced to 2. The sails flapped about in confused purposelessness. We really should have appreciated the slow days, for when the wind finally did return, it did so with vengeance. We were moving so fast (11.6 knots) that even daring Kirk outlawed swimming. It's not as easy as you might think to *furl* the jib, lower the main, start the engine and about-ship to rescue fallen sailors. It's a general belief that if you fall overboard, you're forever lost to the clutches of the ocean. Which brings me to the third rule of boating: *"If you fall overboard, you're a goner!"*

One hand was constantly clinging on for dear life, whilst the other caught falling people, produce and toilet seats. Objects learned to magically fly every time we heeled at the mercy of a giant wave. Our bodies glimmered blue with bruises. There was no rest. There would be no sleep. It was impossible to even clamber onto my bunk in those conditions. (Fortunately, I found a stretch of Kirk's floor to foetal-up on.)

The challenge of making and drinking a morning cup of coffee was made harder by a gybe. When we gybed back, we ripped the newly stitched sail and all hands ran on deck to bundle up the flapping masses of fabric.

The waves are mammoth around us. I think it's normal that I feel scared, even if Fiddler *is designed to flip herself back around if she does go over. Land lies hundreds of miles away. We have over 4500 meters of water below us, and it's just us and our little private "island" home. We are the only ones basking in these bright indescribable blues aboard this crazy rollercoaster of life.*

The dolphins were lost in the 3–5-meter swell. *Lee cloths* went up because life became a constant 30-degree heel to starboard and it's hard not to roll out of bed at that angle. We saw one bobbing coconut and a plastic bottle, but for all we knew there may well have been treasure chests lurking nearby. The seas flamed fiercely as a furnace.

The sea was too rough for movie night. Instead, Kirk dictated [from memory] *Being John Malkovich*, as we sat staring at the stars munching popcorn. It felt like we'd always been on the ocean.

White waves mesmerised us by day, shooting stars awed us at night. Our trusty swivel stove kept our stomachs well sated.

￼

At sea, you have many long talks. You sit up late into the night discussing anything and everything. Sitting under the infinite abyss of stars, your mind tends to wander. You remember a lot of weird, wonderful and random things that were stowed away in the forgotten *bilges* of your subconscious. There's something about all that water, the incredibly epic sunrises and sunsets, the motion, and the fact that you have so much time, that really fiddles your cerebral cortex.

Being at sea tends to have some other effects on your physique too.

James and I found ourselves changing shifts one night and got talking. Deep and meaningful kinds of talking. "So, I suppose we shouldn't do this." We both agreed. But seconds later our faces had neared and our lips had locked and it happened anyway. We were busted only seconds later when Kirk, somehow sensing something amiss, had ventured up to check.

Day 12. *Karma's a bitch!* 17 50 379 S; 086 45 777 E. I had just finished my night shift and was waddling back across the boat to the safe(ish) confines of my bunk (which used to be, and I quote, "a glorious wardrobe") when a rogue wave hit the boat hard. I flew across the galley and hit my lip on the "safety" handgrip, just above the sink. I held my hand up to my mouth to feel if I'd lost a tooth and it returned pooling blood! "Kirk," I cried up to the cockpit – "I hit my head!" Before I collapsed in a heap on the stairs.

Now, head-knocking is a very regular occurrence on a boat. You tend to be more surprised by the days you don't almost concuss yourself than by reapplying a new whack to an old lump for the umpteenth time. So I'm glad Kirk actually came running. Fortunately, there were no mirrors on hand because my tooth pierced straight through and jutted out just below my lip. A little white island in an ocean red. Kirk got out the first aid kit and cleaned me up. Then came the real question, who did the stitching?

I'm glad we decided to wait till daylight to do the wobbly boat stitch because I now know that mouth wounds heal really quickly. The boys made me don a motorbike helmet in the kitchen anyway. They wanted to ensure that there were enough first aid supplies to finish crossing the Indian.

Needless to say, it took a while before there was any more kissing to be had! But I did abandon my wardrobe bunk and moved into the luxurious confines of James' princely bed. It was nice to have a warm body next to me. I felt safe curling up in his arms.

Day 13. 14:04. We hit the halfway to La Reunion mark – 1756 miles. Pop-pops and tom thumbs went off and a message in a sweet potato wine bottle went out. We also had the honour of a double beer o'clock, as we finally acknowledged the changing time zones and set the clocks back. We then all sat back down and carried on being mesmerised. We still had a very long way to go!

"When I grow up, I want to be a pirate."

- Former me, age five[ish].

And I really did. I wanted to rope swing from boat to boat waving plastic swords (all swords are plastic when you're five[ish]) demanding cookies and cake.

We had just celebrated our furthermost point from land[23], when a fleet of small boats suddenly appeared on the radar. Not having seen anything for weeks, it was a strange occurrence that gave us the creeps. We'd heard all the horror stories. We knew what could happen. We didn't want to be pirated! We sat nervously watching.

The morning's chat turned from pirates to medical discussion. It was decided that I was probably safe from contamination caused by licking the furry Komodo dragon poo. I was however still at risk of rabies and even more prone to death due to the excessive blood loss through my lip. We all agreed that the likeliness of me making it home alive was slight. We then continued to discuss the legality of sea burials.

WHAM! The *gybe preventer* came loose. I yelled to Jim, who abandoned his *epoxy* and came running to the rescue. In a flash, he had it in his hand and was trying to reconnect it to the *boom*. In another flash, the boom had him airborne as the mainsail pushed him in a trapeze swing back

---

[23] 902 miles away from Cocos Keeling and 902 miles away from Chagos.

and forth over the deck. It was amazing to watch, but there was that ever-present danger of him being thrown overboard. Memo and I grabbed his feet. In a team effort, we managed to secure both the American and the boom. With his heart still racing, he returned to his chores and I returned to pretending to keep watch. Exhaustion had clasped me in its grip. I had Mo in stitches as I kept dozing off and toppling to the ground from the pilot chair.

Week 3, and still we hadn't caught up to the drowning sun. The heavens still had balls of fire to fling about. The ocean still held suicidal fish to die upon our decks. But we finally saw the southern cross and it felt like we were getting somewhere. Almost.

Kirk informed me that my bum was darker than my mum's face. He proved this by showing me a picture of my bum[24] and a picture of mum's face. I think he used this to cushion the question that followed, because he then swerved the conversation to inquire how long I'd be on board for. That was a difficult question. I'd only committed as far as South Africa, but I knew they were heading onwards to Brazil and the Caribbean. I didn't know what home would hold. I didn't know what that thing going on between James and I was. I didn't know how much more the contents of my stomach could withstand... I told him I'd think about it.

Rain. Shine. Snuggles. Food. Beer. Sunrises. Sunsets. Books. Pizza. Art. Writing. Poetry.

With Reunion looming
I feel my heart glooming.
How will I stand

---

[24] ...while swimming off the stern.

On dry stable land?

Three weeks of wobbling
On every wave's throbbing.
Holding on for dear life
Catching falling sugar and spice.

With every windful gust
Forward Fiddler *is thrust.*
Sailing from rise to sunset
And still, we're not there yet.

For each item we break,
Something new Jim must make.
And whilst we sit alurk,
Kirk's always hard at work.

A hole through my lip
A big bruise on my hip.
Even my halo's gone tarnish
And the boat really needs a varnish.

Deaths aboard have been plenty
At this rate, soon the seas will be empty.
For while flying fishes astound,
On deck, it's only their corpses to be found.

Computers keep dying.
People's hands keep frying.
We fall left right and centre
And soon may need denture[s].

But someday we'll arrive
And our challenge will be land to survive.

My vocabulary increased profusely as both Kirk and James fed me words for the day: *Barratry. Simony. Belligerent. Matins. Yokel. Merkin. Edsel. Regent. Mellifluous. Moot. Shuck. Reconnaissance. Libel. Hellacious. Hijinx. Pugnacious. Sobriety. Confederation...*

"Hey Kirk, didn't you teach me some new words yesterday?" I called from the cockpit as I tried to update my vocabulary list.

"I'm sure we spoke."

We celebrated Mo Day[25] with a puppet show and a game show (and presents too, of course). Under the influence of a cheap glass of whisky, I had a revelation:

Flying fish are the shooting stars of the ocean.

My mind was at sea. While watching *Brazil*, I found myself in awe that people could put things down on a table without them falling over. Dreams went from crazy to mad. And I started wishing that land wasn't approaching so quickly. I was addicted to the solitude and simplicity of sailing life.

And then there was the day when I was mindlessly staring into the oceans' abysmal vortex, when suddenly a Coke can floated by. I ran to awaken the others. Sadly, they didn't quite share my joy.

The other [less exciting] things we passed were:

One boobie on a plank (the bird, not the breast).

One tsunami warning buoy.

---

[25] With Memo being the only crew member not to have a birthday aboard, a celebration in her honour had to be created.

One soap cover.

One coconut.

One blue plastic cup.

Six aeroplanes.

Twelve tankers/ cargo ships.

Mauritius.

We were 24 days out when the yell arose from the cockpit, "Land Ho!" I ran to the deck and found Mauritius on our Starboard side. She was still miles and miles away, but she jutted magnificently out of the water. We were so accustomed to seeing only water, that seeing land was an anomaly. Familiar scents began to drift in our general direction. At sea, the only things you smell are fresh air, kitchen, and bodily induced fragrances. To smell plants, grass, beach break waves and kelp was perfume to our senses.

The sight of the French island was commemorated with French toast. Let it be noted though that you do not crack the eggs into the pan and hope that the bread absorbs them.

We stared at the island all day. Bobbing along slowly, waiting for the wind. But we weren't stopping.

The thing about running away from cyclones is that you can't predict them, and you generally don't see them coming. You're a fugitive from something that probably doesn't exist. We were so late in the season that, on the off-chance that we were being pursued, we'd decided to do only one Indian Ocean stop: **Reunion.**

12:04, Wednesday, 21 November 2012.

What a mammoth journey we've just undergone! 46-knot winds, and no winds at all. 16-foot swells, and glass waters. Billions of dolphins at some points, and then days on end with none. Schools of jumping, flapping flying fish, and 54 dead corpses on the deck. We've only lost one veggie peeler, one knife, and a paintbrush overboard. Two computers have died (although we are still hoping they might be resurrected). There are far too many reasons for celebrations: nobody's lost a tooth, a limb or a soul. There have been no mutinies, no keel-haulings, *and we even avoided scurvy. Life is awesome, and it is good to be alive!*

26 days (619 hours and 37 minutes) after licking land farewell, we stepped ashore on La Reunion, France. A blip on the map littering the Indian Ocean somewhere between Madagascar and Mauritius - technically in both Africa and Europe. We had a welcome party too: customs, immigration, and a friendly Canadian South African Peter, who the boys knew from their Thailand days.

I finally licked land hello again!

REUNITED

It was strange being back on solid ground, and my body didn't know how to handle it. Land sickness set in as I wobbled about trying to counter-program my brain.

Four men boarded and began paperwork while a boat search ensued. Instead of just a routine check, they opened and examined everything. Every bag I owned was undone. Every plastic bag I'd kept perfectly folded inside every bag, was rolled out and inspected. Every box of feminine hygiene product was carefully scrutinised. It was a scary feeling I hadn't had in years. We didn't have anything to hide, but man do I have a guilty conscience! Mo was next to be checked as they moved their way back through the boat. Then Jim. I suppose in the end, there was reason for the worry. He left in handcuffs.

I strolled the marina aimlessly all afternoon. I had that sick feeling in my stomach that nauseated life to the point that it was unbearable. I was finally on land, but I could think about nothing other than James. Actually, my burning feet too. The sun was so hot that my walk back may as well have been on coals. By four, I'd claimed his bed for a power nap. When I awoke, he finally returned! It was quite a relief. What would *Fiddler* be without a beer buddy?

They'd let him off with a substantial fine and kept the gun for forensic testing, only later to be destroyed. Despite its noble purpose, the unlicensed firearm was packaged so well and deep in the transom of his bed, that it would have taken at least an hour's notice to be ready for uninvited guests.

We took the time to breathe land in properly. Peter joined us as we strolled into town to find pizza. We paused to sniff flowers, stroke puppies, and "Bonjour" the friendly eclectic mix of islanders. After a year in Asia, it was odd being back in a more Western world. We didn't see whole families and their livestock on a single scooter. We didn't have to use squat toilets. People didn't yell out "Hello Mr, where you go?" or "Masssaaaaage-a?" or "You want boom boom? Dr Bob? You want to fly to the moon?" We didn't have an endless mob following us around trying to sell us wooden frogs and chicken giblets.

I woke up on the wrong side of the bed, which is quite strange considering boat bunks only have one side. Nothing worked! Simply trying to get onto the internet to find out what I'd been missing out on in the real world was a failure.

I started the following morning in better spirits. I made real coffee, and that made all the difference. Before noon I'd shot out emails to friends and family all over the world. I took the time to escape and do some soul searching. What was next? What did I want out of life? Was it time to grow up and try and be a responsible adult? Was I ready for it? No, I probably wasn't... but maybe? At the same time, I needed to give Kirk an answer. Was I sailing onward to Brazil with them? Was I wanting to see more of this extraordinary planet? I kept mulling these thoughts over in my head as I did an OCD clean of the bathroom. I'd lost my toothbrush to the bowl a few days earlier and I'd started to value a clean toilet. Wanderlust got me through it; but was wanderlust a distraction from what I should've been doing in life? Or was it healthy and necessary?

Carnivorous Peter took an immediate shining to me, purely based on my diet. The 74-year-old Canadian South African solo sailor was a retired English lecturer and a wonderfully lively fellow you couldn't help but love. I got to know him rather well as the five of us explored the island's volcanoes, beaches, mountains and waters in his rental car. Reunion held such strong contrasts of green and blue. The people came in every shape, size and shade; but they all carried the same unmistakable smell of pot. Having Peter around allowed me to detour from my vegetarian ways. If the others seemed to be offended by our pallets, we'd abandon them to enjoy [as Peter called it] "real food."

The little marina was a fascinating place. One boat had been compounded for running weapons (an enthralling tour as we walked between the walls), another for human trafficking and another for drugs. It was no wonder searches were now so thorough! There weren't a lot of distance sailors, but the locals were a friendly lot!

Catching up on emails and news of the world was an adventure in itself. A lot [and nothing] happened in a month. I wanted to know all of it!

Karen sent a wedding invitation. Carryn looks like she might be the next to tie the knot. This makes me wonder about the last of my single friends. What is happening with Dan and Ben and Megan and Moo and Simone? Is my return to Africa going to be strange and third-wheeley? I've changed so much and learned too much in the years I've been gone. Will I fit back in? Am I too Asian? Too American? Or worse, too Aussie? Will anyone else have changed? Will they understand who I am and what I've been through?

The weird dreams continued. And this time I found myself a serious surfer (Like I said, weird). I was riding a mammoth never-ending tube, thinking I should be topless because I was worried about getting tan lines with all the hours spent on the wave. It was one of those dreams where birds circled around you, dolphins abound alongside and a friendly shark yelled out: "Nah, not hungry today mate!" The next thing I knew, the board was on the roof of a car and I was surfing the highway. People started pelting me with trash and someone threw a banana at me. I caught it and remembered thinking, "I should save this for Memo." At first, it was okay, but then they started assaulting me with cans of beans, cod liver oil and spirulina. I thought, "I have to get out of here!" I looked up and there was a comet that I confused for a shooting star. I wished upon it and it came swooping down to rescue me. It turned out to be a superhero. I was very glad to be rescued! But as I gazed upon my knight's face, I saw it was a woman. I got bummed. Still, it was good to be safe, and even better to be flying plane-free. She put me down safely then slapped me across the face. "I've been waiting to do that all day," she said.

I'm still trying to work out the meaning of this dream.

I dreamed of vegan slaughterhouses. I dreamed of having to decorate cupcakes through scientific experiments; and natural disasters. I dreamed of pole dancing on the mast and having very close encounters with flying swordfish.

"Joi de Vie!" I tossed my worries aside and sat at the pilothouse feasting on olives, cheese, baguettes and wine in the setting sun. I loved my life! I loved my crew!

Peaches, the Ewok-like poodle, was another favourite. He joined me on morning runs and even helped fight off a mob of angry dogs who were eyeing out the remains of my manly calves. I learned that dogs could smell my fear. I started staring and stomping back at them as they ran for the attack. It worked, every time. Just in time too. A new year was dawning and I wanted to begin it living fearlessly!

The sails were returned, the stocks were replenished. The island was explored and enjoyed. It was time to get moving. The crew was nice enough to postpone departure just a little longer so that I could commence my 28th year on land.

AS WE GO SAILING HOME

20:57, Saturday, 1 December 2012. I was slightly hungover and rather sad to be leaving the friendly island, but this was the final leg and I was homeward bound!

There were only four knots of wind as we exited the port. Half an hour later, as we marvelled at the hills ablaze with Reuniony lights, there were eight knots. As the half-moon rose, there were twelve. And when we exited the lee of the island, there were twenty-five! We raised the main. Within the hour, we'd left Peter in our wake.

Fortunately, I cut my leg while shaving. In the rush to find a band-aid, I stumbled upon my seasickness stash. I swallowed a precautionary pill and almost instantly, the swell began to tango.

In turmoil and torturous seas I had crayons for hands. The others had pizza with a seductive temptress. Komodo dragons nearly ate me, but instead engaged in *Star Wars* like combat to defend their reputations. The crazy dreams continued to plague me as we danced upon the water.

The first few days were rather uneventful. We busied ourselves with the general mesmorisement of blue, while constantly pole dancing with the sails as the vacillating wind blustered. When conditions were too overpowering for the autopilot, the others took shifts on the manual helm while I served as temporary relief, runner, and [most importantly] entertainer.

Worries about life plans still consumed me as I relocated to the deck for a nudie tan. James almost had me fly overboard as he popped his head out of the hatch. My normally overly-conservative self was tamed as I shifted over and made space for him to join me.

I sat with Mo that evening and tried to explain to her what the word "debauchery" meant. I smiled as I did it. I liked debauchery. A lot.

I tried to add new scintillating veggie dishes to the menu and, when even more excitement was needed, I introduced Africa Day[26].

It kicked off with a quiz which included questions like:

1) How many wives is a South African president allowed to have?

2) What is the basic objective of *Bok Drol Spoeg*?

3) What is the South African name for a traffic light?

4) Which of the following is not a South African national dish?

   a) Hoendervleis

   b) Pap en sous

   c) Bunnychow

   d) Bobotie

5) Correctly pronounce the word "*k-h-a-k-i*"

6) Which African animal translates directly from Afrikaans as "lazy horse"?

Other Africa Day celebrations included starvation and a native dress evening. The wind had died and instead of being thrown about, we now bobbed back and forth at under four knots. Pod after pod of dolphins came to greet us. I eventually decided that I'd boycott the "starvation." For the first time in five years of them owning the boat, we used the BBQ and had *Fiddler*'s first vegetarian braai.

---

[26] Another invented celebration intended to both educate and entice the others for what lay ahead.

"When buying an elephant, do not simply consider the tail."

-Kirk

I never knew if it was a grey sky or jib sail that I was seeing through *Fiddler*'s only transparent fore-port. But I hoped for the best and headed out. Rain greeted me and I quickly retracted to find more appropriate attire. Thunderous bass echoed across the ocean and the show was quite remarkable. Jim had taken manual control and the wind started to pick up. In seconds it escalated from 16 knots to 51.3. The boat heeled over so much that we flew off it, desperately clutching for anything to stop ourselves from tumbling into the waters below. The jib proceeded to disintegrate as we tried in vain to furl. Waves crashed over the main and the mast as the sky became a bubble-like blaze of white and blue. The shrapnel of material floated around us. Thousands of dollars of material. The winds diminished but the rain continued as we deployed the *staysail* and inched onwards. At least we'd be reaching the Aghullus Current soon. That was set to carry us all the way to **Richard's Bay.**

The miserable day continued, but just after the others crawled to sleep without dinner (it was too rough to eat), I saw the lights: South Africa was shining at me! It was nearly 05:00, and I was still trying to fall asleep when there was a sudden strident sound. James bolted from the bed and I followed. We brought in the sail before the storm could claim our last one. It poured so hard that we couldn't see the bow, let alone land. But nothing could kill my enthusiasm. I danced in the rain, jumped and sang as I inflated the fenders and readied us for port. I was coming home!

We entered the small craft harbour of *Tuzi Gazi*, and circled it aimlessly until someone pointed us to a spot just in front of the fuel dock. We tossed the lines to some friendly yachties and seconds later I'd jumped ashore to kiss the earth.

The flag. The accents. *The Dros*. The people: black, white, Indian, coloured – the whole rainbow! After 741 days of sampling and savouring foreign soils, I was back!

8.

GUMDROPS AND ROSES AND WHISKERS ON WOMAN

RRG! I am a pirate, I've come to take over your ship!" Kevin from Home Affairs swung aboard. We'd been waiting for him for three days. I radioed my crew who, after two days of solid sleep, had finally disappeared to explore. "Welcome home!" he said with a big hug and a passport stamp.

We were so late in the season that we thought we'd be the last to arrive. But for the next few days, our community of salty ocean crossers continued to grow.

Americans. Australians. A Spanish single handler. A Canadian boat. Chad! He'd tried to buy cocaine and got screwed over. He proceeded to throw up on the bad-dealer-bartender before we all got kicked out of the marina bar. I was trying to work out his moral system and wondered where the youngster had found the money for a beautiful boat like his (let alone the cocaine), when *Sayonara* arrived. It was good to have Peter back!

It's 03:00 and I've given up the sleep quest. I'm sat on the deck staring out at the moonless sky as the marina creatures splash about the hull. Kirk's sleeping in the stairwell, so I snuck out of a hatch, beer in hand. It's my last night aboard, the beer is a necessary evil. I desperately wish that James would wake up and join me, because things need to be said and discussed. But I suppose I also need this time to clear my head...

I forced all my belongings into my pack and was busy tidying up the boat when customs finally arrived. The neighbours began boarding too, including a new fluffy-bearded single-hander, who'd just sailed 80 days straight from Australia. The cockpit was a happy buzz of beer o'clock. By my second one, my friends Moo and Drew had arrived too.

Burritos. Birthday wine. Pumpkin soup. More drinks, too many to drive. I casually gave Moo my bed, "offering" to share with James. I was exhausted but stayed up chatting with him late into the morning before settling in for a last cuddle. He was off to The States in a couple of days and I was off to Jo'burg, still uncertain if I was to return.

It was an incredibly sad round of goodbyes. Firstly to Memo, who was headed back to Turkey and then on to Finland. Then to Kirk, who would be staying on *Fiddler* in Richards Bay for a couple of months. And finally, to James. I'd feigned indifference and pretended like I didn't really care. But it doesn't matter how casually you treat a relationship, there are always feelings involved. I might be slow to commit, but I'm very easily attached.

As I drove away that morning, I couldn't decide if I was ecstatically happy or devastated. One thing I did know for certain was that I was flying! After months spent moving at 6 knots (+/-11 km/hr) to now being on the highway at 120, it was exhilarating. I was rather relieved when we stopped at the Wimpy for a "real breakfast." Drew began interrogating me, and I finally came clean about my coercions with said crewmate. I hadn't spoken to anyone about it and needed some outsider input.

ƒ

I'd forgotten how tedious long bus rides were. After the third Rowan Atkinson movie in a row, I couldn't tell you how excited I was to be arriving in **Johannesburg!** The conductor prayed and thanked God for our safe arrival and then added a casual, "For those of you who have been away a while, welcome home!" I cried!

I threw my arms around *Ouma* who had come to collect me from the station. I adore her. If I grow to be half as cool as she is, then I'll have lived a most exceptional life! After feeding me and throwing me in the shower (to wash all the gypsy off), she sentenced me to an early night. She loaned me her car and a hairbrush; and I made it to a friend's wedding just in time.

So many smiling familiar faces: old friends, new friends, even some of the kids I used to babysit. People had changed – they'd all become adults. I stopped to pick up hitchhikers on the way back and then continued the reunions with school and varsity friends. Hugs and catch-ups made it feel almost as if I'd never left.

In less than 100 hours of arriving, I was back on a bus on my way to **Cape Town**. Fortunately, I was tired enough to sleep through a good portion of the 22-hour ride. I probably should have been doing other things seeing as it was December 21: the day the world was predicted to end.

Jeandré picked me up and whisked me away to surprise my bestie, Dan. Then Brendon arrived from the U.K. and I finally got to meet his Chloe. We had a prolonged siblingly hug and wandered down the road for happy hour. It was the first time in our 25 years of coexistence that we all drank together. We waddled back to the squatter settlement we'd set up in Daisy's unfurnished apartment. It was 03:00, the world never ended.

We were all rather miserable the next morning, but a hearty breakfast and a dip in Cape Town's icy waters fixed that. By the evening, we were ready to tackle anything and found ourselves climbing Lion's Head mountain in drag. I looked around at the smiling faces – Jeandré, Brendon, Chloe, Daisy and Dan. What I was blessed with in friends, I lacked in fitness levels! When we eventually reached a back-log of other hikers (who were all on their way down since my slowness had made us miss sunset), I was rather relieved for the breather. Instead, I found myself being coerced up the cliff face by the boys' pushes and pulls. We had the whole mountain top to ourselves. We sat down and cracked open [now] warm beers, as the last colour evaporated into the sparkling city lights that shimmered below.

After a corner street *boerie roll*, there were more reunions with happy faces of days long gone. The beer was so cheap that it was very detrimental to my health. And the angry rock music acted as a conduit to continue drinking it.

Later I sat on the porch, white wine in hand. We stared out at the lights, the sea and the mountain that made Cape Town so astounding. "Ad, this is going to be weird," said Dan, before he leaned over and kissed me.

❦

Dan, my best friend of ten years and favourite human, was something else. I'd fallen in love with him the very first time I saw him at a random braai that neither of us belonged in. Within a couple of days, we'd started a band and made too many plans to overthrow the world. He was the inspirational enigma that you find fun, motivational, and able to talk you into anything. It was thanks to him that I ever left on my first adventure! For four years, I'd worshipped the grass that grew on the ground that cushioned the shoes that he walked upon. We spoke about anything and everything. But we never talked about romantic feelings. Neither of us dared to ruin the friendship. After four years of pining, I finally decided that we were just good friends, and left it at that. This kiss changed everything.

❦

There was only one day till Christmas and preparations were furious. Christmas Eve was celebrated on Dan's veranda and Santa-Jeandré dished out the presents. He disappeared inside for a while, returning with a beam and a gift for Daisy. "It's soft. It has a tail. Is it a squirrel?" asked Daisy, trying to guess the gift and avoid the mandatory shot of *mampoer* that Santa dished out for failure to predict. My brother had wrapped his own faeces.

Chloe proceeded to tell us how she had been in the bath while Brendon had come in to take a dump and started flinging dirty toilet paper into the tub. She told us how she'd been stung by a jellyfish on their way down to Cape Town. Brendon had thrown her in the shower, peed all over her, and told her that she had to wait 24 hours before washing it off. There never was a jellyfish. I come from a strange family alright. But I'm proud of it. And despite all the chaos, it was by far the best Christmas.

We joined Daisy's family for actual Christmas and, knowing him[27], I couldn't believe how laissez-faire they were. As we stood in the car park debating the beach, karaoke, and what to do next, my phone beeped. It was Dan. He'd accidentally let it slip to his entire family that we were together. I looked up at the brothers and made the announcement. As a 28-year-old with her first official boyfriend, this was big news. But as someone who'd never had real commitments or responsibilities, this was terrifying!

---

[27] Yes, "him." We think he may have had another name once, but "Daisy" is more fitting. The details of how we adopted him are a little shady, but we like him, so we'll keep him, maybe even legally adopt some day.

With Chloe and Brendon off to London, things calmed down a little and I finally sat down to contemplate all that had just happened:

Three days ago, I was more or less single and ready to sail off to Brazil or to cycle across Africa. Now I'm thinking about relocating to Cape Town, grounding myself, starting something with Dan and seeing where it takes me. It's a crazy mind-screw. This is probably exactly what I need, even if it doesn't work out as it does in the fairy tales... I still have a mother to break it to and I still have James to deal with (Flip! How do I do this?)

Settling down might actually be good for me even if I haven't got an inkling of what kind of job I might do. I'm still not sure if I'm ready to adult. ...But it is probably all going to be alright. Possibly. Maybe.

TAKE ANY OLD YEAR, TURN IT STUPENDOUSLY EPIC

Cape Town, South Africa. 30 December 2012

I'm not sure how I've survived 2012:
I've fallen 869 times, crashed 3 motorbikes, blown 17 bicycle tyres, licked any and everything, hitchhiked 2687 km, cycled 2953 km, motorbiked 3214 km, sailed some 13 060.8 km, shipwrecked and probably contracted rabies. Today marks 396 days of unemployment...
Not to mention surviving the predicted world's ending.

I've always pretended to be ballsy.
But I'm not particularly. I'm a woman - we don't have balls.
I think my could-be-any-race-group complexion, calloused bare feet and mangled mop of gypsy hair gives me that caveman-style untouchable aura.

But I bruise, I bleed, I have sleepless nights of worry and I'm generally
just as scared as the chickens who live across the road from the KFC.

A year ago today, I sat on a friend's balcony in Singapore staring
worryingly at the world map wondering where to go next.
My goal was a flightless mission to Spain.
But the terrified little girl inside had only a giant teddy bear and an even
bigger backpack to cling to.
The bank account wasn't very happy.
A pep talk with myself, and excessive amounts of prayer later,
I missioned off into the abyss and let life unfold.

It's easy to have a good year when you play it safe.
You know what's going to happen.
You know who and where your friends are.
You have a secure job where you can budget and plan bonuses.
You have a cellphone contract and internet access.
You know that when you walk into a local supermarket or a restaurant,
that you'll find the brands and the flavours that you're looking for; and if
you don't, you can at least speak the language and ask.
But an excellent year involves a bit of roulette.

"Never try, never know" is one of my favourite Asian catchphrases
(normally used to promote drug sales and prostitution).
You don't.
Think back to the year that's just passed and how many times you turned
down offers that made you nervous, conversations with people who
smelt funny, travels to places you'd never heard of…
How different would life have been if you'd said 'yes' more?
(or, in a few selective cases "no" more.)

Our lives are short enough, so we really ought to be seizing every
second.
Doing instead of just talking about it.
Running away from regret.
Attempting the impossible.
Frequently facing fears.
Making sure you have good stories for the grandkids someday.
Making sure you have grandkids someday.
Always going to bed happy [when you have time for sleep].

I'm about to give the realer world another shot [GULP] - but this doesn't
for a second mean that the adventures are over.
It simply means a new sort of gypsyism.
I'm both excited and terrified.

Happy 2013!!
Go crazy. Be awesome. Say "yes" a lot. Come visit. Don't die.

❦

Fiddler was a mess. Kirk had been left to his own devices for months and
chaos reigned. Still, it was so good to see the boys again! I reclaimed my
old bunk and was grateful to James for not making things awkward.

While we waited for the new sails to arrive, I busied myself by trying
to eradicate all the critters that had moved in to keep Kirk company. I
carpeted Kirk's floor. Did some cleaning. Did some polishing. Continued
job hunting.

Most yachts had moved over to the yacht club, so *Fiddler* was now in
a lonely spot still tied up on the visitor's dock.

Finally, the sails returned; but the wind was howling so hard that we
had to wait till after dinner to fit them. First the main. Then the staysail.

The brand-new jib was twice the thickness of the old one, and almost impossible to fit into its narrow slider. After hours of perseverance, we finally succeeded and cheered. But when we tried to furl it in, we found that there was something majorly wrong. The *furler* wouldn't budge. We tried everything we could and finally dropped the sail again. It was 03:00 and we were exhausted. We sat down in silence for a very long time. Then one by one we burst out laughing.

I took a long morning stroll on the beach and bawled my eyes out. I was a mess of emotions. I'd worked so hard to get *Fiddler* on her way again, and now I had to give up on her. I'd made other commitments and didn't have time for any more delays. It was Valentine's Day and Dan was in Cape Town. I didn't even care about the day, but I needed hugs, love and just about anybody to tell me it was all going to be okay. But was it?

❦

After weeks apart, Dan and I reunited in **Durban**. We beached, attended weddings, chilled and caught up with many friends; and broke up. We sat in silence staring out at the stars, sipping beers, as the waves crashed around us. It wasn't a bad thing. We were definitely better as friends.

It was only the next morning when Dan's mum came to check if I was okay, that the tears came. It was 04:00 and we had to be at the airport at 05:00. Dan was flying to Port Elizabeth for yet another wedding and I was off to Cape Town to start my new job. Once the tears were there, there was no turning off the floods. In true humiliation, I cried all the way to the airport. I cried through goodbyes. I cried through all four cups of coffee while I awaited my flight. I pulled myself together for the check-in.

Five-year-old Abby sat next to me. She chatted incessantly and braided my hair, oblivious to my tear stains. She even let me win at rock paper scissors once.

I'd almost forgotten my torment by the time I landed, but Jeandré called. The waterworks returned. It didn't help that he was off on a film shoot and everyone else I knew had gone back to work (outside of **Cape Town**). Dan had flown from his family to his best friend's. I was giving up gypsyism and restarting life in a whole new city, where I knew virtually nobody; and I'd already committed to a job that I knew nothing about.

Daisy picked me up figuring that I simply had a traumatic flight. When he eventually translated my sobs and discovered that it was not the fear of flying, but rather heartbreak that was driving the tears, he spun the car around and took me for a breakfast beer. He then gave me a big hug and returned to preparing for his impending final exam.

I went for a long walk and returned to the balcony where I sat drinking all the alcohol in the house. I was feeling surprisingly good when I went to bed.

Tomorrow I will be a new person: Employed. Single. Able to function again.

9.

MURDERING THE GYPSY

I found a tap and tried to tidy myself up a bit before the other employees arrived. Cycling to work after a big day of heavy drinking with sea legs and no sense of direction was less than ideal. Especially when your new job is 25 kilometres away, at the top of a mountain. Daisy had a half marathon at six. We left at the same time, but I'm sure he was home and showered before I was even halfway. A tall skinny old woman with a stooped back and a petrifying glare came out screaming, telling me to get off her private property before she called the cops. I tried to introduce myself, but she stormed off in a huff.

I had a sneak around the property before venturing back to the office to meet my colleagues, an awesome bunch with colourful personalities to match. They stood up pretty straight when they realised I was coming in as "the boss." It was such a crazy first day that I didn't have time to think about anything other than the job. "Putting people in trees," what a satiating vocation.

I returned home exhausted. I thought I was fixed, but that night I allegedly got up, turned on every light in the house, walked into Daisy's room, stared at him, and then went back to bed. My *Psychology 3B* classes taught me that some of the highest scorers on the stress scale were:

Starting a new job.

Breaking up a relationship.

Moving to a new city.

Moving to a new house.

Not having a support system.

… I may have been suffering from a little bit of stress.

In desperation, Daisy dialed a friend. Anri arrived minutes later with two bottles of champagne and sophisticated goblets. Anri got me through Cape Town!

DEAR MOM, I'M AN ADDICT

Cape Town, 1 July 2013

Dear mom

I know you've always told me to steer away from drugs, but I got really really high the other day and had one of those epiphanies that only really happens under the influence of somewhat very illegal substances.

Life suddenly made sense.

As I soared through the air and the world swirled around me and I floated about in a dream, I saw clearly for the first time in almost forever…

Now mom, before you go and hop on a plane back to South Africa (which you will probably do regardless) and come sentence me to a nunnery, the indoors, and a diet of barley green and carrot juice [or worse]; I'll try to explain…

I've been living in one town for almost four months, working the first full-time job of my life with the fewest housemates (1.25 and a giant dirty teddy bear) I've ever had. I'm sure you can understand how, under these dire circumstances, escapism might be necessary?

I tried living real life on the wild side – brushing my teeth extra vigorously before milk, breaking into the neighbour's house [over the third storey balcony] to use their washing machine, and doing my grocery shopping in my PJs… but it wasn't quite enough.

And for what I am about to say, you need to remember that you are partly to blame as I inherited your genes…
… Mom, there's no easy way to say this but [make sure you are sitting down for this one], I'm an adventure addict!
And proud of it.
Adrenaline and adventure are the drugs that make getting up in the morning worthwhile.

The first half of 2013 has vanished in a blink of mediocrity, but part two will be epic! I have decided to get high for a living.

I love you so much and hope you're up for more adventure yourself.
Your fully living [and planning on staying that way] daughter
X0X0 Adeena

PS: I bought a scooter. Sorry.

Six months later I sat on that same balcony, contemplating life. A couple of days squatting in Daisy's lounge turned into permanent residency. I made good friends and, despite working weekends and public holidays, life was good. Even if I felt like I was living a lie, as if I'd murdered my inner gypsy!

When Kirk and James finally made it to Cape Town, they sat in immigration on the phone to me, rather adamant that I was going to Brazil with them. They assured me they'd bought copious amounts of burn ointment and had purchased a whole new first aid kit and...

But I couldn't... I shouldn't... I had commitments...

I said "no."

I started seeing someone I'd interviewed for a job at the company. When I sent him a rejection letter, he sent me a dinner invite. I couldn't reject him twice...

He was a lot of fun. But when things got serious, I opted out.

James emailed from the other side of the world to let me know that he wanted to move to Cape Town for me. I broke two hearts in a week.

And then I quit my job to make the hattrick. I had no idea what to do next!

I agreed to stay on at work until the chaos had calmed and a new manager had been sourced. There were some difficulties with the inscrutably malicious landlady. I didn't want my employees (all of whom I loved) to lose their jobs. I had gypsy blood. They had families to feed.

It was a busy day at work when my phone rang and I wasn't sure exactly how they got my number. "Is that Adeena?" ...My life was about to take another turn... I called HR to see how exit plans were coming on and let them know of a proposal that had just come up.

On Saturday, I broke the news to my staff that I was leaving. On

Sunday [after a particularly heavy night's drinking] the new manager arrived. On Monday, I was off.

BRINGING GYPSY BACK

Cape Town, 25 September 2013

Yes, it's the sequel... It's time to finish what was started...
My old friend, Unemployment, has returned to me and it's now or never
(so obviously, it's now).

Back in 2010, I began my flightless pilgrimage to Spain.
On Sunday, I handed over my responsibilities, left my remarkable team
behind, and officially resumed my mission.

I've packed up my life and said some goodbyes.
Tonight, I jump on a bus to Port Elizabeth where I hop on a yacht with a
bunch of 60-something-year-olds I've never met...

Their destination: Spain.

Tonight, I become a gypsy again.
Tomorrow I will meet my crew and remember how awful seasickness is.
By December this mission may well be accomplished.
But whatever happens, it's time to lick, live and be awesome.
I hope you're doing likewise!

ʕ

I sat somewhere in **Port Elizabeth** waiting for a reasonable morning hour to arrive. It's a terrifying thing sitting between life chapters. You have no idea how the next one will unfold and are almost too afraid to step into it. Half the time you really aren't ready for the current one to finish; and so you linger in it longer than you should, worrying you made a wrong decision, petrified to turn the page.

David, the captain, was the first to greet me. He looked nothing like Kirk. He didn't even bear a beard. Then there was Diane and she didn't have a beard either, look sixty, or sound Aussie. Dick grunted a "hello" and didn't seem particularly friendly as he stomped off the boat. And Simon, Di's other half, simply smiled. Dave could see my confusion and invited me in for coffee.

Nereid was a Beneteau 47, sloop. Skinny, modern and plastic. There were three cabins and three heads, one of the luxuries that come with ex-charter boats. David had kitted her out to be both functional and homey and I was quite smitten.

In the time it had taken me to quit my job and arrive in Port Elizabeth, the crew had changed from an average age of 65 to 47.5. The all-Australian contingent had become 75% South African. One couple had left because their marriage was on the rocks (and seemed as if they may steer the boat in the same direction). Another couple had to fly home in a hurry. And Dick had just been kicked off "because he drank." I was rather concerned when I heard this because I was a drinker too, and probably next to be expelled. But Dick had been pouring Jack Daniels on his cereal in the morning. Personally, I preferred milk. As a replacement, David now had Si and Di (aspirational Capetonians, who had just finished their Yacht Masters) and myself.

Now, all we needed was good weather. I didn't mind hanging around Port Elizabeth for a while. There were good friends to catch up with, and it gave me time to get to know the crew. Besides, all the rocking about was good training to get my sea legs back! The catamaran next to us was shooting a documentary on how great white sharks can be your friends (the footage was exceptional). Sam from down the dock invited me to his mountaineering club for a talk on Vanuatu. The Springboks beat the Wallabies. P.E. was a good stop, but we were all glad when the wind stopped howling!

The neighbours woke us up at 05:30 with Italian coffee (as promised) and we were off. We set the sails as soon as we rounded the lighthouse and I basked in the ocean freshness. I'd missed ocean life, even if the swell was still all over the place, and the wind hadn't quite stabilised yet.

It didn't take long till we had whales. And the day finished with an exquisite sunset!

The ocean was littered with sunning seals that increased in number the further South we sailed. The South African seas teemed with life! When we started beating into a headwind, the autopilot failed. As nice as it was to have other South Africans on board, we quickly realised how little experience we had between us and all turned to our captain for orders. The mist was so thick that we couldn't see anything. It was freezing, and I found myself wearing everything I owned, including Dave's daughter's clothes. Hot drinks got us through it, but I received my second verbal warning for forgetting to add sugar to the captain's coffee.

We rounded Cape Agulhas, the "Cape of Storms" and the most Southern tip of Africa. Despite the masses of traffic showing on our *AIS*, we managed to steer clear of collision as we bid the Indian Ocean goodbye; and said hello to the Atlantic.

CONFESSIONS OF A
SEA GYPSY

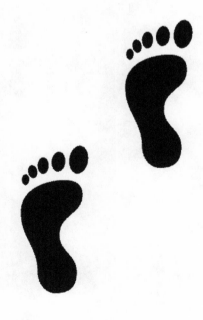

10.

HE initial excitement of the launch quickly dissipated into the realisation that I was losing something special to me [and a hangover]. **Cape Town** had been a blur of farewells and festivals and I probably pushed too hard in the few days that we'd been back. Table Mountain shrunk into my past as we inched West.

With sails set on a starboard tack, I stared back and reflected on my ridiculous attempt to adult. I was going to miss the country a lot!

Di was the first to puke, so we de-commissioned her and covered her watches. With seasickness tablets rich in my blood and many sleepless nights to atone for, this meant four hours of sleep interspersed with two-hour shifts spent shivering in the cockpit. Fortunately marine life still abounded.

The fog became so thick that we couldn't see anything. Sunrises and sunsets were swallowed by the mist and we kept consulting the charts to make sure we weren't steering towards Antarctic waters. The AIS wasn't working, so we had to scan the horizon extra vigilantly for boats. We were still close to shore, and still in the shipping zones.

A pigeon joined our crew 650 miles out. The paltry creature must have been exhausted, regardless of where it had flown from. It stuck with us a day and then, quite suddenly, vanished. We were adamant that it was washed overboard. But a day and a half later we watched it launch from the bow, leaving us a radioactive-green deck decoration.

On the fifth day, I finally saw the sun rise, and life started to pick up. The throng of relentless waves turned to calm seas. The fog subsided so we could actually see the dolphins frolicking in our wake. Di was doing better too. And because we were almost halfway to *Saint Helena*, we made a communal decision to celebrate life with a braai and a couple of beers. We were finally settling into the simple, beautiful sea life.

Both Dave and his wife, who wasn't a fan of long ocean passages, and the South Africans, had met when they had been thirteen. They'd married their first loves and made it work. Si and Di had kids young. Now that the boys were all out of the house, they were free to explore, take risks, and try something completely new. The Australians had done copious amounts of exploring first and then slowed down to propagate three daughters. Much time was spent discussing the merits of their ways, but either way seemed to work. And while I tried to take notes and learn from their examples, I had to remind myself that even though I acted like it, I wasn't thirteen anymore.

On the seventh day, we finally saw the stars and watched the moon rise. But it was short-lived as the clouds returned and more rain bestowed itself upon our watery world. On day eight, we crossed the *Prime Meridian* and found ourselves on the other side of the world. *Fiddler*'s crew celebrated this momentous occasion by hopping from their right foot to their left while calling out their favourite prime number. *Nereid*'s crew slept; and at dinner, we were still discussing how to celebrate. It was too cold to celebrate.

By day nine, I could no longer fight the need for a proper personal hygiene session. Di was already on her second and Dave was busy boasting about his. Si and I were battling it out to see who was the most feral. My leg hair had grown to a forest and my dreadlocked head more than needed a wash. The thermometer showed that the water temperature had increased by six and a half degrees since Cape Town, so I took the plunge and hung off the stern ladder. It was both colder and more forceful than I'd anticipated, but I was a renewed human being afterwards. So new, that I stopped sleeping in all my downtime, and remembered what I had set out to do. It was time to write. I wanted to finish the travel novel I'd begun years before by the time we crossed the Atlantic. I had a lot of work to do!

The autopilot seized up again, and once more we were subjected to hand-steering. David told us how the autopilot had failed him in the Pacific. They'd spent four days hand-steering two hours on, two hours off. Day and night. Night and day. They'd lived on muesli bars and coffee. Fortunately for us, it was short-lived. At 02:11, on the tenth day out, we arrived in *the most extraordinary place on Earth.*

THE OTHER SIDE OF THE WORLD

James Town, Saint Helena, 25 October 2013

Obviously one ocean crossing isn't quite enough, and that's why I opted
to cross the Atlantic too.
Sunshine, tropical waters, stars, phosphorescence, and sunsets…
I missed the simplicity that life on the Indian Ocean had held.
But the Atlantic, blimey it's cold!

Sunsets, sunrises, and the stars have been censored by rain clouds.
Since Cape Town, I've had no less than three layers on my bottom half,

six on the top, three on my head and constant socks on my feet. I was even willing to compromise my standards and wear shoes, but I didn't bring any…

And this is meant to be *the tropics*?

It's not all bad though – we've had a plethora of whales, dolphins, seals, coffee and good food (not all to eat); and that's almost made up for the temperatures.

In fact, being the optimist that I am, I assured the crew that good weather was only a day away. I have officially received another verbal warning (bringing the total to nine), after falsely getting the crew's hopes up.

Anyway, back to the question: what do we do all day?

It's easy – between morning and afternoon naps, morning and afternoon teas, meal times, the normal evening snooze, adjusting the sails (every three or four days, if we have to), and our allocated watch times (which do get quite stressful at times); there isn't nearly enough time for reading, writing, contemplating life, talking and chilling.

How could we possibly get bored?

Di spends some of her spare time being seasick.

Si's spent four days trying to catch a fish.

And the captain is constantly smiling.

We crossed the Prime Meridian (Longitude 00'00.00) in the early hours of Tuesday morning and now officially find ourselves on the other side of the world (The Western Hemisphere).

But none of us are particularly impressed quite yet. There seems to be an excessive amount of murky-grey sky and water, and not a lot else.

To quote the crew: "Next time you want to complain about Cape Town's weather, just think about the poor buggers that live in the tropics."

After 230 hours and 47 minutes, 1750 miles of sea, we finally find ourselves back on solid ground in Saint Helena; a third(ish) of the way to the Caribbean.

❦

THE MOST EXTRAORDINARY PLACE ON EARTH

We weren't very good at mooring and had almost drowned Simon when he tried to secure us to the giant mushroom float. When David decided that we needed to do it again (because we weren't exactly where the *South African Coastal Guide* book told us to be), we all groaned. It was 07:00. The second attempt was even worse than the first.

While we patiently awaited immigration, the captain cooked up a full English breakfast (we were in English territory after all) and brewed three pots of filtered coffee. Finally, their friendly smiles arrived and welcomed us in.

Diane and Si were off to the showers while Dave and I began the research. As sailors, we knew the drill. We started at The White Horse where we found a Windhoek and met a plethora of people whose mumbled articulations we failed to understand. Moving on, we found The Standard Bar where a jukebox box played and the sun finally decided to make a brief appearance. Everyone was 16 or younger at The Continental Hotel. We caught up with the freshly scented couple at Anne's Place before we returned to the boat for a braai and some more beer.

On the second day, after far too many cups of coffee, we took a casual stroll up the impossibly steep 699 steps of Jacob's Ladder before winding the narrow green rolly hill roads back to Jamestown for lunch. I finally went for a [cold] shower and the timing worked out perfectly so that we were sat back in the Continental Hotel for the *Super Fourteen* final. The Sharks won.

Saint Helena had only ever had two celebrities: the infamous Napoleon (who even in his death gave us a hard time by not letting us into his house) and Jonathan, the oldest living land animal (179 years old at the time). I'm proud to say that I licked the latter (in a semi-illegal stint that was performed just in front of the governor's house).

Saint Helena's an interesting place where the volcanic terrain changes around every bend. The locals are all lovely; and quite fittingly named "Saints," even if you can't understand a word of what anyone's saying. Everyone drives a Ford Escort, and there seems to be more of them than people. It's beautiful. It's friendly. But 122 square km only keeps you entertained for so long. 1750 miles from South Africa, 1812 miles from Brazil, and a million miles away from reality. The only way in and out of the island (apart from private yachts, of course) was on the monthly *Royal Mail Ship* (RMS). Definitely give it a visit, but make sure you don't miss the boat!

❦

Plans had changed quite drastically. Originally, we'd planned on sailing straight up the African coast to the Mediterranean. Instead of beating into the wind, we opted for a far more comfortable, yet ever so "slightly" longer trip by crossing the Atlantic twice. Ascension was only a brick's throw away so we re-routed even further out, to give the island a visit. It wasn't far, but man was it a frustrating sail!

I'm in one of those weird phases of life where I drift between exhaustion, panic, confusion and ecstasy. Sat on watch with clean hair, freshly clipped toenails, and a cup of coffee in hand, I have intense desires to go for a run and give a big portion of the world's population a hug. I want to go for a quick snooze and have a long bike ride or take my scooter out for a spin. I need a rush. I need adrenalin. I need a nap. I want to skydive. And paraglide. And surf. I want to beat drums and dance on a table. I don't like this. I don't like feeling confused. I don't like being in a place where things are physically impossible. Being on a boat right now makes most of these things just that.

I don't know what to do anymore! In the past week, three people have tagged me in posts about Dave Someone-or-other who's been the first person to visit every region on earth. It's inspiring me to up my game. Should I try and make inroads as one of the most travelled people on Earth? No, I like going slow. I like learning about cultures and immersing myself in them. I love new places and new adventures. But I also love the idea of being part of a community, of knowing my neighbours, and having good friends nearby. I even like the notion of maybe actually finding the fabled "one" and starting a family...
Life is very frustrating like that. I can't have everything at once. It's an either/or kind of game and I never know whether to "either" or to "or."

Insomnia is my constant companion as billions of thoughts race around my troubled head. I want to make a difference. I need to do something great. Meaninglessly meandering around the planet is a life-changer, but it's also very selfish.

Frustrations were fought by butchering a butternut for Halloween. I wrote incessantly because at least that way I didn't have to think. I tried to do small workout sessions, but that was easier said than done on a heeling sailing boat. Nothing could appease the anguish inside. That's part of doing life at four miles an hour.

❡

We stared out into the abyss, squinting our eyes to try and work out what it was sparkling in the distance. It couldn't be, no? As true as Larry King, for the first time since Cape Town, we finally took our jackets off at sea. We'd found the sun. The flying fish returned to the waters. The night sky was littered with stars and our oceany world had been completely transformed to perfection. It might have been a November thing, but I collapsed with a smile on my face and finally slept for the first time in days.

Blue skies, calm seas and a rainbow. Someone up there was trying to make up for the lack of exquisite scenery we'd suffered. And someone down there was making filter coffee. I liked November already. Sun-rain. Rain-sun. Sunny-rain. Rainy-sun. Sunny-sun. It was a peculiar sort of day. 38 miles out, we spotted land and it beautified as we encroached. The last hundred meters were spent surfing our way into the bay where we anchored in the last light. We cracked open a beer and a bag of Doritos as we basked in life, hoping our anchor would hold and that immigration would remember to visit us in the morning.

AND THEN WE FLED

We spent the morning watching an impressive display as the *RMS* was offloaded. As we patiently awaited customs, we busied ourselves checking the rigging, replacing *shackles*, and launching the dinghy. When that was done, we entertained ourselves by feeding the triggerfish who swarmed in to eat everything, including our toes. It was 13:00 by the time Dave was taken ashore. The rest of us were collected just before 14:00. Despite having everything packed and ready, we were told not to bring anything. This turned out to be bad advice.

We didn't have enough money to pay immigration, so they held our passports while we wandered off to explore the island. The turtle-egged beaches, the trigger-fish-skeleton shores, the strange hues of sand and sea. It was an interesting island. In staunch contrast to Saint Helena (where nobody did anything productive), **Ascension** was a working island, not a tourist destination.

We took our own dinghy the following day, braving massive breaking waves and a very sketchy landing. We finally cleared in and went for a proper reconnoitre before sitting down to a rather American burgery lunch. None of us were prepared for what happened next.

Hearing a gurgling noise, we spun around to find a man pouring a can of beer down the drain. On closer inspection, we established that he had been tasked to discard three cases of Guinness into the gutter. In desperation, we ran at him and tried to stop him. He paused and looked up at us with guilty eyes, fully knowing the gravity of his sin. We tried to reason and negotiate. We pleaded. We begged. We assured him that we would take them off the island with us and be gone. Hope sparkled across his face and through the air as all the by-standers willed our mission to succeed. We were so close to saving the expired liquid of the gods... We held our breath... But his boss wouldn't have it. We failed. We sat down speechless, decided we didn't like the place and fled.

PLENTY OF FISH IN THE SEA

I found the Bible I thought I had left in Cape Town and finally spent some time with God. It made all the difference. Instead of sleepless nights and worry-filled days, I had peace and my writing suddenly flowed. It was as if I didn't have any control any more. My head was clear and I finally knew how to tell the story I'd been trying to tell for four years.

"Do not worry about anything, instead pray about everything. Tell God what you need and thank Him for what he has already done. Then you will have God's peace which exceeds everything we can understand." - Philippines 4:13

As a crew, we all knew our duties and worked together brilliantly. We'd become a team, a family! There was much to laugh about, and much to teach each other as we bobbed along in our floating home.

We were almost 1000 miles away from land when three boats popped up on the horizon. We thought they must be fishing boats, but there was something eerie about them. We gathered on the deck to be extra vigilant. We weren't taking chances. But they continued to linger longer than we were willing to. Eventually we disappeared to our respective cabins, leaving Dave alone in the cockpit. We hoped for the best.

When I awoke for my morning watch, the peculiar vessels remained but didn't seem to be wanting trouble. I let them be and sat back to enjoy my coffee while the great eraser of the sky rubbed out the stars and the darkness; leaving streaks of red, yellow and purple, before rising majestically out of the ocean.

There were so many flying fish on the deck this morning, that I contemplated canning and selling them as a future business initiative. But the thought quickly escaped me as I noticed that we were exactly 729 miles away from our waypoint – I looked up and saw the sign: "You are halfway. Drink beer now!" I ran to call the others, and we did. I'm glad there was a sign! - Di, our voice of moral reason, always needs convincing that beer should be allowed. And while we drank, we almost caught a fish. We'd long forgotten that we were trying; and the sneaky critter escaped with the reel.

A little over 200 miles out, we caught a silver barracuda. Si fought for ages to bring in the beast as we stood ready with a bucket, knife and gloves (for lack of a gaff). He gave it everything he had. We were just about to lift it into the cockpit, when it pulled itself free from the hook. For more than a month he'd been trying to catch just one fish; and now this. We were devastated. He simply shrugged it off and said, "Oh well, there are plenty of fish in the sea!" and threw his lure back out.

Inside I brought years of work to completion. I had finally finished editing my first travel novel. I had quite literally just written "The End" when there was another yell from the cockpit, and all of us arrived to find Si battling the reel again. This time he brought the mahi-mahi home. After spending so much time on a vegetarian boat, I couldn't watch the slaughter process. I returned indoors to back up my writing while the bloodbath ensued. The others were nice enough to bring the fish indoors inside a Pick n Pay shopping bag, pretending like it was supermarket bought. That fish's death was not done in vain. Four sailors found all too much joy in devouring it.

There were ships everywhere, and we were playing a tacking game trying to dodge them. Being under sail, we might have had the right of way; but our collision with them wouldn't leave anything more than a scratch on their hull, while we'd be annihilated.

The *water maker* broke. Shackles failed. Lines broke. The last miles were madness. The waters turned from deep purply blue to violet-turquoise sea-green. Excitement was building. Ahead of us lay a whole new country. A new continent even. A world of unknown…

There might even be clean laundry!

We watched a spectacular sunset before a mass of confusing navigation lights hit us at the same time as the dark. We dodged wrecks and unlit fishing boats with astute eyes. We anchored once, only to realise that we were freakishly close to some unidentified dark matter, so we ventured closer to land.

We cracked open the last beers to wash down a feast of left-over fish and roast vegetables. We'd just completed an ocean crossing and were in South America at last. There was much reason to celebrate.

And then we all went to bed. It's a tiresome life being at sea.

11.

A GOOD NAME FOR A DEAD FISH

WHAT do you want from us!?" I thought I was dreaming when I heard Di yell. But then she screamed it again. "What do you want from us?!" I knew something was wrong but lay there in a daze trying to scrutinize the situation. "Just put it down." Portuguese? One voice? Two? Four? "Take everything and let us be!" said Si. More mumbles. Definitely Portuguese. My mind was racing. Where was David? What was happening? How many people were on board? Do I go and see what's happening?

I mentally scanned my dark room to see if there was anything that I could use as a weapon. I heard Si's voice again: "No!" Deodorant? Plastic pirate sword? Where was my knife? Dave's voice. The others were all together. I didn't want to be alone. Did they know I was in here? I really didn't want to be alone.

There was nothing to fight with so I started praying.

"Just put it down!" "No!" It carried on. I listened to the boat being ripped apart. The crew sounded stressed. I prayed harder. Why weren't they coming into my room? Was I a coward for not going out? I still had the element of surprise to work with. If Di screamed, I would run and put on a fight. But who was I fighting? I carried on praying. The rummaging continued. "Put it down!" "Take what you want!" Things were being lugged across the deck. Heavy things. The voices went quiet and I pictured bodies being dragged.

GOD HELP!!!

It felt like hours before they finally came into my room. I lay motionless, propped up by the pillows that had formed my lee cloth at sea. I couldn't breathe. I didn't dare. My mind feared the worst. I'd joked about losing my virginity to pirates, but this was terrifying. I didn't want it to be like this. For the first time in my life, I was glad that I was having my period, it may have been a deterrent.

They were on my bed. I could feel their bodies touching me. And then a light shone on my face. Portuguese. Rummaging. More Portuguese. The light returned to my statued being; eyes still closed, praying. The door shut. Why had the door shut? I could still feel a body on the bed next to me. I forced my mind to recall rape prevention techniques as I held my breath. Tried not to shake. Not to shiver. Not to move.

An engine started. Di called out. I force-opened my eyes. There was no one there. My bed was vacant. I opened the door and found the others tied up in the saloon. Dave and Si on the sides, Di in the middle. They were badly shaken. They'd had a gun, a knife and a spear gun pressed to their temples and throats. The four Brazilian men had taken turns guarding them while the rest pillaged the boat. Di had almost lost her finger when they hadn't been able to get her wedding ring off. They'd been on board for over an hour.

We started surveying the damages. The lights wouldn't turn on. They muddled with our circuit board, but the captain eventually brought them back. The South Africans had placed their jewellery on their bedside so that they'd remember not to take it ashore in the morning. Diamond earrings, watches, necklaces, wedding bands - they were all gone. They'd taken all the laptops, cameras, cellphones, clothes. They'd taken food, but only took one swig of my soy milk and decided to leave that behind. The satellite phone was stolen too.

I checked the cockpit. The *Chartplotter* was gone. So was the GPS. Both of them. The outboard engine and all our fishing gear had been taken. Miraculously, they'd left Dave's camera and my iPhone. They were too obviously placed to seem valuable.

In my room, I found they'd stolen my jewellery (all sentimental, none valuable). They'd taken my makeup. They even stole my tampons.

Di had managed to conceal our emergency grab bag behind her feet, salvaging our passports and wallets.

I'd come off lightly. Not only had I been left in my bed, with no weapons to my head; but the others had thousands of dollars' worth of losses. I had... I then realised what I'd lost... my book... GONE! I couldn't believe it. I'd only finished writing it the previous day.

ƒ

We were shaken and petrified that they'd come back for more. We found make-shift weapons: knives, the fire extinguisher, a wrench and the boat hook. We sat in the cockpit watching. Waiting. They'd muddled with the *VHF* and we tried to bring it back, but there was no calling for help. We put Dave's Australian sim card in my phone and succeeded in getting a hold of his wife in Australia. She managed to contact the Brazilian police and notify our embassies.

Light came and still we sat there, an angry mob armed and ready. Any fishing boat that neared was stared down with vicious eyes taunting them to come closer. We wondered how we'd get ashore. We wondered if things would be even more hostile once we got there.

The nicest smiles of the harbour police came on board. They didn't speak any English though, so we translated through [expensive] calls via England and South Africa. After scribbling down notes about the incident, they had us follow them to a safer location.

Fortunately during the morning clean up, we'd managed to find the boat keys so we didn't have to sail the precarious route into the "marina." We passed three wrecks on the way, and with no instruments to check depths or charts to lead us, we half expected to be the next. Docking in front of a private hotel in a tight-fitting barnacle-laden dock when you're exhausted and still shaken up is hard work. The Italians off the neighbouring ketch came out to lend us a hand, and still we had to do it twice.

It was 10:00 by the time we finally let ourselves eat something. Then it was all systems go:

Get permission to use the dock – Failed. We'd try again later.

ATM – We stood in the queue for half an hour and almost screwed up our cards by entering the wrong pins.

We grabbed a taxi and wound our way through the hefty trafficked streets of **Fortaleza** to immigration. When we arrived, Dave realised he'd forgotten the boat papers on the ATM.

A very expensive taxi ride later, we got ourselves stamped in.

We tried [in vain] to debrief and talk about emotions while we waited to clear Customs.

Captain du Port was slightly faster.

[We took a very necessary lunch break and had some Brazilian beer.]

The Tourist Police didn't seem surprised. They were apologetic, but it had already happened. It was too late. These things happen in Fortaleza. People deal with them. One by one we had to go in and declare all the details of what had happened, and what had been lost in the incident. They heard the same story four times, and we weren't allowed to spare any of the details. I used their internet to notify my travel insurers. Fortunately, I still clung to the belief that you can't die when you have travel insurance and had taken it out as a last-minute precaution, the others had nothing!

I'd tried all day to be optimistic: "These guys need to feed their families and survive..." "At least nobody got hurt..." "...we even found another six-pack in the clean-up!" ...I was trying to make myself feel better too. We were lucky! The boat before us had had 17 bandits clamber on board and even the floorboards had been taken as the crew had been left in only their underpants. On other boats, the crew hadn't survived to tell the tale. But my crew couldn't take it anymore. They'd had enough of my optimism and told me quite plainly to "shut up."

The police gave us a lift back to the marina and, after a very emotional day, we headed straight to the bar. We weren't ready to go home.

GROUNDED

We scrubbed *Nereid* clean. She was dirty. Violated. But no matter how hard we tried, the feeling stuck. They were still there with us!

Contacting family was next, it had been weeks since any of us had been online and we had a lot to catch up on. Seeing that word had spread about our predicament, we had a lot of people to appease.

We attempted to replace the things that we needed to continue to the Caribbean: some form of GPS, some form of Chartplotter. I needed tampons as I was all out; and the situation had just turned dire. Did you know that they neither sell navigation equipment nor tampons in Fortaleza?

I ventured to the bar, diary in hand, to find a quiet spot to sit and contemplate life. I tried to recall the emotions and feelings life had just thrown at us. The boat still carried bad vibes and nervous crew. It was allegedly too unsafe to leave the confines of the hotel "prison" we'd docked at. Even the staff warned us to be vigilant after guests had taken a stroll down the road and returned scantily clad when someone knifed them for their clothes.

...That dirty teddy of mine seems to have saved me the worst of it. Acting as my doorstop, the pirates must have thought that I was a child (probably reinforced by my plastic sword, snorkel mask, and rubber fish handbag). Allegedly, they kept picking him up and down as they discussed my cabin... What did they see when they shone their torches on my face...? Why did they not take me out and tie me up with the others? I'm more than just lucky!

I hadn't been contemplating long when a friendly bleach-blond smile approached and introduced himself as Roelof. He'd docked two boats down. The Dutch sailor was travelling around the world and writing a book while he tried to find a new home. Life had been ever so cruel to him. He was trying to rebuild himself and restart his life without the pain and heartbreak of all his past losses (wife, kids, finances, and his dad). My little pirate incident suddenly didn't seem so bad. I'd been so blessed all my life; a bit of evil was probably long overdue.

The following night, I awoke with every creak. I got up to ensure no unwarranted guests had boarded. A couple of times I bumped into Di, who was doing the same. Dave's light just happened to turn on a few times too. We were nervous wrecks on the floating vessel, even in the safety of the marina compound and its many cameras. All exhausted, we attempted to bring joy back to our life. We treated ourselves to the hotel's buffet breakfast. They even served an assortment of chocolate!

Brazil was not at all what I expected. The variety in body size, hair colour and skin tones was vast. It was as colourful as I had imagined, but man was it dirty! The dingiest restaurants and bars often turned out to be the most expensive. The posh places lacked vibe. It was a strange place.

That night we began a watch. We were pretty certain we were safe; but for the sake of everyone's sleep, we decided it would be best to have one person keep a watchful eye so the others could relax. Night watches were long. There were no boats to scan for, no course to correct, no sails to trim, and no stars, for the city lights swallowed them all. Instead, we took two-hour shifts sitting in the cockpit to watch either the water, where nothing was happening; or the hotel, where glimpses of romance and debauchery could be spied through curtains undrawn.

I finally met with the marina manager, a colourful character with whom I had to guard my negotiations carefully. He'd lost 63 kilograms purely by excluding coke from his diet. I was amazed, until I learned he'd been drinking eight litres a day, and then even more amazed at how that was possible!

We cleaned the boat again and hand washed our clothes (laundromats cost far more than my rags were worth). Quite quickly, the morning vanished. The rest of the crew returned to the mall. I could think of nothing worse, so I stayed behind to tour *Debonair*, Roelof's boat. The tour turned to us braving the very discouraging walk into town. The extreme contrasts between rich and poor were everywhere: skyscrapers and shacks, happy and sad, flash cars and bare feet.

"And what about dinner?" he asked. Over a seafood feast, he shared more of his story. On the way to find a taxi, we found live music and stuck around for one last drink before finally returning to the marina.

He tried to kiss me as I dropped him off down the dock. I couldn't! There was far too much going on in my head and I wasn't sure how I felt about him. When I got home, it was nearly 02:00 and Di was sitting in the cockpit worried sick. She grounded me. I went to bed very perplexed, feeling very guilty indeed. I never slept.

As penance for my transgressions, I was given the 04:00 – 06:00 watch. This was not only great thinking time, but the perfect time to rinse and hang up the washing I'd left soaking. At six, I went for a run to clear the last confusion from my cranium. I did some push-ups and sit-ups then lay on the grass staring up at the mighty palm trees that towered over me. It felt good to be active, it felt good to be alive! I jumped into the pool and then found the shower. I bumped into Roelof on the way. He apologised for trying to kiss me. I apologised for not.

ᚠ

We decided that we'd leave at the same time as the Italians, that way we could keep in radio contact and check our chart navigation with them leading the way. Silvano had already cleared out of Brazil; but like every other boat in the marina, they were playing the waiting game looking for parts. He agreed, on the condition we could keep up.

The others went supply shopping while I checked us out with Roelof as a bodyguard. First immigration, but they were closed till two. The tourist police still hadn't done a thing about anything. Customs would have been fast, but Silvano's part had just arrived and they wanted to charge him duties of R$1500 for a R$300 part. The smiling coast guard was the first to welcome me to *Capitan Du Port*. He led me through to smiley number 2 who was very disappointed that we were leaving already. We hadn't had enough time to experience the good side of Brazilian life.

Roelof excused me from dinner. He asked permission to take me out dancing. Di let me off the grounded hook. I was nervous as I wasn't much of a dancer. He had a good point though, this was my last night in Brazil and I couldn't leave without dancing.

He asked me to seriously consider his offer. He had already whispered that he loved me. He was willing to go anywhere in the world to find me. Roelof had donated us a hand-held GPS, had given us charts and had set up our new computer. As a leaving present, he donated us a whole assortment of lures, making me promise that we'd name the first fish we caught after him.

CARRIBEAN BOUND

08:06, and we'd hauled up the anchor and were under-way with only a hand-held GPS directing us. Roelof stood waving off his bow. He hadn't been to sleep yet, for fear of missing seeing us off. I bucketed the deck to wash off the anchor mud as Fortaleza drifted out of sight, hoping that happier (or maybe I should say "less pirated") times lay ahead.

We caught the first fish a couple of hours out, while I was napping. It wasn't particularly big and we don't know what it was; but it bore mad fangs and withered and writhed until one of its eyeballs popped out. I went back to sleep until my 14:00 watch and woke up to a crew of seasick sailors. It didn't take long before I joined their ranks.

As soon as my watch was done, I crawled into bed, hoping to sleep off the nausea. I crawled out again for dinner and looked around. Everyone remained pale, everyone looked dejected. We were all very literally in the same boat. Spirits were low. Fishing boats were plentiful. Both the engine and the water maker were playing up. It was as if the negativity on board was attracting more problems. But with the sunset, the problems dissolved and we finally feasted on Roelof (the fish), who was rather delicious even if we'll never know what species he was.

My pen died, so I stopped writing for a while and started reading the book Roelof had given me. He'd signed the front page "You have the most beautiful smile I have ever seen."

Ting ting ting. Ting ting ting. Ting ting ting ting. "This is your captain calling." *Ting ting ting.* "Four minutes to the equator!" It wasn't even

05:00, but we all crawled out of bed. I grabbed the mampoer and the party hats as we scrambled onto the deck to bid the Southern Hemisphere goodbye and greet Neptune in the North.

The mampoer was vile and burned so much that we had to wash it down with a couple of beers and some cheesy chips, while we took turns to make sacrifices to Neptune. It wasn't exactly what we wanted at the crack of dawn; but we were sailors and it had to be done.

Being in the windless *doldrums*, we decided to raise the *spinnaker*. This turned out to be quite a lot of hard work. Made harder still, for Dave was the only one to have ever used one before. I suppose it might have even been worth the struggle. The magnificent green-yellow sail added two knots to our speed. A swim, a braai, and a couple of beers. It was a whole day of celebrations under the canopy of the light wind sail. A simple word of warning though: be ready to bring it in before bad weather hits. Otherwise, like us, you'll get the whole crew soaked and miserable in the early hours of the morning!

We stood looking at our sail configuration. Things weren't holding together as well as they ought to have and the squalls kept sending us off course.

"Should we change the sails before the next squall?"

"Yeah, make the most of the wind push!"

"I don't know, the squalls only last a few minutes."

Silence.

"Some of them last a while," I added. "How far did you say you took us over?"

"50 degrees. 215"

"That's South"

"Yeah"

Silence.

"What do you think? Should we do it?

We all turned to contemplate the sky.

"Why not?"

Simon inched towards the bow. Only it wasn't just a little squall. Lines were twisted all over the place and as we tried to take the *genoa* over, the dinghy was flung into the air and almost went overboard. I ran to the bow to try and tighten it back down and almost got whacked in the face by the jib sheet as it broke free. We almost had everything under control when I noticed a rip in the sail. "Bring her in," I yelled after witnessing sails self-destruct on *Fiddler*.

"Why?" the others asked.

But by then it was too late and we watched it shred apart.

We dropped and changed the sail.

I tried to survive the last 15 minutes of my watch in wet clothes, but it was too cold. As soon as I returned to the deck, another line broke loose and I got soaked all over again! My bed had been flooded, so I took up residency on the saloon couch. A small drip, not much different to Chinese Water Torture, would not let me have the satisfaction of rest. I was still up when Si called me for my 02:00 shift. The storm continued to rage.

I woke up to the smell of pancakes. The storm had abated, and we found ourselves back in the doldrums bobbing up and down. I suppose that's where that whole "all or nothing" saying comes from. The day vanished all too quickly. When I finally finished my watch, I crashed hard and awoke with a startle as something hit my head and then jiggled around in my bed. A flying fish had wangled its way under my sheets. I've never met a fish quite as smelly as a flying one. The scent of scales stained my bedding and kept me awake all the way through till my 02:00 watch when it poured with rain; again!

The inverter broke and the captain announced that there would be no more music on board. We made the halfway mark and cracked open a beer each; but spirits were low, and nobody was really in the mood. Di slept through it.

The hum of the engine makes me angry. Why are we rushing our arrival to a destination we know nothing about? Why aren't we enjoying the journey? Surely we should be making the most of the abyss of blue? We're sailors, aren't we? ...I suppose I want land too; I need hugs!

I curled up in a ball and cried.

I woke up a whole year older. It was too early for my watch, but I couldn't sleep anyway. I crept onto the deck and happened to be just in time for a full-blown meteor shower. When the sun arose, there were dolphins, rain, and ten dead flying fish littering the deck. Two massive rainbows lined our path (as did a big ship). That was all before 08:00. A birthday at sea wasn't all bad I suppose. But I was still disappointed that we were missing out on the festivities we'd planned for Tobago. Now there was no time; and with the ever-present threat of pirates, *Nereid* was taking no more chance locations.

The general consensus was to turn the boat 30 degrees to port so that we could have a braai to celebrate. But even on the wrong course, we were still heeling an awful lot, and it took all four of us to make it a success. The dolphins returned a second time as we feasted, and again for the sundown[28]. By nightfall, Di and I stood poised in the cockpit, chopping boards in hand. A game of "tennis" ensued as we battled the ocean in an ultimate challenge. The flying fish flew at us from every direction; we mercilessly whacked them back to sea. It might not have been Tobago, but how many people get to celebrate their birthday in the middle of the ocean?

---

[28] There were too many clouds to watch it set.

166

December. There was a faint light arriving in the sky, so I put on the kettle straight away. At least with coffee, this whole lurching and bobbing thing feels a little less real, a bit more movie-like. It's liquid food for thought. Only two more days till Guadeloupe. Can we stand two more days of this? Everything is a battle: teeth brushing, dishes, weeing, even just sitting still is hard work. I want land, stability and hugs. We are only ten days out, but I'm falling apart!

Eventually, the wind shifted to the rear and life became bearable again. We lost some speed, but it was completely worth the comfort. Barbados glowed in the distance. I wished I hadn't mentioned that I had friends who did private security there, otherwise we might have been tasting land already. Instead, seeing as I had finished reading my book and caught up with my diary entries (rambling on about my need for hugs) I sat on the stern using the light to make shadow puppets on the water. I wondered if the others had reached similar levels of boredom.

The clouds glowed pink, and finally abated into stars. The engine fired up again. I prayed for the wind, and it arrived out of nowhere. It was like God did still care about us! We'd wrongly estimated our position, so it seemed that the early morning arrival would be in the afternoon. But I was okay with that. I suddenly realised that I had no plans and was wanting land to be further away again. Dave had decided to leave *Nereid* in the Caribbean and fly home for Christmas. Si and Di were all-qualified and off to find jobs. I didn't know what to do next or how to even start thinking about it. I hoped that land would be as beautiful as we'd imagined. I hoped that it would be cheaper than we'd imagined. I prayed that it would be colourful, safe and fun. I prayed that we would all find exactly what we needed: a safe mooring, spare parts, an affordable flight back to Australia for Dave, jobs and replacement electronics for Si and Di. I didn't know what exactly I needed, but I prayed for fresh fruit and veggies [because I couldn't eat any more meat!] and for adventure, hugs, friends and direction. The most beautiful shooting star that I'd possibly ever seen shot across the sky and broke off into an almost firework display of smaller flickers. I smiled. With everything in God's hands, I had an excellent night's sleep.

I woke up with a loud thud followed by two smaller ones. I flew out of bed and raced to the deck to see if we had gybed or if something new had broken. Everything seemed normal, but what was that noise? Who was on watch? There was nobody around. I checked the time, 01:51 – David's watch. I checked the cockpit again – there was no one on the helm and nobody on the deck. Had he gone back to sleep? I checked his cabin. "David? David?" I called as I tried to find his light switch. There was no answer. Louder. I found the switch. No luck. I checked his head – not there. Di and Si's – not there either. He definitely wasn't in mine. I checked the deck again starting to fear the worst. Nothing. We didn't have a man overboard alarm anymore, so I ran downstairs and woke the others. My whole body was trembling.

"Have you checked the water maker?" asked Di. Sure enough, there was the captain, locked into the soundproof stern box, toying with his tools.

I arose with the engine's hum. It drowned some of the sunrise's splendour and then proceeded to splutter and die. The others were horrified. Had we run out of fuel? Or was this something more serious? I went for my daily walk of death to clean the carcasses off the bow. Only one fatality, it had been a quiet night. I prayed again. I knew God had us and there was nothing to worry about. Seconds later the engine roared back to life. The water maker that had gone on strike days before started up. Even the 220-volt power supply returned and I could finally put some music on. As I fried up sweetcorn fritters to celebrate, I heard the captain's cry: "Land ho!" There was a lot of it!

Almost effortlessly we found ourselves in port, docked stern-to amongst a throng of yachts. Our world of solitude was suddenly overpopulated.

Simon wandered off to find beer. Dave wandered off to find the internet to let his wife know that we had safely arrived in **Guadeloupe**. Di got the boat in order. I just wandered the land, being mesmorised by everything. We all reunited back on *Nereid* and cracked open celebratory beers and wine. Red and white. Of course we had a celebratory braai!

f

I lay in bed trying to keep my eyes open scrolling the plethora of birthday messages I'd received whilst at sea:

"I'm not saying you're Wonder Woman, I'm just saying I've never seen you and Wonder Woman at the same time."

- Vicky

"May no more pirates be found along your wonderful journey. May many new lickable joys be found along your path and may it be the best year ever."

– Brian

"I wanted to wish you a life full of happiness, adventures, and good people; but I came to the conclusion that all that would happen anyway, regardless of my wishes. So instead I want to wish you a life without demons, pirates, muggers, and weapons. Hope this year will only bring smiles to your face and maybe (hopefully) meeting up somewhere down the line. Miss you like very few people miss someone who they've only known for three days"

- Adam

"Greetings from Guadeloupe."

I was going to hold off replying till the morning, but I had to check if they were still around!

At 02:04 I had a new message:

"We've just anchored in the bay outside the marina."

12.

AYE CANDY

IT was like I'd never left. The cockpit seemed bigger and the dodger seemed bluer. The curtains were down and the spice racks were up. Everything else was still all over the place. I felt right at home!

Kirk had purchased me for a pack of cookies on condition that he cleared *Nereid* of all rice cakes and soy milk. David drove a hard bargain.

James was nowhere to be found as I sat catching up with Kirk, while Ewa sat quietly at the helm. I assumed I'd pissed him off already. It had been the greater part of nine months since I'd last seen him and I hadn't had a chance to ask how he felt about me hopping on board.

Despite their own challenges, life had been more good than bad. There had been three on board for the Atlantic crossing, and Ewa had flown out from Poland to join them on the other side. As the four of them sailed up the coast of Brazil, they collided with one of the plethora of wooden fishing boats and had to fork out far too much in damages.

En route the bus station to visit a friend, their Australian got mugged and lost everything, including her passport. They'd joined forces with some locals and managed to get most of her belongings back, but their time in Brazil had been expensive with mixed feelings and rollercoasters of emotions. After that, they'd stayed away from the mainland and explored all sorts of island paradises before eventually rounding the South American bulge and sailing up to the Caribbean.

James finally appeared, beer and cigarette in hand. He sat down quietly by himself looking aloof. I felt guilty for spoiling his last few days on board, but I was glad to see him again and wanted to know about all his adventures and inner workings. When Kirk took a breather, I took the plunge and chanced conversation. "So, James, tell me about the last few months? Where have you been? How have you been?" He too took a big breath and told me all about Brazil, Ecuador and Machu Picchu; and eventually cracked a smile and walked away.

He resurfaced with another beer and handed it over. I smiled too. Maybe this would all be okay? Maybe there wasn't too much resentment and hard feelings? Kirk cooked an exceptional curry and before long, we found the navigation lights leading us into **Les Santes**. We'd arrived already.

I held James by the feet as he tried to poke a line through a ropeless mooring ball. I laughed so hard I half dropped him in the water. Dry and showered, he returned on deck, dropped the dodger and grabbed more beers. We sat on the deck discussing life. It was good to have my friend back – even with our colourful history.

"So..." he started "...do you want to sleep up here, or should I move all the shit off your old bunk?" I didn't mind and disappeared inside to find my toothbrush. My bag exploded on opening. As I sat looking in vain for the forgotten necessity he added, "Or you could just share my bed?" My thoughts raced as I remembered moments in that bed and the no-touching sign that he'd hung to make my carnal treasure feel safer. I thought about his past, mine and life altogether... I thought about how I'd crushed his heart only a few months earlier... I was interrupted "...no pressure, no nonsense. I might accidentally cuddle you in my sleep. No strings attached! Anyway, it's up to you."

f

"We've moved around in some strange circles - us," I said as we sat sipping espressos and munching croissants at a beautiful French café since *Fiddler* no longer had coffee on board. "And the timing's always terrible!" he added. We both laughed. I'd slept so well curled up in a warm safe body. I liked having James around. But our relationship was doomed from that very first kiss. We both knew it.

The island, with its quaint streets and electric cars and scooters, was rather pleasant. There was a tiny grocery shop and a plethora of beauty. We took a morning dive followed by an afternoon snorkel. The day concluded with yet another spectacular sunset as we set sail again.

DOMINICA

I loved the country immediately! Green rolling hills and small villages. The people were laid back, chilled, smiling and colourful. Music came from every direction and it carried with it the strong sweet scent of marijuana. Nobody seemed to be doing anything in any particular hurry (including customs and immigration). We sat on the dock watching the sun go down before returning to *Fiddler* for Polish pizza and James' last night at his home of almost six years.

"Have you ever read the inside of a tampon box?" I shot Jim a strange look and shook my head. "Did you know toxic shock syndrome is a real disease that affects both men and women and...." he made sure I was paying attention to this vital piece of information: "...tampons can kill you!" I shot him a puzzled look. "What? I was stuck on the john without a book, and that was the only reading material I could find." Somehow this laid out the perfect foundation for the deep and meaningful conversation we'd avoided. It was a hard topic, but necessary; and it was good doing it face to face. All our previous confessions of love were done either via Skype or email; and the heart breakings were returned in the same manner. This had a sense of finality to it. For both of us.

James left me to care for his dive watch, underwater camera, and wetsuit. He left me a new diary, a decision-making spinning top, and a necklace (now my only piece of jewellery). He handed me his bed, the responsibility of caring for Kirk and Ewa, and ultimately his life on *Fiddler*.

We sat and savoured one last beer before we dinghied him ashore and found him a cab. One last kiss goodbye, the very last; and he was gone.

❦

Fiddler had visited before and Ewa knew the terrain well. Everyone greeted us as we explored the petite town. The [omnipresent] one-armed marine man educated us on the island and assured me that it was much safer now that they had patrol boats. I heaved a sigh of relief until someone nearby reminded him that they were both broken. "Armed robbery doesn't happen all the time," the new man tried to assure me. We paddled home with mixed feelings. I only got up once to check for pirates. Kirk had locked us in.

While Kirk continued to tinker with the outboard engine, we rowed ashore and went exploring. We veered down a dirt road strewn with corpse cars and lost ourselves in a swamp of rubber trees. We found a small beach. There was only one fishing boat lying on it: *Roelof.* I fiddled apprehensively with the shells I'd assembled in my pocket.

The further we ventured, the prettier Dominica became. We clambered up cliffs and meandered through small villages and goat-strewn valleys before winding our way back.

While Ewa went shopping, I sat drinking an ice-cold Kabuli at The Purple Turtle. "Are you single?" A friendly local asked. Without giving me a chance to reply, the local continued "...now don't you go running off with the wrong guy... take time, find the right one... make sure you find a guy with a heart of gold." His monologue continued as he told me about the woman he had married, the mistakes he had made and the things he had learned "...but I could always be happier. Now I'm looking for the right woman…" Ewa appeared out of nowhere and I managed to get my first words in, "Thank you. I'll remember that. Good luck, and have a nice life."

I sat staring at the stars contemplating life. I had everything I wanted and everything I needed; but still, something was missing. It had been a tough year, but I'd learned a lot. It had been a year exactly since I'd arrived in South Africa and bid Jim farewell and Dan hello. It had been a year since I'd decided to live in Cape Town. I'd taken my very first full-time job and quit prematurely. I'd officially broken my first hearts and had mine broken too. I needed to turn my life around. I wasn't going to wait till New Years to do it. The rain appeared from nowhere and I battened down the hatches and fled to the safety of my bed.

We set sail just after 13:00. The dolphins swarmed from every direction and brought with them the wind. I relocated to the bow to get a better look and discovered that the anchor had come free. I almost spewed thrice trying to bring it in, but I couldn't stop laughing. Life was beautiful.

The seas remained rough and the evening brought with it heavy traffic from every direction as we steered into port. This time the anchor was well and truly stuck, so Ewa took us on an hour-long joy ride while Kirk and I combined forces (his brain plus my brute strength) to free it. Exhausted, I collapsed on the deck and cracked open James' last French beer. We were back in their territory.

MARTINIQUE

It's remarkable how different places look in the morning. Last night it was all big ships and city lights. Today all I see is a single alluring island looming and begging to be explored.

In staunch contrast to the tranquillity of Dominica, the village teemed with French tourists from the mainland. It pumped holiday vibes. The people weren't particularly helpful, but they were all friendly. The underwater world didn't disappoint either. It swarmed with turtles, eels and colourful fish.

"We're moving ship and going diving," were the instructions I was given. So, I sat patiently waiting on the deck. Nothing happens quite as scheduled in life, but it always works out how it ought to. I alternated between writing and reading *The Alchemist.* In-between I sent good vibes to *Nereid*, James, Roelof and people back home. There was so much going on, but nothing at all at the same time...

It's such a simplistic book, but I think this is what life is truly about. Even with its senseless circles, annoyances, unpredictableness', heartaches, pains and haphazard happiness – in the end it works out. Even if it makes absolutely no sense at the time!

Kirk finally resurfaced and told me he was going to bed. I had needed the time purely to get my head straight. By sunset I was buzzing; and after

Ewa's gingerbread cookies and Kirk's curry, we were all set for a night out.

I said a silent prayer and hoped for a good night; but we found the place rather inert and far too quiet. A man stood stagnantly singing to conservative-church-style backing vocals and a girl was half-hitting the pans. I was hesitant, we all were; but we had come ashore for live music and I suppose this was the best we would get. I sat down and ordered a Leffe. They were out. Duvel, they were out. Lorraine, out. It was either a Stella or a Desperado. Ewa and I took the Stellas. Kirk went with a very pretty cappuccino. I scanned the room. A couple was sitting silently at a table with a drink between them. A man sat sipping Bourbon and Coke trying to look busy. Two girls sat contemplating their cocktails. A couple wandered in, sat for five minutes, then left again. I thought about doing the same but ordered another beer instead. It was a painfully awkward venue.

A small group of French women wandered in and onto the dance floor. Suddenly life breathed into the room and the band started playing like they meant it. Ewa and I got up and joined them. People began pouring in from the streets and soon the dance-floor was packed. I had the best night I'd had out in a long time! When the band's encores eventually ended, I wandered over to the bar to settle the *Fiddler* bill. The bartender said something in French and smiled. I didn't understand, so I asked him again: "How much?" He repeated himself in French once again. My new friend Marie, came to my translation rescue: "No problem, you have danced enough to pay. You are too delightful." I'm not quite sure how that works, but I made a mental note to always be "too delightful!"

❢

I did an emergency shore run for coffee and Floop[29] before we raised anchor. It was such a short sail that we barely had the sails up by the time we had to bring them in again. We moored and went diving. The French waters had something exceptionally magical about them. Morays, octopi, life-filled coral and lionfish. Every dive got better. Lobsters, trumpet fish, sea stars, nudibranchs... My first night dive was so otherworldly that I imagined I was in space.

Five dive-days later, after we'd sailed back to the town, we sprawled in different directions. Kirk went straight to buy more data. Ewa went for a walk and I went for a beer. Such different personalities, yet we fit together so well. Nevertheless, I asked Kirk for a drinking buddy for Christmas.

SAINT LUCIA

Only a few hours of sailing, and we found ourselves in a whole new country. A land abundant in both English and rabies (as all the welcome signs seemed to indicate). It was the day before Christmas, but I had more success than I'd hoped for. I found presents and treats. I even managed to make friends before heading back to *Fiddler*. The only thing I'd failed at was buying beer. It was catastrophic!

I'd planned to head back out in the evening, but a storm struck as I sat painting Christmas wrapping (I'd apparently forgotten to purchase that too). It turns out that it was a good thing I got stranded on *Fiddler*. The 24th was Polish Christmas and Ewa too had been brewing. I ventured out of my cabin to put presents under the painted tree to find the table laden with all twelve dishes of Polish Christmas: pierogi, borscht, barsczc, piernic... (being "vegetarians," we skipped the codfish, of course). What

---

[29] Frozen ice-lollies.

a feast! Keeping with the culture, there was an empty seat set just in case a vagrant dinghied past.

"życzę Ci wesołych Świąt Bożego Narodzenia![30]"

Christmas morning: I bounced out of bed, wished Jesus a happy birthday and began making pancakes. It was still pouring, but we braved a visit to the local village to deliver bags of James' leftover clothes. We watched the last Atlantic Rally Crossing (ARC) boat arrive and observed how the people swarmed to welcome the sailors in. We contacted our families and shared hugs with strangers. We donned our hats and pop-popped our pop-pops; and then feasted on leftovers before experimenting with Ewa's Dominican gift.

The problem was that none of us had ever rolled a joint. It had a sort of inverse effect as we laughed in hysterics before we even had a chance to smoke it. Feeling responsible, I braved the rain to chain up the dinghy. Somehow I managed to get ropes twisted around my neck and found myself hung by a noose. I fought myself free and splashed into the water. The night finished with coffee, dessert and [of course] more hysterics. Presents would have to wait.

Finally, the torrential downpour abated and we returned to shore. While we had sat safe and [mostly] dry celebrating Christmas, islanders had fought for their lives. By morning, over 30 people were dead. So many had lost their homes, their possessions and their lives!

I never got the drinking buddy I asked for (and I'm still waiting for Santa to deliver on the wish list in a bottle I floated him last year); but I sure am blessed with life!

❦

---

[30] We wish you a merry Christmas!

The solitude of yachtie life had me subdued. I took a long walk leaving Kirk and Ewa to their own devices. Strolling the honeymoon beaches had me both laughing at the ridiculousness of humans and longing for a deeper connection with one of my own. Rain dumped down on me. As the beach dwellers fled for shelter, I found myself suddenly liberated; dancing and singing and free! I wandered back to town and found the others still busy, so I sat down for a happy hour drink. That's when I met the Irish.

My heart was won over by Irish accents. Over meaty dishes, the tales were told: How sharks had bitten off their hydro-generator. How sleeping Fin had first been hit by a flying fish, and then by the marlin that chased after it (fortunately the porthole had been too tight for the beast to stab him). It was the easiest catch of their passage.

I was introduced to *skurfing* and had a lot to learn about skiing the tender wake on a surfboard. I also had a lot to learn about selecting the right swimwear for the occasion. I was proudly welcomed to the Beer for Life Club which sounded fantastic, but really just meant you had to do a lot of beer downing when you forgot to mark your bottle. We wobbled back to the Irish vessel where beautiful voices and an assortment of stringed musical instruments strummed me to sleep.

New Year's arrived all too quickly: Sundowners on *Fiddler* and a pub crawl along the many watery docks. We'd just made it to solid ground when I watched Kirk fire off seven gun flares from 1983, two parachute flares from '87, and a hand-held. There were hugs. There were kisses. There was happiness everywhere. 2014 had arrived! There was much to celebrate; and every friendly Rasta had a better [and stronger] infusion for us to try.

"I wish you a callous free 2014. May your gypsy heels be smooth, your tongue be ever at the ready, and your laughter ring hauntingly in the ears of naysayers"

❦

I saw a familiar boat as we sailed into **Marigot.** My heart thumped. How was I going to deal with this? Kirk and Ewa had already watched me jump from James to Fintan in just a few days. How did I explain this one? I really had become a sailor! By the time we'd dropped anchor, he had dropped into the water and started swimming.

I did the only logical thing. I started debugging the boat and had Kirk fend off visitors to buy me time to think. In retrospect, this was a bad call; but I wasn't ready for Roelof!!

I kayaked over to apologise, giving him both a hug and a dinner invite. I needed time to get to know him again. He's such a sweet soul and I didn't want to hurt him. But I also had my heart in other places as well as no places at all. I wasn't ready for love. I craved affection and cuddles. But love was too foreign of a concept!

"Can I kiss you?" he asked as we sat up late into the morning sipping Piton. It was even more terrible than the first time I had rejected him in Brazil. I wanted to cry as I watched his heart shatter. Watching him row away was one of the most painful experiences of my life!

Dear Adeena,

Now I have to change my email. What can I say, you do not know. Spending more time with you will mean falling more and more in love with you.
You do not have the same feelings for me, so it is difficult and beautiful at the same time.
...but still, it is very confusing for me. I feel so stupid telling you the truth about my feelings, which I will never receive back from you.

Forgive me. Let us say I probably see something I want to see. That will explain it in the easiest way. I am just a sensitive and stupid man, who feels too much and really enjoys spending time with you.

The best thing for me would be to go very soon. To be rejected time after time is not a hobby of mine. Again, thank you for the really beautiful experience you have given me. I really enjoy all the feelings I have when you are with me and when you are not.

So I want to stay and I want to go. Better to run... The different feelings you give me... Wonderful, crazy. I ....

I hope you will find love because it is a beautiful feeling. You want to do and you do not want to do. You want to see and you do not want to see. You see a future and you think it is not possible. You feel how a person can have such an impact on you, and it makes you crazy. Different thoughts, different feelings. So alive and wanting to see more and more. Addicted to spending more time and at the same time, you do not want to. Because it frightens you. Warm feelings, getting lost in the eyes; and in her smile, not knowing what to say or think. It will throw you off guard from your normal doing. That is love for me. It is scary. Glad you did not answer it positively; and at the same time feeling as damn. What a pity. To find someone so nice and have to let her go.......

Just want to describe what a little bit of love does to me. Thank you for letting me feel that I am alive.

X
Roelof

Sorry.

❦

Luckily, boat life was back to normal. We had our first problem-free sail through to **Soufriere**. We braved the scores of snake eels and snorkelled ashore to explore Bat Cave. Teams of tourist boats arrived. While they were awed by the bats, they seemed to be far more impressed by the humans who had crawled through the guano and clambered up the rocks at the back of the creature's lair. Swimming home, I finally found a vacant flamingo shell; but as I picked it up, I got stung quite painfully by a creature unseen. Seconds later, a jellyfish stung me and then returned with vengeance to wrap itself around my arm.

We ventured into town. It looked rather quaint in the setting sun as music drifted through the air. We were greeted by swarms of money hunters, grumpy people, and angry eyed dogs that sent us running. Over-sunned, stung, and carrying much emotional guilt, I crawled into bed. I didn't like this place. The chaos ashore mirrored my inner turmoil.

Insomnia ensued and that night I lay awake fretting. Strange calls came through on the VHF. The next day we heard that *Magnetic Attraction*, a boat just one bay over, had been pirated in the night. He had attempted to fight off the invaders and had sustained a blow to the head that left him unconscious as he dropped into the water to drown. She was beaten and robbed, and left a widow.

We untied our mooring line to move to a more beautiful and potentially safer anchorage. Despite the Rangers' adamance that we'd find a spot, there was nothing available. While we were debating what to do, Kirk's phone beeped: "Just arrived in Marigot Bay. Crew exhausted." I looked at Kirk who looked at me and then we both turned to look at Ewa. Instead of a mile and a half relocation, we did a 17.6-mile beat into the wind. We'd finally started working as a real crew. We all understood *Fiddler*'s peculiarities. We laughed and giggled, and enjoyed the bumpy ride while my first-ever attempt at a banana bread baked in the oven. It was good. All of it.

We dropped anchor 25 feet in front of our previous spot, launched the dinghy, and sped over to say hello to Peter and meet his wife. There was no Roelof to be seen.

I've become quite the engineer greasing fans and derusting showers. I fixed my self-induced flag issues and changed all the burned-out light-bulbs. I've fixed our language too. Inspired by the local favourite chocolate, I've had the captain agree to decree that all swear words will now be substituted with "Oh Henry."

Fiddler was long overdue a wash and I was feeling very sick after a day spent bobbing up and down in the dinghy. I was just about to finish up, when Peter rocked up: "I've come to kidnap you. Get in!"

I wish all kidnappings were as pleasant as mine. I was taken to the Do-Littles where I was forced to drink Pina Coladas with the *Sayonara* crew! I kayaked back whilst they prettied themselves in preparation for a formal pumpkin soup and pierogi dinner. As much as I hated being prim and proper, I rather enjoyed playing the perfect hostess. I relished pretending to have my life altogether that night.

The year was a week old, and I had yet to find peace or sleep. I tossed and turned and then watched the seventh sunrise in as many days. I had a long meaningful chat to God and asked him to sort me out. I realised that I had no reason to feel guilty and that life was what it was. Every man [and woman] has their own decisions to make and their own hearts to follow. I'd barely finished breakfast when the radio crackled "*Fiddler. Fiddler. Fiddler...*" and the Irish came out to play.

"Drinking rum before 10:00 does not make you an

alcoholic, it makes you a pirate"

- A wise anonymous soul

It was hard work standing up in the morning, but I was on breakfast duty and we were having guests. A ship's galley is no place for a hung-over sod. Seeing as Peter's family had left and he was single-handed again, it was decided that I really ought to learn more about other boats. While Kirk and Ewa were left with the dishes, I hopped on board *Sayonara*.

The ketch rig is an interesting one and I liked Peter's set up. After schooling me on the purposes of either mast, he educated me on the efficacy of the *wind vane*. With very simple adjustments we could hold course using only the wind. The next lesson was in *heaving to*. We "stopped" the boat by turning the sails inside out. We set an *anchor alarm* to mark our position and sat sipping gin and tonics until eventually we'd drifted too far, and the alarm reminded us that we were in fact meant to be sailing. *Fiddler* breezed past, doing just fine without me!

Trying to explain to Peter that I needed to go ashore to say farewell to the love of my week was easier thought than said. But eventually, we headed ashore for a beer without me having to say anything. We found the Irish "parents" following suit. They were sweet enough to let me know that their vessel would be off at five and I'd better hurry up and say my goodbyes. The boys felt so bad about leaving me without any drinking buddies, that they left me the last of their Eastern Caribbean Dollars and Euros. But, only on the condition that every last cent of it got spent on alcohol.

Lessons learned in 2013:
- Shoelaces are not suitable for human consumption.
- Not all pirates are friendly.
- Tampons can cause death in both men and women, and are a

favourite amongst the items that pirates will loot when they pillage your boat.

❦ You can make as many perfectly formed plans as you like, but life will lead you down a very random path regardless, normally in the wrong direction.

❦ You can't die if you have travel insurance (just in case you forgot[31]).

❦ Life's always better barefoot.

❦ Vegetarians are people too.

❦ It's better to be heartbroken than to be the one smashing up other people's hearts.

❦ It doesn't matter how many times a day you accidentally rub chilli in your eye, it hurts EVERY time.

❦ The more you lick, the more you live.

❦ Every good day begins with [chilli] coffee and ends with a sundowner.

❦ Beer pong is more fun when you play with your mum.

❦ Cape Town is the most beautiful city in the world.

❦ Get as many hugs as you can every single day. Be careful when in French territory, because when you go in for the hug and they go in for the mandatory double cheek kiss, it ends awkwardly.

❦ There is no cure for the travel bug.

---

[31] Once again, please do not in any way try to prove/disprove this!

13.

DON'T KILL THE COCKROACHES

*S**O**, what am I doing next? I can't float about on* Fiddler *forever! Should I head to South America somewhere? Or continue my quest for Spain? Or maybe the Pacific? Should I go home? Or adventure onwards? Should I be looking for gainful employment?*

I met with several yachties to discuss chartering and had several run-ins with Roelof, as if it had been preordained for him to continuously see me with other men. He avoided me and fled, but I always felt his eyes. How could I tell him these were business meetings and that romantic notions were as far away as the answer to world peace?

Between boat work and various invitations to cheat and eat meat with Peter and other friendly sailors around the anchorage, there wasn't time for much else. Ewa's Passport was about to expire and we weren't sure what to do about it. Plans were being bounced about like a basketball.

Skypes with people at home revealed that Jeandré was in hospital with tick bite fever and septicaemia. Brendon and Chloe's car had broken down and their house [as well as their relationship] was falling apart. Ouma had given someone a lift and had her purse stolen as gratitude. The cousin's Rottweiler had fallen on the other dog and paralysed it... It wasn't a happy time, and I really should have been praying more for my own family rather than fretting over frayed hearts and future plans! But, on the positive side, Mom and Ouma were excited because they had met a missionary who lived in Brazil and was [probably] single. Simply the fact that he was Christian and adventurous made them adamant that he was my "one."

Kirk, Ewa and I made a communal decision to get off the internet and head home.

"You look like a crazy bunch of Gypsies," called a friendly face as we walked. I spun around to assure whoever it was, that's exactly what we were!

❦

We were cleared out of Saint Lucia and about to head off on *an adventure*. Time to go was long overdue. I needed something new, and I needed it desperately! I woke up at the crack of dawn to prepare for sea and was probably overly fecund because by 06:00, everything was done and I had already had my second cup of coffee.

Kirk kicked me off the boat. I was being too productive. I managed to stifle the tears until I was drifting far away in a kayak. There are far worse things to be kicked off a boat for, and I knew that Kirk was not the reason for my waterworks. A long walk down the beach did me wonders despite the friendly Rasta who yelled "Hey you! Come over here and touch me." I thought I'd misheard him, but he yelled it again. I walked faster.

A friendly familiar face walked past me for a third time. I finally stopped him and asked if I knew him. That's how I met Dutch Luc. His boat had been overtaken by hippies who were currently sprawled out on the beach trying to make a living by busking, baking, and doing massages.

"So, I met a bunch of hippies and they're all chilling out on the beach..." I started. "Make sure you're home by midnight," Kirk replied from the depths of the *bilge*. I kayaked over to the furthest corner of the bay and sure enough, there were hippies everywhere. A nice bunch too! They'd filled up two tiny boats and were merrily trying to get through life however and by whatever means they could. The afternoon disappeared and the sun started setting. A bonfire was made and Luc was trying to talk me into jumping ship. I laughed. Firstly, there was no space; and secondly, never before had I been through a phase with so much male attention! I wondered what I was doing wrong!? Or right perhaps.

We called it "The Curse." Of my closest school friends, there were five of us who were all relatively normal [awesome] human beings with a sense of humour and all our limbs intact. We were all mildly intelligent (well, the others were near geniuses. I lowered the aggregate). We all made it onto the school's leadership team as head students and prefects. We were also the only ones who made it through high school without as much as a look from anyone of the opposite sex: The Curse!

Our teachers and parents prayed for us regularly - for the protection of our hearts, lips and carnal treasures. It must have worked because we couldn't work out how else we were alienated so viscously from the norms of the teenage flesh. Of the five of us, I was the first to experience even the joys of kissing. This came at the tender age of 21.

"Mon, either you kiss her, or we're gonna have to do it for ja." The Rastas were giving us a hard time. I assured everyone there would be no kissing going on. My lips had done just about enough damage for one week.

After too much coconut and star fruit, I realised midnight must've been fast approaching. I clambered onto the kayak and started my long paddle home. *Fiddler* wasn't anywhere to be seen. I paddled circles around the anchorage wondering if perhaps they had left without me.

"Work is progressing well. Underway in the morning - FOR SURE! - Please carry on having fun," said the note on the table, when I finally clambered aboard. I had started the day in tears and then cried again when I got chilli in my eye. I cried from smoke at the bonfire. And now, I was crying because life was so freaking awesome. Luc cried every week for his daughter. It's amazing what stirs up emotion inside us human types!

Two and a half days after checking out, we finally set sail.

I threw up once, twice, six times. Then we tacked and I got to relieve myself four times on the port side too. The jib sheet tore and had to be replaced. We heaved to and replaced it before we tacked back. I allowed the involuntary detox to resume: 22 spews through six tacks!

By morning I'd managed to keep down an apple and a glass of water, found my Stugeron[32] and Gaviscon[33] and managed to pull myself on deck to relieve the others of their watch. The flying fish silhouetted the rising sun.

ANTIGUA & BARBUDA

I awoke to find the sea littered with kite-surfers. **Nonsuch Bay** looked like

---

[32] The only sea sick tablets that have ever worked for me. They give you an amazing night's sleep too.

[33] It's the only solution for when you have nothing left to throw up.

a dream and I was ready to explore it! I launched a kayak and ventured over to the cactusy *Green Island* where plastic bottles seemed to grow from the ground and crabs made the pilgrimage to die. The day disappeared as we went snorkelling, diving, kayaking and swimming. Whilst I still lacked purpose, I made up for it with happiness.

Barbuda was too beautiful to be good for us. I got up to watch the last sunrise of the Chinese New Year. After a swim and a kayak, we dodged coral heads and anchored a few miles north. In contrast to the Caribbean islands that I'd visited, we'd finally found a secluded spot, far enough away from the bustle of charter boats and mega yachts. We went for a walk on the conch-shell-infused pink-sand picturesque beach. It seemed to get more beautiful by the bend in the shore, and we returned laden with shells and sunburns.

You might ponder the name "11 Mile Beach" and then go for a stroll. And then quite suddenly, after about 11 miles, you might discover that not all names are deceptive.

The Year of the Horse began with a plan. We loaded up the dinghy with snorkel gear, an umbrella, extra fuel, oil, and lunch. After exploring the underworld, we crossed to Goat Island for lunch. While dodging the mangroves, we marvelled at the millions of nesting frigate birds that filled the bay. We burned through four full tanks of fuel and were just about to pull into **Codrington** when the engine cut out. Ewa and I paddled us in.

Warmly welcomed and banana chipped, we set off to explore. Holy Trinity School claimed to be "Child-Friendly." The bottle shop sold everything but alcohol. Every person who had a bicycle was riding one that was far too big for them. Every tree was littered with people nesting in its shade. A friendly fireman led me to a back-alleyway gate where I finally managed to buy three Wadadlis for 10 EC. Kirk assured me that I'd be alright: "Many of the world's most interesting people were alcoholics."

People loved Kirk! "Barbuda" means "bearded man" – they welcomed him home. We bumped into a local drunk at Madison Square who tried to convince us that we should hire him as a guide purely because he spoke French. When we finally got rid of him, he mumbled off cursing us in English, forgetting that we were not French.

It began raining and we took shelter under the roof of a red bar. The sign outside read: "Frig-it Birds Live Tonight. Entrance: Good Behaviour." The sun was low in the sky and plans were changing fast. At the mention of "home-made banjos," we were sold.

The bar was packed with both locals and a colourful array of expats, who all had interesting stories about why they were there. Apart from the Brazilians, all I could get out of them was dancing. The band was a little on the Hari Krishna side, but were amply amusing with their banjo, drums and triangle. Getting home was even more interesting.

Eventually, the day came to set sail when we could put off departing no longer. Ewa had a flight to catch. With all our billions of shells carefully stowed for sea, we set off back to **Antigua.** We battled winds in the high 30s and again made 11 knots. Phone reception came and went. I managed to contact the homelands while I dodged a cruise ship I mistook for an island; and some similarly sized mega yachts. An hour out, I awoke the others and we sailed into **Jolly Harbour**, anchoring in Mosquito Cove.

We checked ourselves out and were quite disappointed that the customs and immigration officers weren't all that "Jolly." As free men (and women) we walked the marina's many walkways eyeing over-priced curious and empty restaurants until happy hour struck. I sat at The Crow's Nest sipping two beers [for 8EC], having to drink them both because I still didn't have a drinking buddy; and abusing the Wi-Fi. Because my blog still hadn't uploaded, I had to have two more.

IMPOSSIBLE IS EVERYTHING

Jolly Harbour, Antigua. 3 February 2014

The very best things I've ever done were all once labelled "impossible."

I'm a 29-year-old barefooted gypsy, intrepidly travelling the world with a ginormous teddy and a cable-tied-together backpack. I stop regularly to gawk at magnificence and occasionally to lick national monuments, weirdness of nature, people of interest and hopefully someday a president.
Not exactly what younger me [or my mother] envisioned for my life.

After a whole morning spent throwing up over the railings of *Fiddler;*
and an afternoon cuddling up with my old friend Buckie,
I was seriously contemplating my purpose and place in life.
I was pretty sure I'd missed my calling
(unfortunately, I hadn't missed the boat, I was on it.)
I was also pretty sure that the next thing to be thrown up was my vital organs and that death was imminent.

I watched helplessly as my crew steered us toward Antigua, knowing full well that surviving the 170 remaining miles was impossible.
But eventually, I found the strength to stand up again. By the following afternoon, we found land.

Antigua is the mega yacht capital of the world. Cruising into Falmouth Bay, we felt like a toy. After all, we were only a 60-footer.

Perspectives changed quickly though. Only a couple of hours later we

watched the first of the transatlantic rowers pull into the harbour.
In light of their 46 days of constant paddling in a tiny raft tossed about
by massive waves and capsizing thrice,
my triumph over a day's seasickness seemed minuscule; and *Fiddler*
seemed massive.

It's all of life's challenges (both big and small) that remind us we're alive.
It's the victories in conquering them that make life worthwhile.

For the sail from Antigua to Barbuda, I was prepared. But after two
months of cruising the Caribbean, dodging yachts left, right and centre, I
was totally unprepared for the raw, untouristed perfection that the island
threw at me.

It was on a long solitary expedition of untamed beautifulness that my
mind kicked into reminiscent action.
I thought long and hard about all the epic adventures I've had,
all the incredible people I've met along the way, the challenges I'd
overcome,
and how much life as a Part-Time Professional Gypsy had taught me.
It struck me how all those times I was staring death in the eye, on the
verge of broke-ness, feeling the loneliest ever, or completely overcome
by purposelessness; that preceded all my lifetime highs!

Yes, impossibility is everything. If it's too easy, it's probably not worth
doing.

You may not feel like you've accomplished much in life,
or you may feel like you're aimlessly floating through it.
But, sit back and contemplate the extraordinariness of your life
accomplishments thus far. I'm sure you'll agree that life is freaking

fantastic; and that in fact, all things are possible!

HOME IN MY HAREM

It was sad to watch Ewa go. She'd be back of course, but I sensed then already that I wouldn't be around to see her. It was the start of a new chapter on *Fiddler,* where we were only two; and two very different souls at that. I wondered how it would work. I wondered how we would get along. I wondered what was next. I wandered ashore for a walk.

There were still some familiar faces lurking about the island, but a whole host of new ones had arrived too. Saint Lucia remained a man's world. "Excuse me miss?" said a voice as I walked past a bar trying [quite unsuccessfully] to cut down my intake of alcohol, "but if you don't wear shoes, does that mean you're not wearing underwear either?" The Irishman I had been chatting to said he was happy to do the research.

Rodney Bay was as strange as ever. One night I headed out with only 10EC. I spent that at a bar before finding another 10 on the floor. I spent that as a deposit for pool cues but somehow managed to get beers out of it too. After a long night out and far too many tasty beverages, I returned home with 20EC. Logic didn't work.

Canadian Jud became a good friend and the only downside was that his boat was called *Cummoniwannalaya.* Calling that on the VHF was rather awkward. He was also anchored too far away for a casual kayak chat, and he never answered his VHF unless you called him properly with the vessel name repeated three times. He'd been in the bay so long that his anchor chain sprouted a garden and had a "pet" turtle that grazed off of it.

One day Kirk was accosted by a German vegetarian who recognised his beard from a crewing website. She was looking for a boat and he didn't know what to say, so he panicked and invited her over for dinner. I'd seen ads for other interesting-sounding boat-seeking vegetarians, so we invited them too. I'd bought dessert just in case they turned out to be nice. I'm happy to say that I baked and served the brownies before dropping the vegetarians back ashore.

CREW-SING

Despite Fiddler *having the biggest and most diverse crew ever [in my existence aboard], I still have no drinking buddies. It's not just global warming we should be wary of these days, there's plenty amiss in this world!*

There's Katrin, a German biologist who was rather surprised to find sauerkraut in the fridge (so were we... I really ought to clean it out someday). She swears she doesn't own lederhosen, but I don't believe a word of it.

Then there are the Bulgarians: Sergei and Radka, whose staple diet is bread and oil (slightly more of the latter). They don't believe in sleeping indoors, flying or in the evilness of cockroaches. Their most favourite pastimes are doing dishes, hitchhiking and repacking their backpacks. In that order.

This time it is up to me to teach them everything they need to know about Fiddler. *I've come full circle!*

Fortunately, it was just a day sail so my "Farewell Forever Rodney Bay!" hangover didn't matter too much. We were **Gros Piton** bound and it was a perfect day out on the water. There was a lot of fun to be had in teaching newbies the ropes. We found a mooring spot waiting for us and within minutes we were in the water enjoying the crazy beautiful underworld. After experiencing the smudginess of the rest of Saint Lucia, I was incredibly impressed! After a three-hour snorkel, I was exhausted. I failed to sleep because we kept getting attacked by mythical pirates and real mosquitos.

Shore exploration gave further credence to the South of the island being a lot nicer than the North. I sat by myself on the bow, staring at the stars when Kirk wandered on over and asked if I'd be interested in a night dive. It was almost 23:00 and I'd been awake for close to 64 hours. It was cold and probably illegal... I kitted up!

The coral gardens were exceptional in the light of our ultra violet diving torches. We didn't see much in the way of fauna, but we didn't need to – there was so much other life! The beauty seemed to dissolve both the cold and the tiredness. I was transformed.

In the morning we finally cut our ties with Saint Lucia, which had held us far too long. We left with a bang, somehow managing to sever the mooring ball with the propellor.

SAINT VINCENT & THE GRENADINES

With Kirk returning from immigration, I orchestrated a shore party and tendered everyone in. The Bulgarians went hitchhiking, Katrin went internetting, and I wandered off to explore. I was quite happy to see a painting of a Merman at the Oasis Art Gallery, giving further credence to my suspicions that they do exist. **Bequia** was the friendliest island I'd visited in a long time. And instead of allowing the rain to dampen my spirits, I danced in it.

"Never get on the back of a snowmobile with a drunken Inuit."

- a Canadian I met at the old fort.

We had a morning wreck dive before breakfast, which came in the form of pancakes and set a perfect platform for a rather pleasant day of sailing! We brought a sandbag up with the anchor.

We leapt into the multi-shaded deep turquoise blue waters of **The Tobago Cays** as soon as the anchor was down. The islands teamed with colourful birds and more colourful iguanas. We'd reached a different planet! The turtles swarmed and the fish swam circles around us as we found ourselves lost in a mesmerizing sea! Flamboyant sea urchins abounded as did a plethora of conch. In-between the pretty assortment of corals, a rainbow of starfish had been strewn about.

The sun hadn't woken up yet as we escaped our calm anchorage. We followed the lee of Mayreau, rounded Bloody Head and Bloody Bay, and deployed the jib for the short sail to **Union Island**. After breakfast, I dropped the Bulgarians ashore so they could get their week's quota of hitchhiking in. Several of the depth-indicating cable ties had freed themselves from the anchor chain so I wasn't sure how much I had put out when I secured us. Kirk assured me that we'd be in the dinghy anyway, "…we can always chase *Fiddler* if we have to." We all laughed.

Whales! We could hear them, but where were they? "Want to go on a whale tour?" asked Kirk after an exquisite dive two bays over. We nodded in eagerness as we threw our gear in the dinghy and headed back to base.

"Hey Kirk, where's *Fiddler*?" I asked as we rounded the headland. He and Katrin looked up and scanned the anchorage. She wasn't there. With dread, we all turned to look over to the far side of the bay, by the cliffs. Our hearts raced as I turned to full throttle. Were we too late already? Time stopped. We were moving far too slowly. It was a bad dream where you just couldn't work hard enough to avoid the inevitable. Nobody said a word.

Kirk leapt aboard while I drifted the dinghy in and followed, leaving

Katrin to tie up. Kirk fired up the engine and I got onto anchor duty. We were in twenty meters of water. How much chain did we have below us? We were only inches from the cliffs, but with the anchor already up and *Fiddler* under-way, I looked up in silent gratitude and we continued on our whale cruise.

Safely anchored with ample chain, we clambered the steep hill up to the road where we found green rolling fields. Kirk masqueraded as a cow, much to the amusement of some locals who snuck past silently pushing a car that may or may not have run out of petrol. We marvelled at the hills teeming with goats and a basketball-playing dog. Frigate Island sparkled in the distance. It was a beautiful island!

This time I pulled up a bucket with the anchor. These anchor shenanigans are getting ridiculous! And even more ridiculous is our departure time. Since when does Fiddler *ever move before eight?*

GRENADA

"You're the girl from the boat, right?" "Umm, yes..." I answered somewhat hesitantly. I'm sure there were many girls on many boats. "The one with the bearded captain?... We've been expecting you!"

They'd prepared a full presentation: Videos, sound-snippets... they even taught me the local bum wiggle as we jived away to *Saltfish*, their latest chart-topper. The phone rang and instantaneously my new friend, Mary, turned professional before continuing her marketing pitch about why we needed to stay in **Carriacou** for Carnival.

After the Grenadines, I'd completely underestimated the size of the island. It didn't help that the people were overly friendly and that I found myself locked in conversations every hundred meters or so. There were remarkable views and fascinating villages. At Windward, I found a boat-building community where, every time a boat was finished, the whole village would come out to launch it before a massive feast would bestow upon its decks. I pushed on to the far west and arrived just in time for a picturesque sunset. I was feeling great about life until I had a run-in with "the creature." This thing was half rat, half dog, and half iguana; it was fully terrifying. I was all alone on the dark dirt roads of the forest. Every time I turned my torch on, goats would stop dead in their tracks and stare me down. The goats who stare at men!

The main island was even more fascinating, and I didn't let the hangover tell me otherwise. People were friendly, the smoothies were delicious, and everyone had something to say about cricket.

We set the sails at 21:44; and after solving all the general problems, I beelined for bed. I woke up when my fan fell off the wall and onto my head. In an attempt to fix it, the puking began. It took me a while to make it on deck, but the starboard railings and I were in for a good night. There were lights everywhere and Katrin seemed mildly panicked. I divided my time between helping her and feeding the fish. We were in oil rig territory.

18 spews later, I lay down in the pilothouse and had a surprisingly good nap until I woke up with a startle. Sergei had a powerboat trying to run us over. Only he didn't want to wake me until the very last minute, when it was indisputable that we were on a collision course.

TRINIDAD & TOBAGO

We stopped in Scotland Bay for a breather and then continued to **Chaguaramas** where the welcome party included both pink and white dolphins as well as an army of tankers. We tied up at the quarantine dock; but our arrival coincided with their lunch break, giving me time to recuperate and meet the Germans we had raced into port. As we sat patiently waiting, we studied immigration's list of forbidden attire: bare feet, mini-skirts, camouflage, singlets, tight clothing, and shorts... Good thing even they didn't adhere to the rules, otherwise, they would never have let us in! In the queue, we met a school teacher checking out her 25 students (brave woman), and a German who was fleeing because he couldn't stand the loud music any longer!

LIFE'S A CELEBRATION

Chaguaramas, Trinidad; 7 March 2014.

It's 04:00 and my alarm's yelling at me to get up.
It's the last thing that I want to do after 15 hours of seasick sailing;
but I pull myself together, plaster on a smile, and let the day begin.
It's carnival Monday, and we are in Trinidad.

The five of us pile into the dinghy and hope for the best.
Previous day's discussions with fellow boat people suggest that transport needs to be pre-arranged weeks in advance and that traffic would be terrible!
But as we step out of the marina, I hold out my thumb and the very first car pulls over and drives us straight to the action in the Port of Spain.

None of us have a clue what to expect, so when we find ourselves in the middle of *J'ouvert*[34], it's a bit of a shock to the system.

Within minutes, our group has been torn apart by the marauding masses of bumpers and grinders (what appears to be the official [and only] dance move of the country). As we pass through the different bands of people,

---

[34] The "Dawn of Carnival". Bands of revellers cover themselves (and everyone around them) in strange substances and dance through the streets until the sun comes up.

we find ourselves coated in layer upon layer of mud, paint, chocolate;
and I dare not to ask what some of the other substances are...
What an awesome welcome to Trinidad and Tobago!!

The streets quiet down in the heat of the day and the German and I head
off to mingle, bar hop and explore the town.
When we return to the carnival scene, we are in a state of shock...
We find the whole island wandering about in the cleanest, most beautiful
and extravagant clothing imaginable.
Nobody warned us that we should be looking like princesses!

Darkness finally descends and our disarray of dirtiness is eventually
masked to the point that we manage to hitch a ride home with some
Biblical characters.

Round two.
And fortunately, it doesn't start nearly as early!
Armed with the teddy bear, we head to land and hitch a ride into town
with the army.

Teddy's a great hit with the ladies
And the police.
He even gets us on the news!

It takes us three rides to get home. But everyone we hitch with leaves us
more enthusiastic about the human race, and how many good people
there are out there.

Trinidad has a bit of a bad reputation. But, from the quality of people we
have hung out with this week, I can only say that this country is rich in
awesomeness!

Carnival's all over for now and most of the country is still lingering with
hangovers...
But the parties continue for no other reason than life being a celebration.

ʃ

With five of us aboard, simple chores went quite quickly. The Bulgarians
washed the windows, Katrin vacuumed and I finished the painting I'd been
putting off; and then had an unsolicited collision with a cockroach. It was
time I poisoned the vessel again.

I was rather glad when Kirk mentioned a shore excursion so that I
didn't have to make a big deal out of it, but Radka didn't want to go. I tried
to coerce her from various standpoints and then Kirk just said it how it
was: "Adeena is going to be spraying some smelly poison to kill
cockroaches and she thinks it's a good idea if you get off."

She cried.

"Just take them ashore and set them free," she pleaded.

She stayed aboard regardless, plonked on the deck so that she couldn't
hear their tiny pleas for help. From that point, I was labelled a murderer.

Time ticked on and it looked like I'd be hopping onboard an American
catamaran to film their circumnavigation. My references had been checked
and former captains consulted. Now I was just waiting for the logistical
part of when I would be flying to Panama.

"Flying?!" I skyped a heartfelt plea to the owner and asked him if he'd
hold off a few days so that I could find a boat and sail there. Carter laughed
out loud and told me I was being ridiculous, but agreed regardless.

Seeing as I was still in Trinidad and it was a Sunday, we decided to find
out what train dominoes were... Unfortunately, Katrin lost and we were

forced to fly the loser's flag from the mast for all the anchorage to see. We were debating on joining the group of geriatrics for ice-cream when my domino "coach" said, "You know, there are some very nice South Africans parked next to me." I followed him down a series of docks where he knocked thrice and introduced me to Tracy and Wayne. The remains of the afternoon disappeared sipping rum on their deck and exchanging salty sea stories. They'd anchored in Fortaleza too and had the police pester them the whole week, begging them to move to the safety of the marina. They never did, they also never got pirated. Life was strange like that.

Katrin was in bad shape and should probably not have tried to keep up with South African drinking habits. When she tried to step into the dingy, she missed, bounced on the dock (twice), and splashed into the murky muck of the infested waters.

ᚠ

I walked circles around the boatyard without any luck before heading into the office to inquire. They didn't have any boat by that name. I returned to the grounds and continued aimlessly looping about. I stopped here and there to greet friends and ask if they knew where I should be headed, but none of them could help me. I tried not to notice the good-looking barefooter lugging bags of garbage to the bins for a second time. In desperation, I found the marina manager and was interrogating him when I heard my name.

He apologised profusely for the state of the boat (which was still filthy despite all the garbage he'd recently relocated). His Atlantic crew had just disembarked, and they'd had a bit of a raucous farewell party. "Karl's an excellent cook," chirped the last passenger who was foetal-positioned on the saloon couch. He'd be flying home in the morning.

I'd expected to find an old man on a shoddy boat. Instead, I found little *Yoldia*, a 27-foot Albin Vega. She was so small that the mere notion of me hopping on board was insane. It made me want to sail her even more. But young Karl was keen to leave in the middle of the following week and would stop off at Isle Margarita on the way. He wanted to take his time getting to Panama. My heart sank, this was the only boat heading my way. I thanked him anyway and said I'd get back to him when I had a better idea of dates for the Panama Canal crossing – the first big step I was required to film.

As I opened my laptop to email Panama, I received a new message: *"On second thought, you have more experience than I could hope for in a crew and I really would like another long stretch at sea. I'd be happy to go straight to Panama. It should take about 14 days."*

Kirk was more excited than I was, but mostly because he loved the idea of sailing on an Albin Vega. He wasn't so sure about the catamaran.

The South Africans, who had come over for drinks, didn't approve of me leaving so soon; so I invited them for dinner the following day. Kirk's logic was rather sound: if we were going to have a few people over for dinner, we may as well have many. So, we did. And I used it as the perfect excuse to get Karl checked out. I wasn't in the habit of boarding boats with just a captain!

The night was a roaring success despite the weird rigmarole of strangers that we'd assembled. Karl was far too quiet and that made me nervous. Who was this guy? Was he safe? Are quiet people more or less likely to be psychopaths? If only I could remember more of my university psychology!

After dessert, the "youth" amongst us dinghied ashore for a party. Much was drunk. Much was spoken. Much was danced. And I felt a whole lot more assured because, when Karl picked up a guitar, much was sung!

Lessons learned in the Lesser Antilles:

- Capsicums and chilli peppers look the same in the Caribbean. Make sure you know which one you are cooking with.
- Vending machines kill more people than sharks do.
- If you're a single woman looking for love, Rodney Bay, Saint Lucia is undoubtedly the best place to start.
- Life doesn't make sense, stop trying to comprehend it.
- There is no home quite as perfect as a sailing boat.
- There's a lot more to life than money. You will always have enough!
- Live in the moment instead of fretting too much about future plans. Everything will be okay!
- Most people are just as uncertain about life as you are!
- Talk to your family and friends as often as you can.
- A little bit of God time goes a very long way.

14.

IT'S 07:51. Kirk and Katrin are our pilot boat to steer us off the dock and on to new adventures. It is all very exciting; and I really hope that I won't need the toilet, because I've just discovered that there isn't one! There is also no wind, so we're using the dinghy's outboard engine to push us along at two knots, tiller in hand.

We bounced along ever so slowly as powerboats of all shapes and sizes sped past leaving us to shake in their wake. Eventually, we found our passage and, on the other side, we found the wind as our speed increased to three. Four... Eight knots. A large unidentified black creature swam over to welcome us back to the ocean (Karl called it a whale. I saw a giant ray. For all we knew, it may have been Neptune himself). Vegetarian-free, we dropped in the fishing line, and it didn't take long to catch a tuna fish. My new captain's first official duty was to cook me lunch. After devouring its deliciousness, I knew we'd be okay.

When I finally crept forward and braved the sailed-off *bowsprit* "toilet," the dolphins swarmed to join in the activities. I officially proclaimed it the best toilet in the world[35]! I'd been so afraid of getting seasick in the tiny bathtub, but *Yoldia* was a flipping comfortable sail and an exquisitely beautiful boat [and Karl seemed quite remarkable too].

The sunrise was spectacular and I was more than mesmerised as I watched waves far bigger than our tiny blimp of a boat toss us forward with the wind. I loved the simplicity of technical-gadget-free life. The wind vane kept us on course and the compass helped us check it. It was that simple. I'd done thousands of sea miles, but being on a little boat made me finally realise how and why things worked the way that they did. I officially graduated as a sea-gypsy.

I had much to learn from the young Swede. At 21, he and a friend had decided to conquer the world by yacht. They'd known nothing about sailing, but had done their homework and found that Albin Vega (small caravan-ish vessels), were sturdy enough for ocean sailing. They clubbed together and bought the boat, and then started preparing for the epic voyage. They'd done a few short sails around their home archipelago, Gävle; and Karl had deemed them ready. Jonas kept stalling until eventually Karl gave him an ultimatum, and proceeded to leave without him. If Karl could make it to the South of Sweden alive, he'd be proud. Once he'd done that, he continued onto the Keel Canal through Germany. Then across the English Channel and the Bay of Biscay to Portugal, Morocco; and eventually over to the Canaries. There had been four aboard for the Atlantic crossing and I couldn't fathom how so many fit on such a tiny boat! The crew had never sailed before and had spent most of their time either throwing up or basking the Atlantic with pleasant melodies. The doldrums had been a bit of a scare, as he worried about water and food

---

[35] And when we heeled enough we didn't even need toilet paper.

supplies; but they'd all made it to Tobago unscathed with only happy memories. The others opted for a life less seasick and had flown to various corners of the globe from Trinidad. That's where I entered the picture. I hoped that I wouldn't disappoint.

Conversation flowed freely and life was care-free and liberating. Karl told me bedtime stories and lulled me to sleep with songs. Insomnia vanished from my life and I felt alive. I couldn't remember a happier time than sitting in the little cockpit at sunset with the wind wisping through my hair. Karl's leg brushed mine and a shiver shot up my spine. I wasn't sure if it had been an accident or not, but I ignored it. We had two weeks together and I wasn't going to let things get awkward. He was an amazing guy – funny, smart, awfully good-looking... but a 27-footer was too small for drama.

The sun rose with Irish tunes belting. It was Saint Patrick's Day, and we may have been well in the middle of nowhere; but it was the one holiday I kept somewhat religiously. I painted the captains face luminous green, and he painted mine. The paint was just about dry when there was no fighting it any more. Our faces neared and before we knew it, they had locked in a glob of tom-foolery that made the afternoon disappear all too quickly. As we sat sipping our perfunctory Guinness, Karl grinned, "I thought you might be a lesbian." I was quite taken aback, but he added: "…It took you three days to kiss me!"

The flying fish attacks were brutal. They flocked from every direction and despite whacking them away with the breadboard, they wangled their way into my hippy pants and tangled themselves into my gypsy hair. They had their target and would swarm around me for the duration of my watch. As soon as Karl took over, they'd behave themselves again. This pattern seemed to follow all the proceeding night watches. They'd lie in wait and time my stepping into the cockpit to take over the watch, with a fishy smack to the head. The waves began following suit. I further graduated to an official sailor by encompassing cuss words (mostly new Swedish ones) into my vocabulary.

I finally followed the captain's example and challenged my insecurities. I stripped off all my damp clothes and tried to live naturally and freely. It was rather liberating; and while I was still very insecure about my voluptuous bags of skin wilting about in the wind, I was on a journey of acceptance. With no mirrors on board and only Karl to tell me I was beautiful, I started to believe it. I came to realise that happiness makes a person attractive, not what they look like.

Time disappeared far too quickly; and when Karl cried "land-ho," I was somewhat disappointed. I didn't want to leave the boat. I didn't want to leave him. I wasn't ready to put clothes back on and be a prim and proper, functional and well-groomed crew member.

We realised how little we had done in the ten days we'd been at sea, and quickly tried to atone for it. I sat trying to mend the broken *sail cars* with fishing line while Karl topped up the outboard fluids, packed away the genoa, fixed the furler, and started preparing for arrival. Dolphins carried us through the sunset and a swallow flew circles around me before settling on the tiller. The evening was too perfect.

Karl took the first watch and when I awoke, there were boats everywhere – massive ones. I was so tired that I struggled to make out which were stars and which were *running lights*. A ship that must have been at least a mile long stood in our way. After tacking back and forth to try and sail around it, I woke Karl up. I was seeing things. He sentenced me back to bed.

When I awoke, he'd managed to get everything under control and had successfully distanced us from the worst of the traffic. He'd put the coffee on and made me breakfast. Karl took a nap while I steered us through the breakwater. He then left me at the tiller while he prepped the anchor. We passed the shallow reef that led us into **Shelter Bay Marina**, the end of our trip and the start of new escapades. Only, there was no anchorage so, in a very sudden change of plans, we found fenders and I successfully docked my first boat.

The dockmaster came running; yelling. We couldn't dock there. He'd been trying to call us on the VHF and was furious that we hadn't responded. We laughed it off and told him we didn't have one, it was broken. He was still angry, but we didn't care. We'd made it to Panama!

FLIPPING PANAMA

We fought the temptation to get beers straight away and visited immigration. They were very unorganised and didn't speak a word of English, but they were friendly enough to warrant patience. We needed to visit Colon to pay $105 each for a visa and the cruising permit would cost Karl $300. At that price, it was unlikely *Yoldia* was going to be crossing the Panama Canal and the dream of the Pacific was fading quickly. There was a three-day grace window in which he would have to decide.

Karl checked *Yoldia* into the marina for the night while I walked over to E-dock and found my new home: *Official Business*. The crew seemed lovely, but Carter hadn't landed yet. I was excited about the new adventure but more excited that Carter's absence gifted me more Karl time. We walked to the shop to buy a six-pack to celebrate. We drank most of it before we stopped infuriating the dock manager and finally moved the boat.

One of the many Panamanian canal agents saw our yellow *Q-flag* as a cry for help. "Every year I choose two boats to help across the canal for free," said the smiling man, "and I'd like to help you." With Pablo, Karl could skip the visas and the cruising permit and would only have to pay the exorbitant transit costs. Pablo would take care of all the other canal logistics and Karl wouldn't have to pay him a cent. Our moods lifted, but it did seem a bit too good to be true. Still, after meeting him, Karl suddenly saw the Pacific as a possibility again. We cracked open another beer and cheered: "To life, wherever it may lead us."

We met a plethora of seasoned sailors and it soon became apparent that Shelter Bay Marina was full of people with stories. These people had a real sense of adventure. Panama is a land of tough decisions: either you cross the canal, or you don't. It's a big step. It's an expensive crossing; and once you make it through, there's no turning back.

We spent the morning stripping everything out of *Yoldia* and onto the docks. She needed a proper clean. Carter arrived at the height of the chaos and seemed more than a little horrified. Fortunately, he was on the rum; so I raised my somethingth beer and cheered to break the silence. He invited both of us over for dinner. Cleaning the boat took a lot longer than anticipated, and by 18:21 we were finally on the way to the shower. By 18:23 I had entered into a conversation with some South Africans. By 19:25 we were just short of an hour late; but we were perfectly on time for the champagne.

Official Business was a perfectly manicured craft. Too perfect. We sat down to some excellent wine before aperitif pizza was served, followed by a home-made pasta. The one thing that Carter would not let fly was the spilling of alcohol, so it was a good thing that he knocked his glass over before I did. The captain drifted off, followed by the cook; and then finally Carter and his very quiet, bodacious bodied, twenty-something Panamanian girlfriend. Karl had to wake me up to escort me back to the cosy confines of *Yoldia*.

Karl was still sleeping, so I sat down in the cockpit to write him a thank you poem[36]:

---

[36] Not that my poetry is in any way a gift!

Welcome to Karl's little den of iniquity
On which only the bravest sail the sea.
His mad Swedish ways
Never cease to amaze.

Tsunamis and storms
Blizzards, too warms
These things are easy
Try taking a pee-pee.

Dolphins, whales and UFOs
So many weird creatures that nobody knows.
The captain is one of them
Without saying that goes.

The seas might get drastic
But the meals are fantastic.
She might only measure 27 feet
But Yoldia really can handle the heat.

The captain's a sailor through and through
Maybe, if you're lucky, he'll make one of you.

It was time to get things moving and we did a slow, sad walk over to immigration so I could be removed from *Yoldia*'s crew list. We may have moved too slowly though because, by the time we got there, they had closed. We paid a visit to the chandlery instead. But it was the worst stocked shop in the world! We gave up productivity and returned to the boat with beers.

It was a frustrating day until Norwegian Bjørn started talking to me in a funny language. "Karl, one of your people is here," I called without so much as greeting the newcomer. The wild Viking had been lured over by the Swedish flag and was a rather amiable character. We had a few drinks with him and when our stores ran out, we followed him to *Chiaroscuro*, where we met Dutch Pieter who had hired him to deliver the boat back to The Azores.

We overslept and had to run to catch the free shuttle bus into town. Carter caught me on the way past: "We need to chat." I agreed to return at 16:45 when the shuttle returned, but we arrived at the terminal to discover we were living in the wrong time zone. We still had a couple of hours to spare. We reattempted immigration before Karl's three-day leeway was up. This proved to be even more complicated than checking in so I returned to *Official Business* to find out if they knew the procedures.

"Plans have changed," said Carter. I looked at the [real] time, 11:15. "Can we have that talk now?"

"Well, we've been chatting, and our captain is leaving. He wants to buy a farm and settle down. With that and a few other worries, I don't think we are ready to do the canal."

"Okay, well, what are you thinking?"

He stalled a bit. "I think I need to delay the trip… by a year."

My heart stopped. Was I really hearing this? Was the valiant, brave Carter actually saying this?

"I need a safer boat. A bigger boat. We are going to, hopefully with your help, sail her back to Florida and take it from there."

I sat staring, blood beginning to boil while trying to compose myself before I replied.

"Okay, so let me just make sure that we are on the same page. You're not ready, and you don't feel the boat is safe enough? [with its multiple *EPIRB*s, three life-rafts, excessive safety railings, personal tracker beacons, and more] So, you are going to sail the boat back, sell it, get a new one, find a new captain and you want me to help?"

"Yes."

The previous night's words came flooding through my head. The Scandinavians told me that I was making a bad decision and that I was selling my soul. They reckoned that *Official Business* was no place for an unofficial gypsy and reminded me that catamarans weren't real boats.

I left with a head flooded with questions. I didn't really want to do a two-month cruise up the East coast of Central America, did I? Not on that boat…

Karl burst out laughing as I gave him the run-down on the shuttle. He knew he and Bjørn had been right all along.

❦

The bus was a whole lot chirpier on the way home. The South Africans next to me were meant to be doing the canal on Wednesday, but one of them had just developed health problems. They scrapped their Pacific plans and were trying to work out what to do next. In front of me sat some Aussies, who were giving up and selling their boat. And an English man told me how he had just discovered a hole in his. I started feeling a whole lot better about my predicament. Yes, my plans had changed – but so had everyone else's.

Besides, there are always plan Bs! I could always ask Karl if I could stay on board? Hmmm…. Or maybe I should do some land travel again? Or join the crazy Norwegian as he delivers Chiaroscuro*? Come to think of it, there are a plethora of boats crossing the Atlantic to Europe. Maybe it's time that I finally complete my pilgrimage to Spain… No, I don't need to worry! The world is my playground.*

We returned just in time for Gary's visit. The resident mechanic's (an aeronautical engineer by trade and boat guru by passion) whole face lit up when he saw that it was a little Yanmar 6.9 Horsepower engine he was working with. Three hours later he left and promised he'd try again. Bjørn gave it a shot too and as thanks, we invited him and Pieter for dinner. We had no cold beers and it was still happy hour, so I ran to the bar to get some. I bumped into friends from Bermuda, who said they'd come for a drink, as did a gregarious German. I bought 18 and returned triumphantly with buckets of iced beverages. Unfortunately, we got stood up on all accounts and were forced to drink them all ourselves.

Despite the hangover, I found decisiveness and told Carter that I would not be joining his crew. He was horrified; and even more perturbed when I mentioned that I might just stay on *Yoldia* instead. He "wouldn't wish that on his worst enemy!"

☙

Fixing a boat in Panama was hard work. It's frustrating and soul-destroying, especially when you need parts. We suffered another wasted morning town mission. Broken, we sat down to an oily lunch. Karl was talking about giving up the dream again. In an effort to lift his spirits, I bet him a beer that we'd find the fuel filter he needed to fix his engine. We sourced it at a Mazda dealership (the very next shop we visited), for only $7. In fact, the Hong-Kong born, Birmingham-raised salesman had just about everything we needed. Karl treated me to two beers to celebrate as he made his definite decision – he was taking *Yoldia* into the Pacific. "Adeena," he said with deliberation in his words, "you know I'd love it if you joined me." As soon as I got home, I hoisted the South African flag. It was official.

Mom took the news quite well, but she skyped me back to ask if she could come with us. She has some time off work and wants to learn how to sail. I saw straight through her chaperone shenanigans and told her I was already pregnant and that I hoped to make it to China in the next eight months to drop off the twins. There was no reply.

Jeandré is stoked and has started making plans to meet me in Ecuador. He'll be in the area shooting a documentary!

Luc, from Saint Lucia, messaged to say that his good Norwegian friend, Bjørn, is in town and that I should look him up...

Bjørn became a regular visitor. I really needed to learn Swedish because it would be easier than having to keep reminding him that I didn't speak it. His American counterpart, Kennedy, flew in to help with the delivery. Between the two of them, there was never a dull moment! Kennedy had lived a hard life of sex, drugs, and rock and roll but still radiated youth!

We were about to take the morning shuttle bus when Bjørn offered us a lift, he was driving in anyway. Kennedy kept me entertained all the way into town while segregation had, as Bjørn called it, "the English speakers" at the back.

We had a lot to do and were ready for a morning mission. The Chilean fixing our VHF was not yet in so we all went for breakfast. We had barely finished eating when Bjørn hung up his phone and we were loaded into a van. He needed medication, and I don't mean over the counter stuff. While he and his "driver" ventured in, we were given strict instructions not to open the doors or the windows. We were in a dodgy area and apparently it wouldn't end well.

I sat jotting down things Kennedy thought valuable for an ocean crossing as an assortment of colourful people and police marches strolled past.

KENNEDY'S SURVIVAL PARAPHERNALIA

Big super-absorbent sponge

Corks

5200 (to stick anything together for more than eternity)

Tarp (for sun, catching rain, fixing leaks)

Sun clothes/protection

Bungees

Strong (90%) spray alcohol (to kill fish with)

Blanket (to smother big/sharp fish with)

A gaff

Hook board (to dry excess fish on)

Bribes (alcohol/cigarettes/etc.)

Scrap material

Scrap metal

Spare rigging (old shrouds from bigger boats?)

Old bike tube (a mobile gym)

Thank you gifts/cards

Paper/pen/stationery

Rehydration capsules

Lots of spices

Batteries

Multivitamins/fruit juice mix

...

(The bottom half of the list dissolved in something green.)

The driver returned us at last. We were about to begin the real supply shopping when Bjørn started cursing in Norwegian. I knew those words well. We all turned to find the car smashed in from front to back on the passenger side: the bumper, the wheel, both doors, and even the boot. Whoever had done it had made sure they'd done it properly. The paint marks left no doubt in our minds who the culprit was – a yellow taxi – only there were thousands of them in Colon!

How were the boys going to explain this to Pieter (who they were already on less than amicable terms with)? Or the cops? They were loaded with illegal substances and Bjørn didn't even have a driver's license.

We attempted to find witnesses and a phone number for the police, but most people were afraid of them and didn't want to get involved. Bjørn tried to hand me his backpack, but finally left it with Kennedy as Karl (who had a driver's license on him) and he walked off to find the station. "The English speakers" started shopping.

With a police report in hand, and the rental company notified, we were permitted to hobble the vehicle home. The day held more drama as a bus broke down on the bridge over the canal lock. We waited for hours watching angry shipping companies yell about how much money they were losing. When we did finally make it home, we were spent.

Knock knock knock. Knock knock knock. 02:13 - We ignored it. *Knock knock knock* "HAPPY BIRTHDAY!" Karl stuck his head out to see what was wanted. We were being summoned for birthday drinks and instructed to follow immediately. We didn't seem to have a choice. We followed Bjørn to the room above the restaurant and met JD, the manager and a handful of other colourful characters. Wine was bestowed upon us and the cocaine [which we shall call "Steve"] decorated the table in patterns. There was a bit of a party, but JD wanted a bigger one. After wandering over to invite the mega yachts [who's lights were always on regardless of the time of day] and failing, because they were all actually asleep, he started forming ludicrous party plans for Karl's birthday. Work started at six, so we left JD to have his hour of rest and went for a skinny dip before returning home. It was good to be naked again.

I woke up before Karl and began wrapping his cheap assortment of crappy presents. I felt desperately drab as I walked off to use the bathroom. Just outside was a Treasures of the Bilge market. "How much do you want for the VHF?" I asked. "$140," said the man while his wife scowled at him. "Okay, $40," she carried on scowling. "Okay, make it $20," and he threw in a couple of water jerrycans too. The perfect gift. The nicest

223

Germans!

When I told Karl that every incorrectly guessed present got him a shot of rum, he made me cook him bacon and eggs first. I then proceeded to get him very drunk before noon. The festivities continued. As darkness fell, there were so many people on board that it was deemed a safety hazard. We were ordered to move the boat.

JD had lived up to his word and there was a serious party in store. He even arranged a marque next to our new dock where he stood BBQing chicken for the whole marina. Beers were unpacked by the crate and people swarmed in for a celebration of Karl's birth. Countless instruments emerged and the docks were lined with dancing silhouettes as the night blurred into awesomeness. The night was a raging success (apart from the BBQ which took so long that people simply forgot to eat).

"He can cross an ocean, but he can't make it to bed!" strangers cheered as they bid him farewell and three of us carried Karl off. What a night to remember! - If only we could! All the captain had asked for, was to get drunk. I definitely gave him that!

I woke up to the Norwegian eating chicken in the *companionway* and the captain lying naked on the floor. Bjørn stood up and spilt chicken all over Karl. "That's a very nice penis you have there," he said without apologising to my dazed skipper. Bjørn and Kennedy moved in for the day. They couldn't stand Pieter anymore and were pulling the plug on the delivery. The instruments and Steve came out. And so did the stories… You know it's been a crazy night when there's a plethora of marriages and relationships on the rocks, when noses are broken from a brawl and when people you think you have never met come flooding to thank you for the best party they have ever had in all their years of cruising. Bjørn jumped on the band-wagon and told Karl that he had proposed to me at the party.

"No. No way. No. No. No. No way. No. Adeena, I'm sorry but I can't... I don't... I..." Karl took the joke so badly that as Bjørn pushed the story too far, my heart shattered. I casually excused myself and erupted into tears.

Maybe I am just a simple fling, a casual hook up?
Maybe I mean nothing to him!

❦

We continued getting the boat ready, but we always had a plethora of visitors. There was seldom a dull moment as people of every calibre and creed would come for coffee, beer or to let us watch them snort. Ours was the party boat, everyone knew it. A night didn't pass where a stranger was not passed out in the cockpit.

We officially enlisted agent Pablo for his services. Despite helping us for free, he also paid me $50 for every boat I referred to him, something I would have gladly done for free. Our marina fees were almost covered. We scraped together the money for the canal through four ATM visits and went to the shady offices in Colon to pay. Another 23-year-old, single-handed sailor sat there counting his cash. When we discovered that he too was on an Albin Vega, a deal was struck with the Dutchman. Jairo would help us through the canal if we would help him.

We waited for days for the canal representative to come and measure our boat. In the interim, Pieter, who was in a very feeble state from cancer and some other medical issues, had flown home. I felt sorry for him having to leave his prized possession in the hands of Kennedy and Bjørn; but they were good sailors and maybe the drugs would eventually stop?

The marina got emptier by the day as we watched friends disappear to the Pacific or back across the Atlantic. Even *Chiaroscuro* snuck away in the dead of night without saying goodbye. We'd been in Shelter Bay for so long that the marina came to give us money back. Apparently if you stay a week, it's cheaper than staying for three days. Two weeks makes it even cheaper.

I told Jeandré it would be safer for him to meet us in Panama considering all the delays. Who knew Ecuador was still 1400 miles and an impossible canal crossing away?

JD mysteriously "quit" his job and said goodbye with a very strange leaving party. We didn't query the details.

Karl sat me down one day and told me that there were things about him I didn't know. With all the recent company, I was fairly concerned. It took a while to say it, but he eventually came clean and admitted to having been a 15-year-old pop star with the hit song "Do you want to touch my penis?" I wondered what sort of trip the Pacific held for us.

The measurement officer finally arrived. Three days late. Before 08:00. On a Sunday, after a rambunctious party the night before. He pretended not to notice the mess and gave us the list of things we needed for the crossing. Our departure date was set for Wednesday 9 April.

To cross the Canal, you needed seven things:

- An engine that can maintain 5 knots
- A crew of 5 (excluding the advisor)
- A toilet
- 38 m lock lines, 23 – 38 mm in diameter.
- Shade
- Bottled water and cold drinks for the pilot/advisor
- Hot meals and snacks for the pilot/advisor

We had none of the above!

We continued to get things ready for the crossing and found it wasn't just the fuel filter that was problematic. The entire marina tried to help our little Yanmar. News spread and everyone wanted to fix the tiny engine [that might]. But there was no luck; and at the umpteenth hour, we called the canal company and delayed departure till Saturday.

Our favourite [VHF] Germans, delayed their trip too. Barbara and Manfred visited us daily with bags of groceries that were supposedly not going to last the year. Things we would never have afforded ourselves! They gave us so much and didn't want a thing in return. I made a treat bag from all the goodies they blessed us with, I had a feeling that their luxuries were going to come in handy someday.

A new generation of people started arriving and we had to introduce ourselves all over again. Every time we needed the bathroom, we had to pass the restaurant, the bar, and several docks. It kept our lives exciting; it kept our productivity low. We met Rupert, a delivery captain, who's still one of the most eclectic and good-natured humans I've ever met (even if he does have a terrible potty mouth). American Josh was hitchhiking on another Swedish vessel. The Finnish couple on *Homeless* were also sailing the world on a 27-foot boat. *Djerpie* housed three crazy Frenchmen. Countless new people flooded into our lives and the little community of iniquity continued to flourish.

"I'm a junkie, but I'm a good swimmer."

On the Friday afternoon, we delayed again. We could get the engine started, but it would sputter and die after only a few minutes. There was no way we could risk the canal in that state. *Plastic* had been scheduled for a Monday crossing, so we opted to help Jairo first.

Rupert found us looking forlorn and told us we had our priorities all wrong. We nominated him for three awards. Firstly, he gave the soundest advice when it came to yachts. Secondly, he had the best sense of humour we'd come across in a long time. Lastly, we awarded him for using the most vulgar allusions to perfectly illustrate a point. For him, we stopped moping and got straight back to work.

Josh dragged me away for a happy hour distraction so that the captains could have their engine time. After dinner distraction, we found Karl and Rupert sitting at the bar. Even though it was closed, we managed to wangle a few extra drinks[37]. Rupert inspired me to want to do boat deliveries. Josh inspired me to be more free-spirited and wild. Karl inspired me to not give a flip about anything except what I'm meant to be doing. Then, the scariest navy woman I have ever met joined the table and inspired me to go to bed.

The seas had gone crazy and the air was brewing something strange. The four of us sat at the breakwater watching the tankers roll in their anchorage with shudders. While Rupert and Karl discussed engines, Josh told me of his former life as a drug addict. His family was still abusing but he'd chosen a better path. His dreadlocked and tattooed (to perfectly match the markings on his box of cigarettes) exterior was quite suddenly softened by his genuineness. We had a "family" lunch that turned into happy hour, at which point Rupert excused himself and the three of us returned to *Yoldia* for dinner. I still can't quite work out how it all happened, but that night I made the worst judgement call of my life. I stepped off the boat and kissed Josh. In front of Karl. And then, in a continuation of bad judgement, I followed him and went for a walk.

❦

I spent the morning trying to wash clean the guilt and save friendships. And then bumped into Gary. "Do you by any chance have an electric fuel pump?" I asked. "Follow me," he replied and led me to a junk heap where a little rusty Yanmar engine lay decomposing. "If it fits, you can have it."

---

[37] While writing this, I'm quickly realising how much we drank. I don't think you'd believe that I did once manage an alcohol-free day in Shelter Bay; but I think I may be the only person in the history of the place to have accomplished such a feat.

I ran back to tell Karl the good news and for a moment we celebrated the fact that we didn't have to order a $330 part from Sweden. All too soon, reality kicked back in and I disappeared to give him space.

Three hearts were shattered: Karl's, my own, and [later] Josh's when I tried to explain myself. He hadn't had a clue that we were together. I don't think many people did. We were still in denial about it ourselves. And subconsciously, after the "fake wedding fiasco," I was pretty sure we weren't. It was simply propinquity that brought us together.

I'd run home to Karl to tell him how I really felt but I was too late. He was asleep on the couch with headphones on and tears running down his cheeks. I curled up and cried.

It's easy to realise your mistakes in retrospect.

𝔣

We were meant to be picked up at 12:30, but Jairo was late. Eventually we stopped avoiding each other and sat down to attempt a serious chat. It was going to take a long time for this to blow over. Josh arrived to deliver Happy Day ice-creams but retreated very quickly on seeing the anger burn in Karl's brilliant blue eyes. We were still waiting at three, so we ventured off to find beer. The restaurant was closed, forcing us to buy a six-pack at the shop. Rupert arrived to help us finish it and purchase a second; and finally, so did *Plastic*. Our goodbyes were said and, seeing as Jairo had thought that we were three, a random backpacker was accosted to help cross the canal.

Plastic was so full of gadgets and junk that you could barely recognise the Albin Vega that lay beneath. Jairo was overly safety conscious and had waterproofed and modified the vessel to ridiculous extremes. He'd also just acquired a cat, making the whole living arrangement even more interesting. Mitch, a gregarious German who'd spent the past few weeks sailing with Jairo, welcomed us in. With all six of us (cat included) aboard, we set off to The Flats to pick up our advisor.

While we waited, Jairo cooked us dinner on his alcohol stove. He had just finished explaining how dangerous a gas stove was and why he would never have one on a boat, when flames coated the cockpit. The alcohol burned out of control. Karl and I stared in disbelief before clicking into firefighting mode. There was so much crap on board that we struggled to find anything other than a towel [that we wet] to battle the blaze. The South Africans anchored next to us found the whole scenario very amusing.

Three sailing boats were transiting that night – *Plastic*, the South Africans on *Kelekele Lady* and *Black Swan*, a mega-yacht who refused to have anyone tie up next to them. Fred, our friendly advisor, hopped aboard while Mitch pulled up the anchor. Being the smaller boat, the locks were very simple. We merely had to raft up next to the South Africans while they did all the work. Or at least that was the plan. The South Africans ended up commissioning Karl and I to do their bow lines, so every now and then we actually had to do something.

The first lock took hours. As we laid on the deck awaiting instructions, a lunar eclipse began to unfold. It would have been the perfect setting: lying comfortably on a sail bag on the bow, staring at the sparkling sky and reddening moon - if the horridness of my previous night's shenanigans didn't still linger in the air. We slowly progressed through all three locks and arrived at the lake in the middle. I'm not sure *Nes-puck*, the catamaran Jairo tied us to, appreciated our rowdy 02:00 arrival. I passed a line over to a crew member on board and asked if we were tied up properly. "I'm not Thai, I'm Italian." I repeated the question and got the same answer. I hoped for the best.

Jairo and the hippy yelled and screamed. They made far too much noise as they splashed water everywhere and spat toothpaste all over me. The cat turned vicious and kept trying to escape to the luxury confines of our neighbour's vessel [between random attacks of fury upon whoever stood in his path.] Karl, Mitch and I bonded together to form a wall of normal, but it seemed to be of no avail.

Things were just as crazy when we woke up, maybe even crazier. I almost killed the cat! We all jumped into the crocodile-infested lake for a freshwater wash. Mitch cooked us an early pancake breakfast because the advisor was coming at six. He arrived just after nine and we set off on the 28-mile cruise to the next lock. It was rather pleasant being on someone else's boat that we didn't feel responsible for. We needed the break. The only useful thing we did was peel potatoes.

Black Swan was informed that if they did not raft up with us, they would be delayed by three hours. A huge fight ensued over the VHF until they grudgingly took our lines. Minutes later they handed us cold cokes and turned out to be quite a good-natured bunch. With no coffee onboard, we desperately needed the caffeine. We finally reached the last lock and the partying began. There was no beer on board either, which made us wish even more that it was *Yoldia* instead of *Plastic* passing into the Pacific.

We'd secured lines at Balboa Yacht Club and were about to hop off and return to *Yoldia* with bags, lines and Pablo's portable toilet[38] in hand. But the unfriendly staff informed us that we would have to pay $25 just to disembark. An argument ensued and Jairo cast off, taking us captive against our will. All the happiness of the successful crossing abated and we turned miserable. We were trapped, he didn't own a dinghy.

After anchoring in **La Playita**, Jairo kayaked off to find us a lift. He forced us to join a party instead. It was the captain's birthday onboard the hippy boat, *Sea-Star*. Masses of food were being prepared and the multitudes had gathered. At the time, at least 13 people were living aboard the 34-footer. This excluded the group from a nearby Mango-Tree squat, most of whom were seeking a vessel to cross the Pacific on. We were not

---

[38] That we had loaned Jairo for the crossing.

ready to be crowded in with that many alcohol-free hippies! When someone mentioned that they were rowing ashore to pick up the ice-cream cake, we jumped in the dinghy and finally made it to land. WE FOUND BEER!

It was too late to return to Shelter Bay, so we sat around a small table drinking away the day's frustrations instead. We hitchhiked back to the vacant *Plastic* and had a rather peaceful evening until Jairo kayaked back, downed one of our beers and raised the anchor. He was in love with a *Nes-puck* line handler and wanted to be closer to her – in another anchorage. It was all a bit surreal, but in Panama everything always was.

In all the chaos Karl looked at me, inched closer and finally gave me the hug I'd been needing for the past two days. Full forgiveness was still far-off, but this was the first step. And just in time too, the *Nes-puck* crew swam over with rum.

"Where are we?" asked Karl. "Home," I replied looking up at the beautiful sunrise unfolding above us. Only we weren't home, we were about as far away as we could possibly be[39].

...There we stood. Four big ropes, two bags and a toilet,
Awaiting Forecast.

f

When we finally did make it back, we found the marina full of strangers. It was as if we had been absent for years instead of days. This time we tried to keep a low profile and get our act together. With all the delays associated with returning from *Plastic*, we pushed our canal date forward

---

[39] It's a story in itself how we eventually made it back to *Yoldia*.

again. We assured the canal company that we would be transiting on Saturday.

The engine was almost running. It just conked out when in neutral, so we took her for a test run. We'd signed a document stating we could maintain the 5-knot minimum speed requirement, but we were sceptical. With the Yanmar full throttle, we could make 3.8 knots. Combined with the outboard, we were pushing 4.1. We stopped, anchored, had breakfast and began scrubbing the hull. I'd never seen so many barnacles! The water was grotesque. It was anything but calm as we scraped, scrubbed and cleaned. When we reached puking-point, we gave up and tried again. We made 4.8 knots. Close enough!

We returned to the marina, had ONE beer and then settled down for the quietest night yet on what was to be our last night EVER in Shelter Bay Marina.

PAN[D]AMANIUM

Shelter Bay, Colon, Panama. 19 April 2014

Three weeks of blood, sweat and tears culminate today.
And to be honest, we don't think we're ready for it.

So, where am I? Panama, yes, Colon in Panama.
Mañana land.
(Where "Man-ya-na" means "probably never" - not "tomorrow").
I sailed across the Caribbean Sea with a crazy Swede to start life as a
photographer/ videographer on board a catamaran...
Plans changed.
In Panama, everyone's plans change.

Instead, I decided to continue aboard little Yoldia.

What better way to cross the Pacific than on 27-feet of pure awesomeness?

Shelter Bay Marina [and its luxuries: a toilet, a shower and a pool] seemed perfectly normal on the outside. But what lies beneath you'd probably never believe.
(I'm not sure that sharing the details here is family-friendly, so I leave it there).

Being the smallest boat in the marina has its perks.
We've had donations of food, parts, lures, rescue equipment, meals and most importantly, hugs.

We have met all sorts of people. Mostly good. All crazy.

We have worked flat out for the last three weeks repairing everything on board, and nothing is 100% yet, but we are ready enough!
(We hope!)

With just over an hour remaining...
We are still awaiting our new crew.
We need to do an oil change.
We need to test the engine properly.
And load up the new dinghy someone donated us this morning.
We're stressed. We're tired.
And we're sweating like gorillas, but we're doing the transit at last.

The fines for delays in the canal are up to $7000 US.
We definitely don't have that.
If you have a moment today and tomorrow, say a little prayer for us/hold thumbs/cross your fingers and toes/post us a hug...

We need all the help we can get!

Let's hope it's more relaxed on the other [Pacific, which means "calm"]
side.

See you there!

❦

By 15:15, Karl began to reassemble the engine. By 15:31 we were still two
line-handlers short and I was in tears. "It will be okay!" said my incredibly
chilled out captain. And right then and there we heard it: "You thought I
was going to leave you behind, hey? You thought I wasn't coming?" We
looked up to see a beaming Jairo.

Michael's version of the story was slightly different:

> *"Light impressed itself on my memory of the moment. I saw* Yoldia
> *still in the docks. I am not sure if the clouds broke or the exit from the
> tinted windows cab provided the contrast I experienced; but at that
> moment I saw the boat I would eventually be underway on to the
> elusive country of Ecuador. The sun seemed to shine brighter than
> any point before that day; and everything was full of colour. The day
> of travel that included biking, boat-hitchhiking, swimming, kayaking,
> walking, two buses, a cab, running and a second cab; finally
> concluded with a pot of gold: my ticket to South America."*

The previous day we had seven people lined up to be line-handlers, but we
decided to stick to the original three: Jairo, Michael (an American cyclist
with a grin that constantly stained his great ball of gingerness) and Cinthia
(a Canadian that we had yet to meet, although her sister assured us that she

was fully awesome[40]). Jairo owed it to us and the other two had agreed to help us through with the view of crewing onward, across the Darien Gap. They'd both been travelling Central America and wanted a ride to the South.

The world was good again. As we untied from the docks we yelled, "So long and goodbye forever Shitty Bay!" We had no idea of the adventure that lay ahead. We had no time to properly meet our crew. All we knew was that we needed to go full steam ahead to The Flats – we were late.

"*Yoldia Yoldia Yoldia* this is Port Control, where are you?" They were nice enough to meet us halfway. Zachariah jumped aboard and we knew that someone was looking out for us, we could not have wished for a nicer advisor. We were the only yacht heading South that day, so we lucked out further and got tied up to a tugboat. To make things even better, it was a foreign tug and the crew were as excited as we were to be crossing the canal.

The sun set, as we arrived in the lagoon after an incredibly fast transit. We were told to tie up to the stern of a mega yacht before Zachariah hopped off. The friendly crew aboard was so impressed by the tininess of our vessel, that they pleaded to be granted a visit when they were off duty. They were very envious of our lives.

Karl cooked up a feast while I distributed beers. Dinner was just about to be served when Zachariah returned and said, "Let's go." Karl and I shot each other disbelieving glances. The overly-kind advisor wanted to help us transit another 20 miles that night, just to make sure that we did make it through the canal in our allocated time. While half the crew slept, the guise of nightly darkness gave us a much-needed chance to pump out our bilge as the engine ran. When it started raining, Zachariah didn't blink an

---

[40] Turns out she was even more than that – she was a tiny free-spirited bundle of mellifluous joy!

eyelid. He simply accepted a raincoat and took off his shoes as he sat smiling and guiding us through the rainy runway of lights. It was after 01:00 when we tied up to a mushroom float and bid the legendary advisor goodnight. We cracked open another beer, had a second dinner and fell fast asleep.

It was weird waking up in a strange land of fields, tankers, and container ships. I made a cup of coffee and sat enjoying the sunrise on a mushroom float before the others began stirring. It was going to be an excellent day. I was just about finished cooking breakfast when our new advisor started yelling that we needed to turn the boat around. I handed over the spatula and ran to the bow to see what was going on. We were three miles away from the final set of locks and there was no way we were turning back!

"You don't have enough *cleats*," he said, "you have to turn the vessel around." I found it strange that an advisor would argue that in the middle of the canal after we had already been inspected before being granted our permit. We had already transited the most challenging locks without Zachariah showing the slightest concern, never mind Jairo doing it on the same boat only a week earlier. It was simple – he did not want to be aboard our little boat. He was on a mission to make our lives miserable. I showed him how we could effectively secure lines to our single bow cleat, but he was already on the phone to the authorities at the canal company. I took the phone away from his ear and put it very simply: "Look, sir, you only have to be on this boat for a few hours to get us to the Pacific. For us, it has taken months of preparation and we have scraped together every cent that we own. You can't turn us around for a cleat. Not after everything we have done to get this far." I had tears rolling down my cheeks. Real tears. I was tired of fighting Panamanian bureaucracy. He still had the company on the line. He looked me dead in the eyes and lifted the receiver back to his ear, "It's okay," he said, "we made a plan."

We were meant to be the centre chamber but, out of nowhere, our friends from the previous day's mega-yacht arrived and we tied up to them. Our advisor ventured over for lunch in a more luxurious establishment, while their crew took it in turns stepping over to *Yoldia* to snap pictures. A huge cargo ship that touched the walls filled the lock behind us and it really did put our lives into perspective. While we waited for the waters to drop (with no advisor onboard), we had a chance to properly clean the bilge into buckets. WE HAD AN OIL LEAK!

By the second lock, we got the instruments out and had an exceptional jam session: Karl on the guitar, Cinthia on her harmonica, Mike on some pots and me on my shaky eggs while Jairo hummed strange melodies. By the third lock, the smiles on our faces were uncontrollable.

The viewing tower was filled with hundreds of enthusiastic tourists watching us head for freedom but this joy was all ours. We'd worked too freaking hard for it! As we watched the last lock open, we leaped about hugging each another and cried a little bit.

We untied from the mega yacht and ventured out, into the Pacific.

15.

SPEAKING OF BOTTOMS

CONTRARY to popular belief, the water was not much bluer on the other side. The sky was not much clearer. The yachting community was of a similar calibre of craziness, and Panama still had the same tricks prowling up her sleeves.

Jairo caught a fish with his bare hands. The neighbours' chicken finally laid its first egg. We ended up on *Sea-Star* for the tail end of *Naked Pizza Night*. We rescued a boat that dragged anchor. We managed to reunite a lost Speedo with its owner. Jeandré arrived.

It was after 23:00 and we were sitting on the breakwater skipping stones on the smooth sea. We had just about given up on being the welcome party when a cab pulled up. I jumped up and flung my arms around my big little brother; and then the masses descended upon *Yoldia*. Jeandré barely had a chance to tell me about his diving accident before alcohol was thrust upon him. Sadly, he couldn't drink it.

We'd planned to set sail at first light but [obviously] Panama had other plans. Jeandré was coughing up blood and we needed to get him to a hospital. I'm not sure why he had taken his flight from Mexico, but I was glad to have him around.

Hospital Punta Pacifico was a pretty snazzy establishment, but that's where his dive insurance had sentenced him. When we realised that he would be in there for a while, Karl and I left him to the doctors and ventured off to explore. It was unfortunate circumstances, but holiday fever had descended upon us. We were off the boat and not even going to attempt to be productive!

Panama City could not be more different from Colon. It was bling, clean and functional. Their mall seemed to only cater to the rich and famous, but fortunately they had a food court that catered to our needs in any form of fast food our hearts could desire.

Back at the hospital, Jeandré had disappeared. Nobody spoke a word of English and there was nobody to point us in the right direction. We took a nap in the lobby to sleep off our lunch. I tried again every half hour or so and kept finding new wings of the hospital to get lost in, but still no Jeandré. When it started getting dark, we started getting worried.

"Only one visitor at a time," said the nurse when we eventually found the allusive ward. I stepped inside and stared in horror; my brother had tubes pinned all over him and was shaking and writhing like a person possessed. "I… I… I…" I completely freaked out before he opened his eyes, smiled, laughed, and said, "Hey bud." He was still waiting to see the lung specialist, so I took on the new mission of finding out what was happening, leaving Karl and Jeandré to get better acquainted.

After X-rays and a bunch of other tests, the doctor gave him the all-clear. He'd ruptured blood vessels around his lungs and while he was given strict instructions not to dive again for at least the next month, there was no major cause for concern.

"Do you have any other questions?" asked the smiling specialist with the best English we'd heard since the Mazda dealer. "Actually yes, where can we find something good to eat?" I asked. The boys gave me a hard time saying I was wasting the specialist's time while other people were out there dying and what not; but the doctor beamed and wrote me a prescription for succulent steaks and beers.

Karl took Jeandré ashore to sort out insurance while I prepped the boat for sail. They took such a long time that I even managed to sit down, make a cup of coffee and trade pictures and music with Jairo, who seemed relatively calm that day (it might have had something to do with his new [female] crew member). Jairo was just leaving when the boys returned; and they did so in style, chugging a whole bottle of wine each while grinning.

Turns out it was a necessary evil. They'd sunk the dinghy and needed the corks to replace the missing plugs. We saw the open bottles as an excuse to keep drinking, and the wine went down quicker than the anchor came up.

We were so excited to be sailing again that we didn't care that we were only making two knots (or which direction we were heading in exactly). We cracked open a beer and eased into life at sea. I caught my first and second tuna. In all the excitement, we sailed straight past our destination, **Bayonetta**. Under the circumstances [and influence] we did very well in managing to read the charts and plan a course that dodged rocks and other islands. We dropped anchor just before 02:00 and Karl prepped the perfect fish dish under a twinkling abyss. We stayed up to watch the sunrise.

The *Homeless* Fins woke us midmorning and were very impressed by the state of our intoxicating cockpit. After a day of adventures, we agreed to race them to Gonzalez the following noon.

"*Yoldia Yoldia Yoldia.*" We woke up with the radio. "Do you have a straw?" We thought it was a pretty random question, but the Finnish are rather random. When we gave the affirmative, Miko sped on over. He had a crab stuck in his ear. We tried to swab it out, blow it out and alcohol it out, but the creature seemed quite snug in his new abode. Eventually, with four cigarettes, Karl managed to chain smoke the critter free. While we sat down to a celebratory cup of Amarula coffee, another one emerged.

11:59 had arrived and we prepared for the race. On "Go," we hauled up the anchor and set the sails. At one point we made a whopping 1.4 knots; and after about an hour of making no progress at all, we agreed that engines might have to be utilised. Miko cracked open a beer, so we cracked open rum. He turned to vodka, so I made us Pina Coladas. Miko was jealous, so I mixed some in a bottle and threw it over to him. To say thank you, he filled a bucket and threw us ice. Johanna slept. It was that fierce of a race.

We had planned to raft up with them and had the fenders out and ready, but one look at the angry anchorage made us reconsider. Instead, we dinghied over with a sparse selection of food and beverages and together we celebrated life. Well, most of us did. Jeandré, still in his element, spent most of the night cuddling the railings as he threw up the remains of his internal organs, which fed the phosphorescent fish. Dolphins, a shark, and even the birds glowed as they dove to the depths to catch their dinner.

After a swim-shower (which unfortunately resulted in me jumping straight onto my brother's freshly dispersed turd), we said our sad goodbyes. We told the Fins, who were carrying on straight to the Marquesas, that we'd see them soon.

"*Woah!* That ray just jumped out of the water!" I yelled, shattering the silence as we slowly sailed back to **Panama City**. Karl was sceptical, but fifteen minutes later he yelled the same thing. A little later, there were leaping rays all over the horizon. A shark drifted past. Jeandré and I sat awed on the bow and had a siblingly deep and meaningful. I'd denied any romantic affiliations with the captain, but he was the wiser. He made me promise to have a real chat about feelings with Karl. He made me promise to see a doctor about the massive tumour-like lump that had suddenly festooned on the bend of my leg. He made me promise I would finish writing my book, again[41].

All too quickly, I hugged Jeandré goodbye, unsure how long it would be before I saw him [or any other family] again.

ƒ

We kept talking about getting up, but finding the motivation was tough. It was hard to accept that our "holiday" was over and that we had to get back to work. Eventually, I mustered up some will-power and became proactive: I put the kettle on. But, it was one of those days where we should have just stayed in bed.

I handed Karl a steaming pot of fresh brew. Somewhere in the exchange, the mug slipped and the whole world slowed down as the captain's cup released bubbling hot liquid onto his lap. In hour-seconds, he was screaming and rolling around the floor in a ball of agony. I thought it would be like a kick in the balls, where the pain would dissipate; but it got worse. He was in serious torment.

He ran and jumped in the water. That didn't help. We tried freshwater – no luck. I thought cooking oil might calm the burn. Still no luck. I grabbed every first aid kit we owned and tore them apart. There had to be burn ointment in there somewhere. After ripping through all four kits (three of them in Swedish) I looked over at the anchorage: *Plastic* – no kayak. *Nes-puck*... I didn't even take the dinghy. I jumped overboard and swam.

---

[41] I'm incredibly fortunate to have a baby brother who perpetually looks out for me and seriously keeps me accountable for my un-serious life!

Unfortunately, he was not home and it was only her. The Ukrainian spoke virtually no English and charades were not as easy as one might think. Eventually, she handed me a tube of sour cream and whispered, "family secret." I didn't think she had understood until she gave me a tub of burn ointment too. She drove me back with fervour. The creams seemed to help, but huge blisters were rising on Karl's legs and he was still screaming. "Okay, we are going to the hospital!" I said with finality. There was no more resistance. I tore the lining out of his shorts and by the time he had them on, the skin was separating from his balls. I found him a shirt and fed him the hardcore pain-killers I still carried from my Malaysian dog attack. We sped ashore to the dinghy dock.

With a nicely wrapped pack of ice in his pants, cigarette smoke heavy on his breath and a coke in hand, I hailed a taxi. The driver stared at us as if we were diseased and put the floor mats on the seats for us to sit on. With tears still running down his cheeks, the taxi sped off to the hospital. I was the worst person in the world. I made the coffee!

There was quite a queue at the information desk at Santa Thomas and I didn't want to wait. We got bounced around all over the place and eventually I left Karl in the waiting room and stormed into the emergency unit to find help. I pleaded the case with someone in a nurse's outfit. She didn't appear to speak English, but she put us into the right queue and disappeared before I could thank her. Minutes later she arrived with someone to attend to Karl.

I checked him in and entered *Urgencia* to find him lying on a bed squirming. They kicked me out, and by the time I broke back in, they still hadn't given him anything for the pain. All the nurses were sitting around giggling and tweeting about the poor guy with the burnt penis. They tried to kick me out again, but I was going nowhere until I knew what was going on. When they found someone who spoke English, he tried to calm me down. They told me that they had to wait for the plastic surgeon and that I could return during visiting hours, which were from 18:00-19:00. "If we find him a bed we will move him, otherwise you can find him here. With this type of burn we probably have to keep him a few weeks." They threw me out again. I walked to the back of the hospital and smoked Karl's cigarettes because I didn't know what else to do.

I'm glad I snuck back in again because there was a long list of tests that had to be run, and they weren't doing any until payments were made. I paid the fees at the various counters and got his parents' details before wandering off to find the internet. The worst part was just about to begin.

"Hi, it's Adeena here, Karl's crew. How are you?"

"Hi Adeena, I'm well. How's Karl?"

"Karl's um, that's why I'm calling, um..."

How do you tell a parent that their child is in the hospital?

How do you tell a mother that you burned her son's penis?

With a few art supplies and a toothbrush in hand, I returned to the hospital with 15 minutes to spare. I didn't have a clue where to go. *Informacie* was closed and the security guards were still not letting me back through into *Urgencia*. A stranger guided me outdoors and I was left with a teeming mass of people. At 17:55, the doors flung open and the crowds swarmed in.

When I finally made it through the narrow entranceway, I was kicked straight back out again for being barefoot. Finally the tears came. I'd held strong all day, but this was too much. One of the street vendors watched my predicament and came over to give me his shoes. I cried some more in the selfless beauty of the moment. I followed the crowds to the second floor, but Karl was not on the patient list. I tried the third. No luck. They sent me back to the vacated information desk I'd tried earlier. Back on the second floor, I gave it another shot. More tears came flooding. An English-speaking nurse, who was on her dinner break, took pity on me. She checked the lists and said I should be on the fourth floor. I followed her, but that was a different Karl. She phoned through to information for me and together we visited three more wrong wards, before eventually arriving at *U de Quimodas*. It was almost 19:00 when I eventually found my heavily drugged captain, but I think he was happy to see me too.

There were three other men in the ward with visible burns far worse than Karl's – their faces, legs and arms had melted in gas explosions and actual fires - but they all agreed that Karl was by far the worst of the lot. The nurses were nice enough to allow me to stay long after visiting hours. By the time I found my way out of the maze of a hospital to where I think the vendor man had stood, I found the spot vacated. I kept the shoes.

Mike arrived back at Yoldia at the same time as me. He got to witness the remnants of the morning's carnage first hand. Medical supplies were strewn everywhere and the floor was coated in oil, sour cream, water, coffee, and yuck! Leftovers still sat on the stove, so I finally had breakfast while I broke it to Mike [and Cinthia, when she returned] that there may be a delay in departure.

𝔣

Jairo came knocking. He had huge shards of glass wedged into his feet and they were now properly stuck and very infected. He could barely walk and asked me to help him to the hospital. *(#RoundThree!)*

I checked in on Karl first (while Jairo followed like a lemming). His doctor had told him that he'd be in for about two weeks! I handed him his phone and a sim card and made a shopping list. I checked Jairo in downstairs and made sure he was okay. Seeing as I was there anyway, I kept my promise to Jeandré and checked myself in too. When it was discovered that I spoke English, the doctors got excited and traded patients so that a man on his last shift could practice the language he had been learning [in almost vain] for virtually a decade. He took all my vitals and

I was happy to learn that I had an athlete's heart-rate, despite the lack of exercise and excessive drinking I had been doing.

I had a bit of time to kill before visiting hours, so I tried to find Jairo, but I didn't even know his last name. I joined the masses outside the door and quite enjoyed the fervent preacher riling up the people. I was the first through the doors, but it still took 23 minutes to find the correct ward.

I tried to return the shoes, but my smiling vendor friend instructed me to keep them. I assured Karl's mum that he was much better and gave her his phone number. I let Jeandré know that I was cancer-free[42]. Jairo was nicely stitched up and seemed quite comfy in the arms of his crew-babe. With everything in order, I came home to an empty boat and collapsed.

After a good night's sleep, I had an exceptionally productive morning before actually taking a lunch break. I made it to the hospital with plenty of time to spare and didn't get lost or cry. Although I did miss the chair after Karl kissed me, bringing much amusement to his roommates.

The rest of the crew had tried to visit too. Mike hadn't been allowed in because he was wearing shorts and Cinthia had been refused because her shoulders were uncovered. They laughed when they saw I was wearing both shorts and a singlet. We walked home together because it was a beautiful night, and Panama City was pretty remarkable.

I was being towed in the dinghy by Jairo on *Plastic*. As he bobbed about from boat to boat to say his goodbyes, I had the perfect opportunity to gather the things I'd loaned various vessels. *Plastic* and *Sea-Star* were finally off to cross the Pacific. Jairo hugged me goodbye and dropped me off. As a final thought, he veered back past *Yoldia* and yelled, "Hey, do you want some garlic?" Inspired by our cooking (the fact that a simple addition, like garlic, could make food taste so good), he had been driven

---

[42] Although I did need to get the bulging lump drained! That could wait a bit – one crew member in hospital was enough!

to invest in 10kgs of the white herb.

Despite my depraved first impressions of the crazy Dutchman, his heart was golden and I was sad to see him go. "Thank you!..." I yelled as he flung us the biggest bag of garlic I'd ever seen! "Have fun and see you later!... Oh, and we're not sinking anymore! – I think you fixed it!" He'd spent most of the previous day teaching me how to stop water leaking in through our propeller.

In the rest of the blur of the week, things were fixed, bought, built and sorted; and broken. At some point, the outboard engine was sunk in the oily zero-visibility water. The harder we worked to get ready for departure, the further we got from completion. I was tired of playing captain. I really missed having Karl around.

The call finally came to collect the captain and I was only a train ride away. I didn't have shoes or "appropriate" clothing with me, but I decided to push my luck. Getting in was easy, getting Karl out was not. In the fourth hour of visiting different departments and trying to wrangle payments, I gave up and climbed into bed to cuddle him. I couldn't take it anymore. I got busted immediately. But it was his favourite nurse. Not only did she delay kicking me out of bed, but she also smuggled me some gauze and a red liquid she called "soap."

Unfortunately, the hospital was in no way set up to accept foreign payments. By 17:30 it was established that Karl needed to spend one more night in his hospital jail. We begged and pleaded and eventually they felt pangs of sympathy and set him free. We escaped with seconds to spare before the security guards swung open the gates for visiting hours.

Karl had been in there for so long that his bagged-up admittance clothes had gone mouldy. As part of the escape deal, I wangled a free set of hospital scrubs for him to wear. I'm not sure what passers-by thought of him standing in his gown while chain-smoking his first cigarettes, or what people were thinking as we walked down the street to a busy restaurant where I treated him to a beer. We had a few more beverages at the marina bar before a giant *Yoldia*-style party ensued.

It was an exceptionally difficult job waking up the captain, but it had to be done. We had an appointment to sort out his insurance. We made it in just before nine and, without a word spoken, they seemed to know exactly who we were looking for: Rosa. She was ready and waiting for us and we thought we would be in for a quick and easy day.

Our new best friend, who oversaw insurance, had never dealt with a foreign claim. She spent half the morning passing me the phone to speak to her Mexican boss who lived in the US. In-between, we were on the line to Karl's Insurers in Sweden and their nearest local branch in Nicaragua. By 15:42 we were finally cleared out of the hospital and ventured out to have a celebratory hangover-curbing breakfast. Roelof was on the bus!

❦

I shoved $40 into Karl's passport ($10 each) as I'd been advised. I had no intention to pay a bribe, but there was also no way we could pay $105 each [and a cruising permit] just to leave. The officer welcomed me and motioned for me to take a seat. My heart pounded too quickly. Almost instantly, the money fell to the desk. I feigned ignorance. The officer scrutinised me carefully and then casually handed it back. I smiled and shrugged. Six[43] stamps later, thanks to Pablo being true to his word, we were cleared out of Panama at no cost at all.

Stowing and prepping everything for sail took the greater part of the day. It culminated in a celebratory dinner on *Djerpie*. We dined like kings and queens and decided to sail back to Las Perlas together. As soon as we got

---

[43] Including the boat and Teddy Bear's passport; of course.

back to *Yoldia*, they started their engine and raised the anchor. We tried, but not only were our running lights not working, but our starter battery was also dead. At 05:30, we called it a night and went to bed in the cockpit. We'd wreaked havoc aboard and there was no space anywhere else.

It was a rough day of engine problem elimination, but we found the source of our woes: a new oil leak. In one of my proudest moments in all my days as a sailor, an "engineer" and a human, I fixed it with a clove of garlic. In perfect timing, the clouds burst open and the rains bucketed down. We danced, scrubbed and sang on the deck. It was the first fresh-water wash we'd had in weeks!

Someone sought to donate us a hand-held VHF, so we sent Mike hitchhiking in to claim it (as well as four beers with the coins we'd found while re-organising the boat), while we stowed everything away again. By 21:15 he still hadn't returned so we raised anchor and headed into the marina to see if we could find him. Sure enough, there he was, asleep on the dock. "Mike!" I yelled, "get ready to jump." He leapt into life as Karl steered, I held us off the dock and Cinthia tossed our last trash ashore. We were off!

It felt so good to be back on the ocean, and it was even better knowing that this was the real thing. We were finally leaving! It was a chilled night sail and an even more *shill* (as the Swedish say) day. I caught a baby tuna and threw it back. In gratitude, the ocean delivered a much larger one. We watched sharks swim by, circling what could only be a disintegrating whale carcass; and there were dolphins. The sea swarmed with life.

We dropped anchor just after midnight in the perfect anchorage, and cooked up a feast under a sparkling Panamanian sky. The tuna was decadent and our new cockpit lights were squeezed into tiny yellow teacups for ambient lighting. We might have missed *Djerpie*, but the phosphorescence was alive and our spirits soared.

When the sun rose, we were rather disappointed to find ourselves in a construction site. It didn't take long for us to up-anchor and carry straight on to Ecuador. We were just easing into sailing when I spotted a boat off the far side of Gonzalez. We radioed through and sure as sugar shards, it was *Djerpie*.

Both boats sailed side by side, headed for distant shores, until eventually we veered in different directions: them to Galapagos and us to mainland Ecuador.

Wisdom gleaned whilst withstanding Panama:

- Catamarans aren't real boats.
- Coffee isn't always good for you.
- The truth is far stranger than fiction.
- Always follow your instincts, but never trust your sense of direction.
- If all else fails, you can always find shelter under the Mango Tree[44].
- When you do finally retrieve your sunken outboard engine, do everything you can to resuscitate it as soon as possible; and be persistent. Otherwise, like us, you'll have to get good at rowing.
- Don't get distracted on your way to immigration and lose the passports! If you do, pray hard! Very hard! And perhaps you will find the entire sleeve of boat papers and important documents lying on a pile of hosepipes in a busy department store, right where you unwillingly left them.
- If you collect empty oil canisters from restaurants to use as water jugs, make sure you clean them out properly first. Do

---

[44] The small bubble of euphoria that dwelled, as the name may suggest, under a mango tree included both Mike and Cinthia, most of the *Sea-Star* regulars, and our Scottish friend Colin.

this before you leave!

SOUTH

We only had a few hundred miles to sail, so we bargained on it taking eight days [maximum], but the wind was nowhere to be found. It was quite cramped being four on board, especially with the bear, the bike and all our Pacific supplies. It started to feel tighter by the day. Still, there was a lot of chilling going on. The ocean basked us with beauty and in return, we filled it with music, art days and plays.

Every day brought with it sharks, dolphins, whales or all of the above. One night, as I started to reel in the fishing line, I told the boys I had something big on the hook. They didn't believe me. They scoffed as I struggled with the hand-line, and joked that it was just the current and I was simply imagining it. The laughter stopped when I pulled a shark right into the cockpit.

We took our night watches in stride and with four watchmen, life was pretty good. Until the rains came. The incessant rains. The new sealing in the cockpit didn't seem to be working, and the floor (which doubled as the third bed) became a constant pool. On one particularly bad night, we scooped 63 FULL pots of water off the floor.

Then we stopped moving completely. The currents were against us and the winds had vanished. At some point, one of the two lines Mike had been trolling actually caught a fish. The fish went berserk and tangled both lines around the propeller and the hull, leaving us stuck in the pouring rain and unable to start the engine. In twenty-four hours, we moved backwards by nine miles.

Mike took a morning dive to free up the lines, getting stung by swarms of blue bottles in the process. And when we finally did start the engine, the boat was filled with smoke and bizarre noises. Something was very wrong. On closer inspection, we found seawater pouring out of the water pump. We used ingenuity for a temporary fix: gasket maker, sticks, and a whole lot of WD40 (the answer to all the world's problems). The pump was not going to last long, but at least it was working.

The nearest port was 70 miles back, but that seemed to have a six-knot current in the wrong direction. Instead, after too much discussion and some beautiful acrobatic displays by dolphins and whales, we decided on Tumaco, Columbia. It lay 93 miles ahead. With the cramped and damped conditions on board, we saw it as the land of milk and honey [and beer]. The wind eventually returned and our little engine that probably shouldn't have, got a break.

It was the fourteenth day and spirits were at an all-time low. We had the rain to contend with when the *clew* of the jib decided to break free. I crawled to the bow with a needle and thread. I wounded my legs around the bowsprit to try and gain the balance necessary for stitching. My hands bled as I stabbed them time and time again trying to push the needle through the thick fabric of the corner sail. I was just about finished when there was a loud bang. I turned to see the main on a mission of its own. It too had broken free. When things go wrong, they go very wrong. Even outside of Panama.

By sunset, we had it all under control and watches resumed as normal. We were so close that we could see the lights.

The current turned against us.

The divide on board arose mostly based on dietary preference. There were those who were sweet-toothed and those who were not. With ten miles to go, Mike used our last eggs to make CAKE for breakfast. By the time the CAKE was ready, the current was so strong that we had to drop anchor to enjoy it. We weren't going anywhere but backwards. It was good to have a breather, but I was quite happy when the captain pulled me aside. He whispered that from now on, that kind of breakfast was outlawed on board.

We raised the anchor just before noon and the wind woke up too. We followed the wrong-sided channel markers and tacked our way through the many fishing villages and shallows. It would have been nice to have a functional engine, but there was something satisfying about doing it all under sail. We rounded the last corner safely and finally dropped anchor, quite amazed that we had managed to avoid collisions with all the hordes of local fishing vessels. We high-fived, hugged, cheered and then started to wonder how we could possibly row ashore with all that current.

We waved a nearby fishing boat over and asked where the anchorage was. The friendly man pointed behind us, and we came to understand that we had passed it miles earlier. We were trying to devise reverse plans when he had a second thought. He suggested his friend's restaurant that lay just ahead.

Friday, May 30th 2014, 16:33, we officially anchored in **Tumaco**, Columbia. We found some corks and launched the dinghy while the restaurateurs stood on the docks ready to welcome us in.

COLUMBIA

After running for a real toilet, I found everyone seated with Filipo, beer in hand. "Relax!" said the friendly owner as he handed me an ice-cold Columbian. Immigration was only a few blocks away and it closed at six. He even went as far as driving us there. When he was certain that we were in good hands, he extended us a dinner invitation and disappeared to prepare it.

Immigration welcomed us with big smiles and shiny stamps. We asked about Port Control and customs, but they assured us that this was all we were needing. Checking in was that simple[45]. We went for a walk and sampled some more of the country's liquid cuisine. It was an exceptional place, even with the excessive amounts of military presence.

We sat with Filipo, his wife and a good portion of their extended family as they related tales about the land and their lives. Each of us had a seafood platter and kiwi strawberry salad set before us, as we sipped merrily on beers, feeling right at home. We could not have dreamed of a better welcoming party. The coastguard interrupted us at some point and whisked Karl off so that they could inspect the vessel. The celebrations continued into the early hours of the morning.

We re-joined the couple for a home-made breakfast in their kitchen: fresh bread, butter, sausages and eggs. Then, because they had a big event that evening, we set off into town to explore, find the internet, beer and other important paraphernalia. Such a nice town Tumaco was too, with all it's strange shops, pastries and alley-way markets. We wound our way through the streets lined with marine and spare-part stores to a small bar that overlooked the water. In the little hideaway, there was a perfect perch to view passing fishing boats and frigate birds. As the tides changed you could watch masses of garbage flow in either direction: clothes, diapers, handbags, pig's heads... it was always exciting to see what was drifting by.

An email check brought heart-breaking news. A radio call-out from a passing vessel had sent the coastguard to check reports of a half-submerged unmanned vessel drifting off the coast of Columbia. When boarded, Bjørn and Kennedy had been found unconscious just above the water-line. It seemed that they had both suffered severe withdrawal-syndrome. They'd been planning on picking up more Steve (and other substances) en route to the Azores, but never arrived. They were rushed to hospital where fortunately their lives were spared. But the boat was lost.

---

[45] Or so we thought.

Pieter survived his terminal illnesses. Instead, he died of a broken heart - *Chiaroscuro* had been the only thing he'd had left to live for.

❦

Our little family prepared for separate life directions. Mike and Cinthia moved into the restaurant where Cinth began the search for a motorbike and Michael started gearing up for the long cycle south. Karl and I tidied up the rigging and replaced the worn-out halyards. We found the cause and changed the blocked pipes that had constantly flooded the saloon. We got the water pump repaired (at a shop that fed us beers and borrowed the neighbour's kids to dance so that we were entertained while we waited). Karl fixed the fragile parts of the wind vane making sure they would hold for the crossing. We sorted out our water woes by taking on 100 sturdy six-litre bags. We were progressing fantastically.

Alejandro! We finally met an English speaker. Every day he would appear in the most arbitrary places and invite us for "one beer." He never had any money with him, but there were far too many parties, random celebrations, and strange bar brawls. Even the fights ended well. The Colombians were passionate, but they never held a grudge for long. Being a town that never sees tourists, we made friends everywhere we went. Even the military was friendly, but I didn't want to get to know them too well. At any given moment, there were at least six of them guarding the bridge that over-looked *Yoldia*. I shuddered to think how many times they saw me defaecate off the bow or the stern in the not so stealthy moonlit sky. It was a lot of poop too, seeing as we had tried to see what the local water would do to our stomachs.

We said our sad goodbyes to the crew, and eventually we were ready too. The tide was changing and the wind was waking up, conditions could not have been better. We had a last beer with Filipo and stuffed our final supplies away. I took the tiller as Karl raised the anchor. Before we knew it, we had cleared the channel and were making six knots in the same bay it had taken us two days to clear. The last buoys were in sight and we were getting ready to celebrate. "Welcome home mate!" said Karl. It was where we belonged, out on the water.

"STOP!" The coast guard suddenly pulled up with their 3X300 horsepower engines. We couldn't really stop. We dropped the main and furled the jib, allowing them to come closer for a chat. They wanted us to return to speak to the Captain of the Port. They requested permission to board. Granted. The fenders went up and two guards hopped over while their vessel backed off to get pictures of the uniformed men posing on our bow. We showed them our paperwork. We did not need to go back, especially seeing as we were sailing straight for French territory. They seemed to understand and were busy chatting it through. Suddenly, for some reason we will never understand, they decided to deliver a third guard. We turned in horror to see the driver ram straight into the bowsprit with a thunderous bang. We ran forward to inspect it. The bow was completely mangled and the forestay was loose. A lot of yelling ensued; but we had no option, we had to go back. There was no way on Earth we would be starting the longest ocean crossing in the world on a boat that was not rigged right.

❡

It took all day to fill in paperwork and orchestrate repairs. With $20 left in our wallet, we went to speak to the coast-guard. They were very apologetic and quite upset that nobody had admitted to the damages earlier. The friendly staff restored our spirits and we left with massive smiles on our faces and pesos in our pockets[46]. We were going to have a good night!

---

[46] Reimbursement for the money we had had to fork out to repair damages.

I woke up hungover. Karl woke up angry. I hadn't let him get drunk. We scrubbed the hull in the murky muck of water as the victory cries of the Soccer World Cup rang out, Columbia beat Greece. How had four years vanished so quickly? How had I still not made it to Spain?

Karl ventured ashore to spend the last of our pesos on supplies while I prepped for sail. He returned beaming with hard bread and crackers as well as a promise that we would say a final goodbye to Alejandro before we set off. The friendly Columbian actually cried.

We had a sneaky wash in the Port Control bathroom and took a final stroll through the row of confiscated home-made cocaine-runner submarines, and then licked land goodbye. We raised anchor and ventured out while the coast guard followed, but this time they really only wanted photographs!

16.

FIRST WE ATE YOUR WIFE

WE sat there staring at each other, speechless, more or less heaved-to. We had brushed aside so many boat problems, but this was a next level ballgame. Neither of us were prepared for this.

We sailed out of Columbia on Saturday, 14 June 2014, at 18:03. We couldn't find any propane bottles small enough to fit into the over-packed vessel, so we opted against a spare. The water tank was full of chlorine, making it undrinkable. Despite the hours we spent scraping the hull, we had more barnacles than ever. The mainsail had a rip in it (thanks to the boot of a posing coast-guard) and the genoa was still stowed away out of reach. But it was one of those now or never situations and we always opt for the now!

There was no wind, so we had the anchor at the waterline, ready to drop. It quickly became evident that we were not going to be able to stay in the designated channel so I handed Karl the tiller, he knew his boat better than anyone. It was touch and go late into the night as we dodged shallows, buoys and a plethora of fishermen, all under sail alone. It was not the same triumphant exit we'd had two days earlier, but it was good to be on our way. My captain beamed his boyish grin as we cracked open our final beers and cheered, "To the crossing of the Pacific at flipping last!" NOTHING could make us turn around now.

We were going to be good sailors and planned to keep abreast of tasks. I used the over-chlorinated water to clean the anchor and its overgrown planktony chain. I cleaned the bilge, the ceilings and then bleached my whites back to their former beauty. The wind picked up in the afternoon, so sail repairs were out of the question. We simply sat down and allowed ourselves to be mesmerised by the Pacific-ness that engulfed us. Karl cooked up a delicious dinner while the stars and phosphorescence set in.

I was already marvelling at how lucky I was to be alive, when the dolphins showed up and illuminated our path. They streaked lights across the water as they leaped, spun and frolicked in our wake. Lightning lashed out over distant land. The world was too beautiful.

I'd been running a marathon and was in first place. Only, I kept getting distracted by familiar faces, stopping to chat to people and pay bills I'd forgotten to settle. The race veered off the land and was now underwater. I lost the crowd with more distractions and accidentally discovered the lost city of Atlantis...

Karl interrupted my exploration and woke me up with coffee. I returned the favour by salvaging the bananas and transforming them into pancakes. I stitched the sail in the rain while the captain attempted to clean and refill the chlorinated tanks. The fishing line went out and, while it didn't catch anything, we were happy enough with a vegetarian curry. The sun sank. The clouds abated. The stars returned.

The wind and currents finally shifted, and the wind vane swung into full operation. We were still setting alarms for the hour, but we were excited that soon we would be in the trade winds and we'd both be able to get some much-needed sleep. This was the Pacific. The calm ocean. There was nothing in our path except thousands of miles of deep blue.

Day 4. 04:31. Karl came in cursing, looking for a flashlight. The prognosis could not have been worse. The bottom half of our wind vane was missing. Not just the rudder or the plastic bits for which we had spares, but the whole thing. Gears and all - parts he didn't even know were removable. Without the wind vane, we would have to hand steer the 3600+ miles to the Marquesas. One of us would constantly need to be at the helm, while the other slept. For 30 days… More maybe! We turned the boat around and got the spotlights out while we followed our track and hoped that it floated. We knew we were playing a loser's game, but stranger things had happened. We searched everywhere. For hours. We didn't want to go on without it.

We began toying with possibilities:

- Ecuador: It was close enough, but we knew they wouldn't have the parts. We would either have to order them in (and, if it was anything like Brazil, import tax would cost far more than the expensive parts that we already could not afford) or fabricate make-shift parts locally.
- We could leave the boat somewhere and Karl could fly back to Sweden, work to earn more cash, and return with a new one.

Sometime after sunrise, while heaved to, we both shattered the silence and blurted out almost simultaneously,

"Let's do it anyway!"

What kind of sailors would we be if we turned back? Even though we'd probably hate each other by the end of this. We poured another cup of coffee and had some hard bread.

01°51.324N, 080°16.824W. We took a deep breath and Karl took the tiller. We began what would probably be the hardest journey of our lives.

Because the engine had been running, the batteries were high enough to be able to "blast some tunes". For lunch, we threw a popcorn party to celebrate life, regardless of its challenges. It rained straight through my 16:00 – 20:00 watch. I collected rainwater like my life depended on it, while trying to hold the course with my butt. Shivering with cold, I handed over the tiller and crawled inside. I can honestly say that that 25¢ tuna spaghetti dinner was one of the best things I had ever tasted. I took over again at midnight and, like clockwork, the rains returned. *What am I doing wrong in life?!* By 02:00, I'd tacked four times in the inconsistent winds, and all the buckets were full. By 04:00, I could take it no more. The last squall had been the most vicious. We were flying six knots, heeling an awful lot. My whole body ached from the hours at the tiller and my spine was tense from the nearby lightning strikes.

How have I got myself in so deep? All I wanted was a hitchhike to Panama and here I am signed up to cross the largest of all the oceans on a 27-foot bathtub. God, you and I are going to be closer than ever after this trip! There is no way I am going to be able to pull this off without You.

Day 5. I traded places with Karl, poured the water in the tanks, and collapsed. He woke me up just to pester me. "I've been through all the lazarettes," he said, "and I found the wind vane." I laughed while I tried to shake the dream I'd been having. Mike and Cinthia had hitched out on a fishing boat to chase us, they'd decided to join us after all.

Back in the [past] present though, I was as happy as Karl was that his "little tiller tying technique" seemed to be working. With a rope and some bungee, we were steering a perfect course at just over five knots without us having to touch a thing. We napped the morning away. I kept saying I'd wake up properly when the sun did, which was just after ten.

Day 6. I clung on for dear life as I attempted my morning bow poo. I then carried on trying to be productive, stringing all our wet clothes out to dry and finally doing the dishes. Four blue bottles pumped themselves through the saltwater tap. The daily cup of coffee was brewing and I was about to wake Karl from his slumber, when a rogue wave swept through the cockpit and drenched me and all the clothes that had almost dried. Life is cruel sometimes.

We fixed my broken bunk, the cupboard, a tiller stick, the dinghy, and poured another 20 litres of rainwater into the tank. We solved the problem of the breaking main sheet, and still had time to read [and write all of this], before watching an unbelievably spectacular sunset.

We instigated *Psychological Thursdays*. We needed some structure to our floating. So, over a cup of coffee and some delicious eggy-mushroom toast, Karl began to tell me the details of his childhood. By 10:09, we were drafting happiness curves and psycho-analysing each other.

The following day hand-steering resumed. We were getting into the swing of boat life, and the dolphins were everywhere. It was the longest day of the year in the Northern hemisphere. I shouldn't have mentioned it to Karl because he suddenly realised that he was missing Swedish Midsummer.

"The day of the year when you must visit seven different fields and pick seven different flowers to place under your pillow so that you will dream of the one you will marry," said Karl. "It's the day you wake up early and visit the woods to collect flowers and branches to decorate your home. The day we feast on meatballs, potatoes, salmon and fermented fish. And schnapps. The day continues with beer and a tipsy day-drunk lie-down shill on the grass before we dance around a giant flower-covered penis, like frogs – with no tails. Everyone moves to the beach for more beer, followed by an evening guitary BBQ and bonfire because the sun only sets after midnight and rises again at three. The fields are full of frolicking figures because if you don't get lucky at Midsummer, you will be unlucky all year..."

We played Swedish music and tried to make our own [corned beef] meatballs. And while there were no stars, the drizzle brought with it schools of phosphorescent dolphins. It wasn't quite a "Swedish Midsummer," but ocean life wasn't all that bad either.

Our hands grew less blistery and our bodies began adapting to tilting at uncomfortable angles. We kept each other positive and only one of us was ever allowed to be grumpy at any given time. We did lots of drawing and reading. Being mesmerized was another full-time job. We tried to catch fish but were rather more successful at having lures bitten off. We reminded each other that this was meant to be fun and tried to make the most of it. The rain had stopped, and the days were hot and beautiful. Still, nothing was easy on the little boat. Drinking water had to be funnelled from plastic bags to bottles and then either into cups or the kettle while holding on for dear life. Cooking remained a challenge without a gimballed stove. The swear words that came from the kitchen shan't be repeated here [yet.] We were very strict on coffee drinking attire, and there was a no naked cooking policy instituted on board. Karl's birthday apron did more than its fair share of work.

We approached the Galapagos Islands, but we weren't stopping. Firstly, we couldn't afford the exorbitant rates. Secondly, we knew our hull was far too over-grown to be allowed permission to anchor in their waters. Still, it was good to see land again. We kept a sharp lookout for the mythical creatures that were meant to inhabit the islands and her waters.

As I steered us between isles and crimson clouds, the orb of the sun found a gap and showed off its sink as it disappeared into the ocean depths. Karl cooked up an asparagus pasta. He then picked up his guitar to sing, before the biggest phosphorescent dolphins we'd ever seen came drifting by. 3... 4... Karl crept to the bow. I tied up the tiller and willed it to hold course as I skulked forward to share the moment's magic. Through the luminous glow, they moved exactly like mermaids racing, dancing, leaping and swirling about the boat. In the bow wake alone, were no less than ten. It is [still] the most beautiful thing I have ever seen.

"The High Life!" Yes, we were feigning rock-star extravagance with a cushioned cockpit. There was still water seeping into the boat from someplace and the starboard mattress kept getting wet. So, in the calm of the day, we moved it outdoors. We were hand-steering, but we were doing it in comfort and style. The mattress had just dried when a massive wave swept over the boat and soaked it again completely. We laughed it off, readjusted to its sogginess, and continued to bask in the ocean's beauty. In Swedish, they say: "Det flyter på[47]."

While we still had no fish on the line, we'd started devising plans to become *real* fishermen. Those fins were chasing something! If that failed, it was probably time to start eating the barnacles off the hull.

Day 13. Karl slept late and eventually, my desperation for coffee and company overcame me. I tied up the tiller, turned on the kettle and the Chartplotter to check our course. 00°00.168N – quite literally seconds

---

[47] "Det flea-ter po-a." - It floats on.

away from the equator. We finished the last of the Amarula in our coffee and then cracked open a bottle of rum. We may have pushed the limits a bit by opening a couple of our little bribe gins too. I was back in the home hemisphere and it was Karl's first time in the South. There was much to celebrate! "Karl, you need to make a sacrifice to Neptune," I laughed. But he was having none of the silly sailing superstitions. With the sails dropped for the festivities, I found myself rocked [quite violently] to sleep, only to be awakened later with popcorn. It was quite the party!

It was time to get moving and because Karl was out cold, I clambered to the mast to raise the main; it was snagged on something. I fought to get it free and then returned to acquire more muscle. It took me over an hour of kicking and yelling to awaken the captain. I shoved him to the floor, and still he didn't wake up. I checked for a pulse, still breathing… When he did rise, he walked out into the cockpit only to fall straight overboard. I flew to the deck and was very relieved to see him pull himself back on board! We went back to bed. Sails could wait until morning.

ƒ

You know life is good when your day starts with German muesli!

We needed a treat. I was feeling low and Karl's second day of hangover had him rather subdued. I found rooibos in the German goody bag and introduced Karl to the fine taste of African bush tea. The packaging sparkled in the light and an idea lit up with it. "Stuff the lures!" he said, "we're using that." So we reeled in the fishing line and made our own sparkly lure, before taking it in turns to be creative by writing poetry while the other steered.

The bluest of oceans
The calmest of seas

The only things missing
Are cowbells and cheese
There's dolphins and whales and sharks
Always lurking
But fish for dinner?
For that, we're still searching

After months of preparations,
We were anything but set
But if we didn't leave then,
We may as well forget
The hull and the water and propane
All a mess
But we are survivors
We could always do with less

Day in and out we've rocked on
The waves
Parties on board are crazier
Than raves
We're not sure where we're going
Or when we'll get there
But I'm sure it will be awesome
And there better be beer.

Still feeling creative, I took to the galley and made our first cast-iron pot, cheese-free pizza. It was so delicious that we had it for breakfast too. While we were finishing up, there was a bite on the line. With one hand on the tiller, we fought the mammoth Dorado in before flinging her into the cockpit. *Yoldia*'s biggest catch yet! I handed over the knife and looked away from the bloodbath. A new day was instigated: Sunday roast!

Now if we could just get that other Dorado to stop following us.

I'd been trying to get an ID book in my dream. I wanted to vote and I needed it in a hurry. I was first rejected for wearing blue, and then for being barefoot. I kept trying and trying until the captain woke me up, pretending to screw me in the ass demanding coffee. The satellite phone credit was expiring, so Karl ordered us to call our parents. We were 17 days out and things were going well. It was 02:30 in China, but mum still feigned excitement at the call. In fact, she couldn't comprehend that I was calling her from the middle of the ocean! With voting on my mind, I asked when the elections were. They'd passed already, Jacob Zuma was still president. I gave mum our coordinates along with hugs for the rest of the outside world. She happily accepted and checked if we are eating okay. She'd spent the previous day praying we'd catch a fish. I asked her to do much more of that kind of praying!

There were maggots in the potatoes. *Damn flies! Damn boat! Damn humidity issues!* We sorted the last of our fresh produce and threw the worst of it overboard, while cutting and washing the rest clean. It was a flipping smelly job. We couldn't look at potatoes again after that, so we decided on pasta for dinner. I ducked to the stern for a quick wee and found another catch. I told Karl it was big, but he was sceptical. He was always sceptical. I fought that fish with all my might, and eventually it gave up and wound its way into the cockpit. It was even bigger than the previous day's catch!

I looked him in the eye. "Are you the husband?" I asked. Do mahi-mahi mate for life? We grabbed the alcohol spray and shot it up the gills. I think if I was a fish, that's how I would want to go: oblivious, drunk and at peace. I cut deep, removing the head before thrusting the knife in to open the belly, using my hand to remove and dispose of the organs. The colour drained from its scales as the bright green faded to yellowy-brown.

It's the first time I watched a fish die. It's the first time I killed a fish. I'd always had the joy of reeling them in before scapegoating the murder onto someone else's hands. I severed the fins and removed the scales before fileting the monster and returning the remains to the ocean for other scavengers to prey upon.

With steaks ready for the pan, we bucketed the cockpit. The red kept running even when no blood remained. I wasn't sure what to say or do, but, "Stuff the pasta!" That night we had fish and chips! And to make things even better, we managed to tie up the tiller and eat together for a change. We feasted under a starry sky as we heeled ridiculously to starboard.

I could still smell him on my night watch. My hands were stained.

Had he continued to follow the scent of his wife's blood in hope? Had he wished to rescue her, or had he known her fate already and decided to share it? Am I reading into this too much? Was he simply a stupid fish lured in by shiny rooibos paper?

With things turning a bit too chaotic on board, we tried to reign life in and have some routine.

Our weeks were going to look like this:

Maggot Monday: Check all the fresh produce and massacre all flies, larva, unidentified critters, etc.

Barnacle Tuesdays: On which we at least pretend to scrape the hull.

Wet Wednesdays: The day we air everything out to try and dry the boat.

Psychological Thursdays: No explanation needed, only professional help.

Frigging Rigging Fridays: Properly check all the stays, shrouds and other miscellaneous boat extremities.

Sat Art Day

Sunday Roast

The sun set even more remarkably than its rising, but everything in-between was shit. The floor had pools of water on it AGAIN. After mopping it all up, we traded places so I could steer while Karl made breakfast. Today, 1 July 2014, marks one year since he sailed out of his hometown, Gävle. He prepped the ingredients, but the stove wouldn't light. 2356 miles away from our next port, and we are out of propane! SHIT! Yes, I swore; but I'll do it again. SHIT!!!

The boat and our mental well-being had been falling apart for ages. The one thing hauling us through was good food. And coffee. Now those luxuries were gone. We both almost cried. I would have given up on the hopes of ever having a warm meal again (until the Marquesas at least), but Karl was not giving in so easily. Especially not after all the effort he put into his one-year breakfast bonanza!

"I wonder if we can make a fire on the stove?" I thought he was joking, but he found a piece of material, doused it in the spray alcohol, threw it on the stove, and lit it. It took hours and several respray and re-lights, but he made us a flipping good breakfast. We had leftovers for lunch and dinner. Then we tied up the tiller and watched a movie. We needed to forget and to focus on other people's problems instead of our own. For a little bit at least. We ate crackers instead of popcorn. BLISS.

I woke up in a bit of a stupor. It'd been a rough night and I was dazed and confused. What time was it? Where was the captain? There was no one on the tiller, and his bunk was vacant. I tried to get up, but found Karl using my vagina as a pillow. Outside, the sun was shining and the sails were shaking like we were the worst sailors in the world. I'd pee first then deal with them. Actually, I'd pee, pump the bilge, drink some water and then I'd deal with it. I was just busy changing course when I heard the fishing line clang as the reel banged against the railing. "Karl," I yelled, "we got a fish." The captain slowly emerged from the cave. "When did you put the line out?" "I didn't." And so began the tale of the miracle fish. Jairo may have caught a fish with his bare hands, but we hooked one through the eye by what must have been divine intervention.

We finally reached the trade winds and dropped the main. We'd been so excited for this! The mainsail was covered in rips and really needed to retire. We figured it would be easier to tie up the tiller in the trades[48]. We could not have been more wrong. With winged[49] foresails, we tried and tried and tried some more to construct something of an auto-helm. And then, we gave up. We were going to have to do this manually! It was much harder work too, a different motion. You had to keep a perfect course to keep the sails full. The noon reading showed that we had 2222 miles to go till port. It was a cool number, but FLIP! It was still a long way away!

I woke up feeling refreshed. It was the normal three-hour sleep, but somehow it felt like eight. Sailing downwind was a whole lot more comfortable than the incessant heeling of the previous 20 days. I took the tiller and watched the sun rise out of the glistening ocean when the first problem of the day arrived[50]: the furler wouldn't furl.

In desperation, Karl offered up a penis hair to Neptune. It was a week late, but rather a late sacrifice than to continue on our path of destruction. Almost immediately, the seas calmed. Over lunch, the jib unfurled itself. At sunset the dolphins were remarkable. They kept circling *Yoldia* until

---

[48] The wind pilot had always performed better in trade winds, leading us to believe that the tied-up tiller would follow suit.

[49] With the wind almost directly behind us, we deployed both the jib and the genoa on either side of Yoldia, like wings.

[50] Apart from the wet, the leaks, the barnacles, the lack of propane and the missing wind vane that is.

the last rays of light disappeared.

Day 21. Karl woke me up for the sunrise and he was the happiest I'd seen him in a long time. But the happiness was short-lived. He was "not the kind of guy who ate cereal for breakfast." Today we had stale corn-flakes left on board from his Atlantic crossing.

Sails needed stitching, things needed fixing. Under the weight of the water we'd loaded in the port side lazarette, it was caving in. It was an exceptionally physical day of trying to move things about. Several of our water bags had burst from the ocean's rock, and several more were leaking. Everything had to be reorganized [while still trying to steer a perfect course] in the little cockpit. Karl proclaimed the day "Shit!" He claims that "happiness is boring" and prefers a life of melancholy. The Swedish word for it is "lagom," or "average." For him, "Lagom is best."

Day 22. We'd moved onto kerosene for cooking and started to cut up the captain's underpants for burning cloth. Karl got braver every time he doused the liquid onto the stove and the flames kept getting higher. I'm sure I'd heard that you should never make fires on boats, especially not inside. But I really was appreciating the one warm meal we were getting each day.

Day 23. We had cold oats for breakfast and called our brothers. Brendon said his life was great because he had cooking gas and shops that he could walk to. Still, it was nice to hear his British accent. Karl's brother had just started a band. There were mild pangs of homesickness, but we were happy enough. It's always better to call home when you're happy.

I used the stern for my morning toileting and got hit by what I thought was a flying fish. Seconds later, the world went black as the entire boat was pelted. Only it wasn't fish at all, it was squid. Hundreds of them. They hit the deck with such force that most of them exploded on impact. There was black ink and rubbery corpses strewn everywhere. It took hours to clean and we couldn't even cook them thanks to our lack of propane.

We just about had our Sunday roast sorted when whatever it was that took the bait, ripped the entire handline with it.

Day 24. We needed to charge the batteries and decided we might as well give the engine a bit of a run, just to make sure it still worked. "Fire her up," yelled the captain. There was nothing, not even a spark! Our hearts sunk. Without power, there would be no music; and worse, we would not be able to check charts and get coordinates!

Fortunately, one of the battery nodes had simply eroded itself loose and our Mazda man had given us replacements. "Let's go," yelled Karl. We held our breath. I pushed in the button. The engine roared to life. We both cheered. But when I went inside to start charging everything, smoke filled the cabin. There was oil everywhere. Doom descended as we cogitated all the worst-case scenarios, but Karl had simply put the dipstick back in the wrong hole. Still, I don't think I'd quite found my happy place yet. On the phone to Jeandré, I had a mini-meltdown, while Karl lay in the cockpit on a soggy mattress living the high life, steering with his feet.

We saw the first boat in three weeks and called them up on the VHF to chat. They were so friendly that we called them again and asked if they perhaps had some spare propane. They laughed. They were living an even higher life than us: they had electric stoves!

The afternoon brought with it three massive whales. With my spirits restored, I decided to brave the evening fire and cooked us some delicious instant noodles. Only, they weren't all that instant, they took a little over an hour to prepare.

Day 26. With the mainsail down, we constructed a sun shelter. All the hours spent in the cockpit were taking a toll on our bodies. I built a new handline and hadn't even finished reeling it out when we got a bite. The sneaky bugger made off with my new lure, half the line and the hook. I cried. Karl was a mess. It was the kind of day where we needed to consult the German treat bag: crackers and olives did us wonders!

"Mate," said Karl, "I think we need to stop pushing for Australia! All we need to do is make it to land, ANY LAND," his blue eyes brightened to match the sky, "and chill out and explore some islands."

All of life felt better after that!

(...Even if our hands still ached from tiller blisters and our butts were coated in salt sores from the incessant splashes that swept the cockpit...)

𝆏

We decided that we had about twenty days left. Actually, we had decided that a week earlier. But things kept going wrong; and with the barnacles growing bigger by the day and slowing us down, we kept having to recalculate. "Tjugo dagar kvar[51]," as they say in Sweden. In fact, the breakages and delays were so bad that we decided we'd keep saying it until we broke the 1000-mile [to land] mark. We still had a lot of "Tjugo dagar kvar" days ahead of us.

A new rule was instigated: if you wanted to read, it had to be done out loud. It was weird at first, but we came to love hearing the accents and the other's interpretation of *Lord of the Flies*, *Oz*, *American Psycho*... [the list went on]. Still, we did wish that we had audiobooks aboard! Music was great to steer to, but we knew the average song was 3-5 minutes long. Our minds had started calculating, in rhythm to the music, how slowly we were moving and how long our watches were.

"Aren't there any stories you haven't told me yet?" It was an everyday question. And it always made us think. In desperation, I remember telling

---

[51] "Shu-gaar dag-aar Kwaar" - Twenty days left.

Karl how a friend had once spilt egg mayonnaise out of her rice cakes and onto my leg as I stood in a queue at school. He took it all in. So deep was our need for hearing something new. If we could conjure up no new stories, we would be forced to create some – entertainment was paramount.

Dreams got weirder by the night. Seeing as we were doing either two or three hour watches, we never got more than two or three hours of sleep. It was tough. But the toughest things in life make you stronger, right?

Day 27. It was a day of random winds, which was actually quite fitting for a Psychological Thursday. From first light, the wind suddenly escalated and took us on all sorts of ridiculous rides. This wasn't good considering we'd already lost two hanks off the genoa.

Despite the foreboding red sunrise, it was a great day. For breakfast, we cracked up crackers and mixed up some powdered milk and sugar. It was surprisingly delicious. The daily routine began: dry floor, pump bilge, try to nap, dry stuff. I even shaved my armpits and brushed my hair. I certainly wasn't a hippy!

There was a loud thud. The spinnaker pole had ripped through a shackle... By noon we were spent. But our spirits soared again when we discovered we'd made a 116-mile day[52]. I sorted out our store berth and was quite excited to find instant mashed potatoes. Sadly, several other subspecies of creatures had discovered it too [and taken up residency inside]. We caught a fish. Unfortunately, it got away; but that's okay because we caught it again, and again. Then we gave up. Our hooks were too small; the creatures beneath, too big. Especially the whale – the one that visited was by far the biggest we'd seen. And it was close too.

Day 28. *The good news is that we made our best day yet, 121. The bad*

---

[52] The best since Columbia.

news is that we lost both forestays in the process.

It was a rough night of strong currents and squalls kept hitting us from every direction. I watched my trusty plastic pirate sword break free from the stern mast and fly into the water. Next, we lost a water jug. Finally our life ring, which I somehow managed to regain without tumbling overboard. On the sunrise watch, I noticed that the jib and genoa looked a bit further apart than usual, but I didn't think much of it. It was probably just the wild winds. At nine, I woke the captain and went for the wee I'd been holding in for hours. That's when I noticed the looseness of the backstay, something wasn't right. It was Frigging Rigging Friday, so we'd be doing a once-over anyway. We both agreed that we needed to reduce the sail though.

The genoa came down easily, but taking the jib across was hard work. Karl took a quick [and important] breather to call his granny for her birthday. I pointed at the next squall that was moving in and he quickly hung up. We had to act before the wind became too strong. We forced the pole loose and tried to catch and pull the jib to the starboard side. Minutes later, it all fell apart. Both forestays came crashing down into the water. We swore in disbelief. We were in deep excretion. More than half of our rigging was gone and the mast was next in line to go. It was a bad movie. A terrible nightmare. Only we were living it.

It took most of the morning and all of our strength to fish the sail back onto the deck. I was put on juice duty as a distraction. We needed distraction. We needed juice. With no sails up, we tossed wildly about in the raging current. The mast was deck-stepped and could tumble at any point. We had only a dodgy backstay left. And toothpick shrouds. How long would they hold? 1346 miles away from the closest land.

WE'RE FUCKED!

We threw out the *sea anchor* to try and stabilise the boat, and then lowered the furler (which was still attached by a halyard) to the deck. Karl wanted to climb the mast to re-secure a stay. That only made me cry more. In those conditions, climbing would be hell and the mast was already shaky. We could never make it to land without the mast, and I would never survive it without Karl. He wouldn't let me climb either. We were still in a physical condition to deal with challenges, even if mentally we were completely obliterated!

On closer inspection of the furler, we found that the entire *masthead* had snapped. Even if we did climb, there would have been nothing to attach the rigging to. We used ropes to try and pull the mast forward and converted the jib halyard into a make-shift forestay. The rest of the afternoon disappeared as we removed the sail from the furler and lashed it down on the starboard side, stripping it of all removable parts.

And then we collapsed.

Locked in the cabin, we shared a can of corn.

We could handle the loss of the autopilot. We could handle running out of propane. We could handle the everyday challenges of a little boat in a great ocean. We have adjusted to everything that ocean life has thrown at us, but we cannot handle this.

TODAY WE FEAR FOR OUR LIVES!

We lay down together and watched *Man on the Moon* because we didn't want to be reminded of Earth. It was the first night in ages that we both had the opportunity to sleep, but neither of us could do it.

Day 29. The turbulent seas tossed *Yoldia* about mercilessly. The drift anchor seemed to be in a bit of a tangle and outside there was no option but to cling on for dear life! Rogue waves keep crashing over the boat. Inside was wet enough already. Some God time was good, but I was still petrified! Even cracker cereal did little to lift our spirits.

The rocking and rolling of the night had caused much of our canned food supplies to dislodge and roll about. Several cans had exploded. I suppose that's why in South Africa we put bricks under our beds [to ward off the Tokoloshe[53]] instead of cans. They don't rust, they don't roll, and they seldom or never implode! We dried the floor, cleaned up the mess and repacked our supplies. It provided some distraction from our present. The noon reading showed that we were at least still moving in the right direction, albeit very slowly! 35.5 miles down.

We talked about setting off the EPIRB or calling a mayday. We talked about leaving *Yoldia* to float off into the abyss. We knew our chances of finding another boat out there were slim, but we'd be ready for it. We had another minor meltdown before Karl stepped up, "Enough! We aren't sinking[54], we have enough food, we still have water, we have each other – we can do this! We have been through so much shit already, we can do anything!"

Our little trip has included a new chapter, and this one is called "Survival." We are both fully committed to living up to that, no matter how long it takes us to get to land. Tjugo dagar kvar!

Day 30. Have you any idea how hard it is to take a shit on a rollercoaster? We were in the worst "anchorage" in the world and it was nearly impossible to stand, let alone lean over the edge. Still, "it" came with an exceptional view of the sunrise. It was Sunday Roast day, so we needed to get the show on the road. There was no way we would be catching fish like that!

---

[53] The "mythical" spirit that visits you in your sleep, giving you bad dreams, stealing your virginity, impregnating woman, and sometimes even stealing lives.

[54] Yes, the propeller was still leaking and the bilge had to be pumped every few hours, but it wasn't a convincing sink.

I reconnected the mainsail while Karl dragged the sea anchor to the bow to turn us into the wind. After two days of stitching, while being tossed between waves like a tennis ball, we were keen to get moving again. The plan was to sail under a reefed main as that would push the mast forward, and it wouldn't put too much strain on the remaining rigging. We paused briefly to throw out our message in an Abuelo Rum bottle. We raised and reefed the main. It was all looking good. We dragged in the anchor and set the course. We were just about to celebrate when we stopped and found ourselves heaved to - stuck at equilibrium with our sail perfectly matching the wind. We stood still, dead in our tracks, unable to steer and take up the course we needed.

Instead of sailing into the sunset, we found ourselves watching it through the tears in our eyes.

Day 31. Both of us lacked the motivation to get out of bed. We had worked so hard to formulate a makeshift-plan. We'd spent every last morsel of energy, and it was not enough.

We pulled ourselves together [a bit] and forced down our salty cracker cereal. We moped about and tried to make alternative plans with the smallest of our sails, the storm jib. But everything was risky, everything was sketchy, everything failed.

"Stuff it! It's all or nothing," huffed Karl. We took a deep breath, prayed flipping hard and wound out the boom pole to raise the whole main, without any reefing. Sure enough, we started moving. Slowly, but at least we were moving. Noon reading: 36.5.

We tried to tie up the tiller because steering at that speed was more boring than watching toe-nails grow. In the process, we gybed and snapped two of the new sail cars connecting the main to the mast. This was an incredibly delicate mission, a slow garrotte. I just prayed that the mast would hold up. Neither of us had the strength to face another blow.

Karl was suffering heat stroke so I did most of the sunshine hours while he took on the domesticated duties of slow cooking. Steering had to be perfect. A couple of degrees off and there was too much force on the mast. When you were on the tiller, you were doing NOTHING else!

My night watch was excruciatingly boring. At least the stars flew and shot and sparkled before the moon rose and illuminated the waves like a foggy day in London. It was pretty but at that rate, we might survive the ocean, but boredom would kill us. This was going to be a long trip!

Day 32. I woke up with a gybe and took over, Karl needed a break. As the morning panned out, I had a long chat with God and felt much better. I looked at the incredible waves as the sun rose and noticed that we'd broken the 1200-mile mark, which in Swedish miles was only 120... Maybe it really was "tjugar dagar kvar?"

We caught three fish that morning, but we needed bigger hooks, they all got away. It was an awesome afternoon, ruined only by a big rip in the mainsail. So, we threw out the sea anchor, dropped the sail, and Karl started stitching. Again.

Day 33. The morning was tough. The only redeeming factor was a big beautiful rainbow. I am probably the only person in the whole world who saw it. I think it was put there just for me!

I eventually woke the captain and he made sweet bread (NOT CAKE) for breakfast. We cracked open a bottle of German peanut butter for the occasion. We started a new book, *The Year of Magical Thinking*. While it sounded quite fitting, it wasn't very good so we threw it overboard.

For lunch, we ate canned fruit. We DESPERATELY needed it. Like clockwork, our bowels began behaving themselves.

The sunset painted magical colours across the sky while Karl cooked up coconut curry on his biggest fire yet, mixing the alcohol with kerosene. I watched 11 shooting stars while I waited but, for the first time since we ran out of propane, we had a properly-cooked HOT meal!

The night shift was a little easier seeing as we were naturally progressing in the right direction. My eyes were heavy and I kept dozing off in the early hours of the morning. While being hit on the head by a flying fish helped to keep me awake, I eventually fell asleep on the tiller and gybed.

Day 34. After a long, rough day, Karl tried to use diesel for cooking, but the only thing he achieved was black lungs. The potatoes (that had to be resorted and rescued again - *ARGH!*) stayed raw and the meal was barely edible. We endured it anyway. Both of us were in bad moods. Hungriness and turbulent seas were not a good combination. I fell asleep straight away and two hours later returned to the helm. The chaos persisted so Karl made the call. We dropped the sails, threw out the sea anchor and both tried to get some rest.

Day 35. We awoke to mayhem. I needed the bathroom, but the ferocious ocean would not afford me the opportunity. We also needed the winds to drop before we could raise the main. We snuggled up inside and watched Karl's favourite Swedish movie. Lying flat while lost in a movie can make you forget that there's a life-threatening storm raging outside.

Noon revealed we had 1005 miles to go. We celebrated this with terrible left-overs and then opted for something a bit more fitting by digging deep in the German bag. I found instant coffee! I can't tell you how good it was. Unlike the quality filter stuff that we had an abundance of, this instant stuff could be dissolved, mixed with milk and sugar, and drunk cold. It was delicious.

The winds lowered and we raised the main feeling like brand new human beings. Karl spent the day at the helm while I rescued leaking water bags. I used the undrinkable leftovers for laundry and cleaning, and eventually cooked dinner. *Talk about being a domesticated woman - Mom would be so proud!* But our drinking water levels were low and freakishly scary, so we started cooking with brine.

I knew it was going to be rough when I stepped outside for the night watch; and it was. Karl had me help him lower the main and I got swept overboard by a rogue wave in the process. Fortunately, I managed to grasp onto something and somehow pull my emaciated body back into the cockpit. We sealed ourselves up and hid inside where I lay praying.

Day 36. There had been no sleeping that night, the noises on the deck were so destructive that I'd stayed awake panicking. The tyrant ocean gave my life new perspective.

We had leftovers and a cup of "coffee" before we dared to look at the carnage outside. The night was so rough that I was certain that everything would be stripped from the deck, including the mast. But in relation to my mind's imaginings, life outside was pretty okay.

At noon, we officially passed the 1000-mile to land mark, 943 to be exact. We celebrated with bread and REAL juice, and the seas calmed for the occasion.

Day 37. I woke up with a gybe. Only this time it was planned, the captain had decided to tack. Do you have any idea how hard it is to suddenly change the way you do things? Especially considering it was 06:00 and I was only barely awake. After 36 days on a port tack, steering with mostly my right arm, I now had to switch and do everything in reverse. My shift went on forever! I was flipping relieved when the winds shifted back. And, after marvelling at our barnacle collection, we tacked.

We craved sugar so badly that our lives seemed to depend on it. I'd torn the boat apart several times seeking cookies and chocolates that didn't exist. In desperation, Karl scraped together ingredients and made us raw dough for *fika*[55]. We ate like savages.

The never-ending sky of clouds finally cracked, and we had the first real rain since Ecuadorian waters. All our pots and pans were strewn to catch water. We grabbed the soap and started scrubbing. It was unbelievably good to shower. (I even managed to condition my hair.) The wild wind gusts and crazed currents finally quelled and "normality" seemed to be reinstated. As I took over for the night watch, a shark swam by.

Day 38. The morning's feeding frenzy was incredible. Things were killing and being killed in every direction. We put on some Sigur Ros and it was exactly like being in a wildlife documentary (we only lacked David Attenborough). Birds, dorado, tuna, flying fish, billfish... the waves may have been small, but I had never seen the ocean so alive. Karl wanted to hunt too. We figured a small lure would bring in a small fish that our little hooks could handle. We made the tiniest lure imaginable and brought in a giant dorado. The sashimi was fantastic; and the steaks, even better!

I took the first night watch and while it was hard to stay awake, I counted 48 shooting stars. The explosions in the sky seemed to echo the morning's feeding frenzy in the heavens.

Day 39. It was so nice to sleep in. The only redeeming factor of taking the first night watch was that you were allowed to sleep later in the morning; until tiredness consumed the helmsman. I even had the pleasure of watching Karl get hit by a rain squall [for a change] before my day even began. I made "coffee" and traded places. I called mom. She was in Cape Town with Jeandré and Ouma. She'd just decided to do another year in China and sounded happy. It made me happy too. She asked if I was

---

[55] "Fee-kah" - Swedish tea time.

homesick. But that day I was not. It was a good day to call her.

Karl suddenly knew what he wanted to do with his life. He was going to become a civil engineer. He decided that he would go to university the following year, and then relocate to Ghana to build bridges.

I was so inspired by his plans that I started plotting my own. I was quite excited about them, and the awesome sunset. And the curry. And the whales. I even managed to stay awake for the whole of my night watch!

Day 40. Fruit for breakfast and our bowels spewed forth in thanksgiving. We caught a fish, but it escaped from the cockpit. Humpback whales came to visit and life was good, until Karl took a nap leaving me bored and *hangry*. Lunch helped, but finding more rotten potatoes and burst water bags wrecked my mood to the point that I had to lie down. It was such a day of mixed emotions that neither of us knew what was going on anymore. We hoped there was some epic sort of goodness ahead, because the raw potatoes we were about to prepare weren't all that exciting!

(There was not.)

Day 41. "Coffee". Bread. Tiller. Two squalls. And then the day turned beautiful and the noon reading showed the incredible awesomeness of 71 miles. It was a chilled afternoon with more whales and an even more shill evening because we reefed the main and heaved to.

Day 42. It was rather comfortable being heaved to, but despite the exhaustion, my whole body ached so much that I couldn't sleep. I crept up to the bow for a wee and got hit by a massive wave that crashed right over me, leaving me soaked. When I finally did fall asleep, a squall arrived and my bed became an outlet for the rain to vent its anger upon. *God, are we alright?* At least Karl got his 11 hours. He looked so happy!

More squalls were moving through, so we decided to hide out and have a coffee break before continuing. The shill restored me. Despite a noon reading of only 41 and having cold canned pork and beans for lunch, things were okay. Karl was singing away at the helm. I may have been 7649 nautical miles (in a straight line) away from South Africa, but I was home.

Things might be rough right now, but they'll get better.
Tjugar dagar kvar!

Day 43. Even in my dreams, I was steering. Karl spent the night laughing as my arm followed the motion of the boat.

We were out of decent books, so we'd started studying the Atlas and memorising world capitals. The rice didn't cook and the sardines were meh, but I was exhausted so I didn't care.

In the distance, I saw a light. I thought I was imagining things - I'd been hearing voices and seeing hallucinations for days. Sometimes there had been singing... screaming... visitations... creatures... But the light got bigger and brighter, green lights glowing. It was such a foreign sight after nothing but sea and sky. I leaned into the cave and grabbed my camera to take a picture, just to prove to myself I wasn't imagining this big ship. Karl owed me another beer – he'd bet that we wouldn't see another ship until the Marquesas!

Day 44. I almost got washed overboard as I had my morning wee. My legs weren't nearly as strong as they used to be. As I took the tiller back, a squall set in and we got locked heaved to - even with the full sail up. I spent hours trying to push us back on course. Just before sunrise, I succeeded, but a bit too vengefully. I gybed, and the last two sail cars holding the main to the mast came free. I successfully rebuilt them with cable ties and proceeded to spend the rest of the morning stressed out, focusing on nothing except keeping a perfect course.

I finally started breathing again when the wind died down at about nine. And at 10:21, when the captain awoke, I was in quite a good mood. We finished the last of the crackers as cereal. The noon reading showed we'd done over 80 miles and the challenges of the night seemed to have been worthwhile. We had just 411 remaining. But it was July 27th. The day we were meant to be meeting *Djerpie* in Tahiti for the World Music Festival.

The batteries were low, so we tried to fire up the engine. The lights came on, but there was no luck. Tired and an emotional wreck, I burst into tears. The skies did too as a big squall approached. "Drop the main!" yelled Karl. I jumped to it and as we locked ourselves inside, I got the nicest consoling hug. Karl tried to make me feel better by telling me that ships never used to have any power, only kerosene lamps; but we'd finished all of that and only had the electronic charts on our computers.

With the power of the hug, the day got a bit better, even though we tacked and I was forced to reattempt left arm steering. The evening brought with it a plethora of shooting stars and pizza.

Day 45. *Today we ate bread crumbs for breakfast.*

It was the captain's turn to have a bad day, so, after forcing him to eat cold pork and beans for lunch, I went digging in the German bag to find something delicious for fika. While we feasted, a massive crab emerged and scurried across the cockpit. We both leapt up screaming as it ran for our toes and then vanished, just as quickly as it had appeared.

I took the first night watch, but with barely any wind, it was impossible to stay awake. My second watch wasn't much better, it involved a lot of voices. It was so tedious that I considered ending it all by jumping overboard. If it wasn't for Karl, I would have.

Day 46. "…Adeena! …Adeena!! …Adeena!!!" The captain woke me up because a storm was approaching and he needed help. At least he was nice enough to feed me canned pears first. When it did hit, we sheeted in and tied up the tiller, put out the pots, pans, and buckets for water collection and hid inside cuddling. And then the day turned *crazy*! A bit of toying with the battery and the engine roared to life. *WE'RE SAVED!*

We had less than 300 miles to go and while it was a windless day, we motor-sailed to charge batteries while we dried the mattresses and everything else we owned. It was the perfect kind of shill! I found a bag of crackers in the German bag and cracked open some pate for lunch. We then climaxed the high life by finishing them with marmalade and peanut butter, while the dolphins came frolicking by.

In the evening the wind was so low that we sheeted in and watched *Monty Python and the Holy Grail*, while cooking up a rice curry on our newest experiment: a petrol doused stove. It was a hot meal. We sheeted out again before three, and resumed watches quite refreshed. It had been a flipping awesome day!

Day 47. The noon reading was less than 40 and there was still no wind. But we didn't care. There were enough beautiful distractions to keep us going. The afternoon withered away and was pretty chilled, until it finally dissolved into a beautiful sunset and some not-so-instant petrol noodles.

Day 48. Fruit, coffee, helm and ludicrous winds. We were making 4-5 knots – we were flying! Morning fika came in the form of buttery chocolate dough. While we ate too much and felt sick, it was delicious. The remaining batter would be conquered yet. The winds died in the evening, but Karl used the last of the German butter and made a pie. Everything could have gone wrong and it wouldn't have mattered because we had pie. We also had less than 200 miles to go!

Day 49. August. The wind came and went and came and went. The sun had reached new levels of hotness and the book we were reading reached new levels of weirdness. Karl turned the last of the dough into a massive cookie. We were going to enjoy these last few days no matter what. Even the dolphins seem to be cheering us on.

Day 50. They say that the closer you get to your destination, the harder it is to get there. Wait, I don't think that is what they say at all; but really, we were so close, yet so far. Time was standing still. We finished the bread crumbs for breakfast and I took a morning nap before noon: 60 miles to go. *We might actually be seeing land today!*

The wind died completely in the evening and we were both flipping frustrated. The breeze whispered a little as we ate the last of our "instant" noodles, and then left. It was taunting us. It was going to be a VERY long night!

Day 51. Sunrise came after a frustrating hour of flapping sails. There was no wind at all. And then I saw it. With the first light, came land. LAND! BEAUTIFUL LAND! To our port side loomed an island; and ahead too. As the sun continued to rise, more and more land came into view. Humongous islands scattered our horizons. After so many days stuck in that watery vortex, the sight could not have been more wonderful. I didn't think it was possible. I didn't believe we'd ever see it again. I'd been almost certain that we would die out there. We weren't there yet, but this was the final stretch. "Land Ho!" I cried [with fervency], and the captain came up to bask in its magnificence. We kissed. We kissed again. We sheeted in and fired up the engine. We made a special playlist for the occasion using every song we had with the word "land" in it. We turned the music up.

Karl decided to make a celebratory breakfast so I did one of my longest shifts at the helm. Hopefully our last petrol meal ever! (PLEASE!) And while he cooked, the winds came. I sheeted out to starboard, and within seconds our speed accelerated from 2.1 knots to 6.5. It was exhilarating, we hadn't moved that fast since we had rigging. It was scary at first because I was not used to moving at such great speeds. Also, we had that whole issue of missing rigging. "At least if the mast comes down, it will be ready for repair work on arrival," yelled the master chef. And then the rains came. I had to use my whole body on the tiller to keep the boat heading 265°, the bearing the Chartplotter gave me after all three islands surrounding us disappeared in the heavy downpour. We were less than five miles offshore, but we could see nothing. It only lasted half an hour, but it probably saved us three. By the time it passed, we were only eight miles from the anchorage and breakfast was ready. The most delicious sweet bread (not "cake") we have ever permitted ourselves, probably the sugariest too.

In the distance birds swarm and fish leap. Dorado swim before and behind us as Hiva Oa gets bigger and greener by the minute. We can smell the delicious scent of LAND! LAND! LAND!

We topped up the fuel and freed up some space on the fore-cleat. In the lee of the island, we lowered the main; and seeing as we no longer had anything to keep the boom up, we removed the sail completely and disconnected the boom too. We looked ridiculous! A sailing boat without any sails, almost no rigging, and a whole eco-system growing on the hull!

Now we just have to hope the engine holds out because there are no other options. There is no back-up plan!

17.

[BA]GETTING BETTER

TEAK and *pomme de frites* never tasted so good. Especially when washed down with ice-cold Hinano beer. Two of them, and we were drunk. The women bore beautiful reefs of flowers in their hair and the men adorned even more colourfully. It was the last day of the month of dancing in **Hiva Oa**, and festivities further scented the fresh island air. The police had been nice enough to lift us into town, otherwise we would probably not have made it. When we first touched land from the eight-meter confines of *Yoldia* only a few hours earlier, we'd crumpled to the ground and had to crawl while our legs attempted to remember how to walk. We made many new friends as we stumbled around on that dance floor.

The long walk home was slow but surprisingly pleasant. The streets were strewn with flowers and fruit trees, some of the nicest smelling things imaginable. For the first time in months, our routine fell apart and we allowed ourselves to go to bed without brushing our teeth.

❦

We were so late in the season that we hadn't expected to see any other boats. We cleared the last cove leading in to the anchorage and the masts multiplied. One became three, then six and ten. We had begun to wonder if there would even be space for us. Some friendly sailors pointed us to a gap we might fit. I held the anchor while Karl guided us in. Somewhat emaciated, I was too slow and we drifted too close to the Brazilian boat. I summoned my strength to heave the chain back up, and we did it again. 14:09 on Sunday 3 August, exactly 50 days and 3 minutes after leaving Tumaco; through four time-zone changes and with only four litres of water remaining, we finally dropped anchor in **French Polynesia.**

We collapsed in the cockpit. Exhausted. Unable to move. It was not quite the triumphant celebration we'd anticipated, but man did it feel good to just sit. WE MADE IT! WE WERE STILL ALIVE! We tried to conjure up a scintillating celebration but neither of us had the strength to stand, even if we had had something worthy of the occasion. Minutes later our neighbour paddled over.

Canadian Liam greeted us with a Pamplemousse (grapefruit) that was bigger than my head. As we became better acquainted, another dinghy paddled over.

"Holy Shit! You guys made it!"

"Colin!" We cried and wobbled to our feet to shower the Scotsman in hugs.

"Martin Dolõcek," said the mischievous grin sat next to him. We were in good company already.

An amazing thing happened as the visitors left. We somehow summoned up the strength we did not have and cleaned the boat.

Everything was covered in soot and ash. Every inch of the ceiling was black, as well as the floor, the cockpit, and even our beds [and us]! The stove got its first wash and we swore we would never again make another fire on board.

I woke up with my arm still steering the tiller. We needed to get off the boat! Fresh baguettes in hand, we sat on the dock staring out at our hobo home. We took a slow stroll into town and checked in at the Gendarmerie, before exploring the superettes, parks and churches. Things we'd forgotten existed.

The rains plummeted down and we were very sceptical about the evening BBQ, but Martin was true to his word and worked long and hard to dry wood for the fire. We sat chatting with the fascinating assortment of sailors that assembled. Martin was on a quest to be the first Czech single-hander to complete a circumnavigation. Canadian Liam and his wife, Ruby, were spending eight months exploring and researching French Polynesia. Brazilian Mauricio was a peculiar fellow. He swore he could fix our boat "Nooo prob-lemmmm." Delivery crews, Frenchies, Dutchies, Americans... I'd missed people!

Mauricio had lost his rudder and rebuilt it from a door before being attacked by an angry fisherman and a giant squid, "No problem!" Others had lost and broken important rigging and equipment. Some were still trying to salvage the tattered remnants of relationships after too much time spent in too small proximities with spouses. Colin had successfully made out with the only he-she on the island (unknowingly of course). A girl sat by herself under the shelter, so I ventured over to talk to her. She was waiting for a pick up. "Oh really?" I asked, "Which boat?" "*Plastic Amsterdam*." She replied. I almost choked.

I lay in bed loving the fact that I was in no hurry to do anything. The sun was just up and the world looked beautiful through the portholes. I closed my eyes again and tried to fall back asleep when I heard a *knock-knock-knock*. I looked up and there stood Captain *Plastic* himself. I threw on some pants and jumped up to greet him. "I never thought I'd see you guys again," said Jairo, "I never thought you guys would make it." I was quite offended, but he reminded us that he had left while Karl was still in hospital and the boat was still sinking.

Jairo had pleaded an emergency on board and had pulled in to anchor in the Galapagos. Here his boat "wife" had jumped ship and flown home to study. The passage had been enough for her to decide exactly what she wanted to do with her life. He had done the rest of the crossing alone. Sometimes he would stay inside for days before he even peeked his head outside to see what was going on in the world. At other times he'd kept himself entertained by singing to the ocean. At one point, he'd had all the sails fully deployed and stood on the cabin roof screaming for hours at the top of his lungs as *Plastic* soared well over eight knots.

Jairo had been in French Polynesia a month already and tried to stay off the radar to avoid checking in. He couldn't afford the fees. We burst out laughing. Being a European, it was absolutely free. Anyway, he was picking up the new crew member and then running off to collect some of the *Sea-Stars* and other hippies who were stranded on distant French islands after they too had jumped ship too. Just as quickly as he'd arrived, he was off again.

We finally did it, we bought propane (well, butane really – same thing). We lit both stoves and watched in awe as the flames came out. That first, second, third, fourth, fifth and sixth cup of real coffee were all amazing. Then we made popcorn. It was perfect timing because the catamaran that had just arrived, almost hit the Dutch boat next to us. A whole lot of screaming, yelling and verbal abuse ensued. Popcorn makes life so much more entertaining.

I woke up in a panic. "Karl! Karl!" I cried, "I can't find the tiller."

Judging from the mess around me, I'd stripped everything apart looking for it. "We're at anchor," groaned the captain. "Are you sure?" "YES!" I didn't quite believe him so I went outside to check and sure enough, we were and there was the tiller, right where it should be, in the cockpit.

By about the fifth cup of coffee, Martin paddled over to ask if he could lend a hand with our rigging problems. We didn't think too much of it, but by noon he had been up our mast twice and we'd drawn up some awesome alteration plans. The boys started cutting up stainless steel scraps while I ventured into town to find new grinder blades and cheese. It was going to be a real pizza night.

Work resumed bright and early and things were going stupendously well, until I realized that our dinghy was missing. There was no way I was swimming ashore after Martin had spotted the two hammerheads feasting on the fish that were indulging on the forest that festooned from our hull. I was carefully pondering the predicament when Colin came over to say goodbye. They were heading to Tahuata, a day sail away. Martin promised to catch up and we hoped we would too. It was a rather nice floating community we had going. I hitched a ride ashore and began the impossible search.

I had planned to turn left toward the beach, but something made me veer in the opposite direction. I'd given up hope before my mission even began, but I said a little prayer and carried on walking to the end of the breakwater. In the distance, something small and white was protruding from the water. I waded in, tugged on it, and was surprised to find a whole dinghy lay beneath. I'd just pulled it up onto the shore when a man walked over carrying our crate. I found one paddle and then the other. As I searched for the corks, I found one of Karl's shoes. The custodian of the crate returned with a stick to plug the holes. I thanked him profusely as he helped me launch, and I paddled back triumphantly [in a very sinking dinghy].

We took an afternoon work break and stumbled upon Karl's other shoe. We hadn't even been looking for it. By sunset, the masthead was ready and we summoned the masses to help lift the furler back into place. Sadly, with the weeks it had spent salting on the deck, it was so badly bent that it would no longer furl.

Martin bid us farewell and the Brazilian accosted us on our paddle home. We had the tenth cup of coffee of the day as he tried to convince us that he needed to fix our rigging. Everything was "no problem." Unless of course, I suggested it; women weren't meant to have opinions. He was a strange creature that Mauricio.

In staunch contrast, our other neighbours, the Americans on *Sunrise*, radiated astute calmness and wisdom. Bill, Laura and five-year-old Isobel reminded us how good it was to be a part of a community again. It was just like family. Sailors, no matter how odd, weird, or deviant they appear, are a good breed. They are very used to solving problems and always happy to help a fellow [neighbour] yachty in need.

In other problems, without corks, we tried various means of plugging the dinghy: candles, potatoes, and an assortment of new sticks… but still she was always either sinking or sunk. We finally gave in and decided to fiberglass her. We bundled everything we owned into the little dinghy and paddled as fast as we could to keep the boat afloat while escaping the sharks. We lugged the overstocked vessel over the waterline and began the production process. Karl started fibreglassing while I began two months' worth of laundry. We took it in turns, stitching sails and reattaching sail cars while everything dried. Finally, Karl painted the dinghy and we left the last of the laundry and the paint to dry as we ventured off to find the internet.

It's odd checking your mail after two months without. So much has happened that our devices didn't know what to do with themselves.

The connection was painfully slow, but we managed to send off a few emails and catch up with the world a little. Seven new pregnancies! Dan just got engaged. Wow! House acquisitions... cancer... and marriages. So many marriages! Official Business *made it to Florida safely, but got struck by lightning in the marina, frying all the electronics aboard. I wonder what else I've missed!? Jonas, the co-owner of* Yoldia, *messaged to say that he is finally ready to join the trip. Karl isn't sure how he feels about that. Neither am I...*

With a blog posted and some vague contact made with family and the homelands, we walked home happy and exhausted. We piled everything into the dinghy and paddled home on wet paint. I'm not sure why Karl decided to paint the inside of the dinghy too.

❧

It was a quiet anchorage by the time we finally left. Apart from inching past the cliffs (Karl loved that whole living on the edge thing), we had a most relaxed sail and were loving life. Sailing with a headsail as sunset approached, the world was a magical glow. We planned on sailing around the island, but with darkness encroaching and a mast light glowing in the distance, we altered course and followed the light to settle in a closer bay.

We chilled out under the stars and had an incredible feast. In the tranquillity of the new anchorage, a peculiar peace washed over us. The night was bliss.

TAHUATA

Waking up to crystal clear waters enclosed by a white sandy beach, palm trees, and jagged cliff faces was perfection. Better yet, we were sharing the bay with the Americans on *Sunrise* and that made us even happier. We leapt into the turquoise waters and finally had a real swim. We snorkelled ashore and started exploring our new-found paradise when an angry man started screaming at us wanting to know what we were doing and where we were going. We were commanded to: "Stay on the beach!" So we did and opted to keep the shore excursion short. As we cautiously returned past his dwelling, he beckoned us in with coconuts in hand. Despite the foreboding first impressions, Cedric soon became our friend. We spent the majority of the day with him learning about the island's history and how he had come to own his cosy corner of paradise. We left laden with limes, mangoes and Pamplemousse.

The Americans came over for dinner and were pleasantly surprised by the quality of entertainment and meal such a little boat could yield. Even if all five of us were squashed in the cockpit under the sun shelter while the rain plummeted down.

After donating charts, wisdom and a new electronic tiller pilot, we watched *Sunrise* sail off to the Tuamotus. Hopefully, we'd see them again. We'd be heading in the same direction soon.

Karl finally called Jonas and had "the chat" he'd been putting off. The Swede wanted to meet us in Tahiti on October 6th. This sparked an afternoon of planning, hypothesising, and freaking out. We realized how far we still had to go before the cyclone season hit (November). The Tuamotus, Tahiti and the other Society Islands, the Cook Islands, Niue and then the 600ish islands of Tonga lay ahead. Was it even possible to make it to safety? We were confused and perplexed but tried to remind ourselves that life always had a way of working itself out. Even if we did have to compromise a little [too much] on the way. That's if Jonas was even coming out (Karl was sceptical... of course). And if we ever managed to get Yoldia in order.

Our new neighbour saw us working on the rigging and swam over to lend us a hand. He was a pleasure to work with after the Brazilian. Coming from a perfectly ordered boat, he swung from our halyards and played aboard our wreck like a pirate. With his help, we raised the furler and reconnected everything before we realised that our new masthead contraption wasn't going to work at all.

While we devised back up plans, Cedric taught us how to spearfish, scrape coconuts, climb palm trees and dig traps for pigs. We kept attempting new rigging contraptions and eventually just tied the furler and stay to the mast (a process that sounds far easier than it was to instigate) using some *Dyneema* donated by a jovial Italian mega yacht that had anchored for lunch.

We tried to leave twice, but minor problems that could have had massive ramifications kept us at bay in the little beach paradise. Eventually, after the captain's third pre-sunrise start in as many days, we were off. Destination unknown, we sat trying to fill the jib with wind in a failed attempt to unbend the furler (mostly due to the lack of wind).

We abandoned plans of a lengthy sail and pulled in at the island's village. It was a pretty spot with green rolling hills and wild horses silhouetting the hills; but it had a terrible landing. **Vaitahu** gave us the opportunity to dump our trash, buy a machete, and restock on mosquito coils, cheese and baguettes. The necessities for life in paradise. The shelves were almost empty and everyone was patiently awaiting the Monday supply ship. The whole island was out of beer!

It was a Friday and we decided to have a party. Just the two of us, and a bottle of rum. We sat listening to music, while watching the ridiculous videos from our crossing. It had been almost a month since we sat stuck at sea fearing for our lives. We cheered each other and then raised our glasses to thank God for keeping us alive!

ƒ

Jonas changed his arrival date to September 13th. That was only three weeks away. The new date fitted better with island hopping, but it kicked our brown butts into action. We needed to get a move on!

We have a lot to do, but I'm still not sure why I'm up so early. In fact, I'm not even sure it is so early... who knows? We haven't dragged anchor, sunk or anything, so that's a great start to the day. But man, this is scary. I have absolutely no idea what happens next. Will another boat take me on? How will I survive with no money? What am I doing with my life? Who am I? It's all too much to handle. Three weeks hey? Three weeks to get this boat sailing and make it to Tahiti.

This boat is in such bad condition that I don't trust anything on it anymore. The sails are all stuffed and none of them are easy to hoist. The engine is flipping temperamental. The mast um... And don't even get me started on the hull... for all we know, the fibreglass may have been eaten through by the crazy ecosystem evolving down there. I suppose that's what you get when you take a 1970s boat designed to be a water caravan in the Swedish archipelago around the world...

Karl disturbed my over-thinking and assured me that he wasn't going to kick me off the boat: I was home. I was the first mate.

I made mango bread to show my appreciation [and save the mangoes]. When I fretted about burning the bread and being a failure of a first mate, Karl did a strip-tease to show me his returned appreciation for my appreciation.

We were scared to be blown in the wrong direction by the sporadic gusts, but raised the anchor under sail regardless. We inched out of the bay and just got the jib up when a massive burst came blustering through. We instantly accelerated by three knots. It was an interesting sail in the wild winds, especially with all those cliffs and reefs around [and no way to furl.] We cleared the bay wondering where exactly it was we were going; we really did need to start checking the charts before we set sail. We arrived in the golden hour and dropped anchor in an uncharted bay. Our most beautiful anchorage yet.

ƒ

Ahh, waking up in paradise! But how to explain the day?

Karl cracked open a coconut and started shaving it to make bread while I murdered mangoes to make jam and fruit salad. We feasted while tiny dolphins circled the aqua blue waters around the boat. Even though mum always said that you should never swim on a full stomach, we went snorkelling anyway. Karl had never swum with dolphins.

The jubilant man standing near the shack-hut waved us over, so we clambered up the ragged rocky shoreline to meet him. Takeo greeted us with coconuts. We took a tour of his picture-perfect abode and garden while he tried to feed us some more.

Adorned in a borrowed t-shirt, he led us to **Hapatoni**, the tiny village on the far side of the island. We passed so many fierce bulls and scary horses that my brave captain (who must have at some point had an insidious encounter with some four-legged beast) nearly pooped himself.

The whole village came out to meet us and welcome us with gifts of food as we went. We stopped to graze and gaze upon the beautiful bone sculptures the islanders effortlessly carved. The last South Africans had left them with warthog horns and an array of African ivory, so they were very disappointed that I was travelling without any bones.

Some friendly natives invited us to go hunting. We gladly accepted the invitation despite them being surprised that we did not have horses onboard. We were told to meet them back at the village at 16:00 with shoes, long clothing, water and torches [were we sure we didn't have horses?]

We strolled back to Takeo's collecting a plethora of fruit as we went. Mangoes, Pamplemousse, chillies ("Tabasco"), sour sap, guavas... he loaned us an old Sikaflex bucket to swim our produce home. We were knackered by the time we got back, but we had batteries to charge, shoes to find, fruit to unpack... you know, stuff to do. We decided to row into the village as it had a real landing. But it was more than a mile away and flipping hard work. Karl was cursing for most of it, but it's his own fault for underestimating my rowing abilities - he wouldn't let me take over. I suppose, if you had seen my first few rowing attempts in Columbia, you would have done the same. We were late, but they were later.

We piled into an Isuzu bakkie and were off. Stopping for no man, only for goats (we needed to feed them, and there were many to feed). Marquesan hunting seemed to be rather different to what we were accustomed to. The most important item was the bong. The gangster rap came second and it was pumping as we drove. The guy in the front had a gun in one hand and the bong in the other, while Takeo sat at the back. He had his rifle cocked and poised as we bounced along the rocky mountain roads to wherever it was we might find pigs. We parked and ventured off into the forest. The two fore-men were armed with guns and Karl and I with mosquito repellent. "I think I prefer fishing to hunting. At least with fishing, especially trolling, you can chill and chat and..." "shhhh!" they motioned. They'd heard something. We could hear the footsteps in the brush, but in the darkness, I saw nothing. Karl and I tried to turn off our breathing while they ventured off in a deafening silence. A gunshot rang out, but they returned empty-handed. We carried on... spotted tracks... fired shots... but nothing. We returned to the town with only mud to show. So much for red meat! We were exhausted when we launched the dinghy and Karl began the long row back. He still refused to give me the paddles.

As I said, it was quite a day!

❦

We reattached the Dyneema umpteen times, trying to get it perfect. We scraped the hull and worked long and hard on the boat. Eventually, it came time for water tanks to be filled. This time, Karl rowed over with our empty canisters and dirty laundry while I swam in to meet him. The village kids helped us with everything, but Karl was a little scared of the islanders. He reckoned they all had "six toes"[56].

I bid Takeo "bonne nuit" and made the shark sign – I wanted to be home before dark. He smiled and presented me with three aubergines as a parting gift and told us to come in at 07:00. Something about a "cheval" and "avocat". 07:00 was early, but for a horse and avocados, I was game. I clambered down the rocks and carefully counted the wave sets. I let the two big ones pass through and crawled forward. Only I had the wave cycle all wrong and got washed back onto the rocks, whacking my head. In desperation, I grabbed at the rocks to regain my footing. An even bigger wave hit and sent me sprawling, cutting up my feet, leg and side. I made it out with no aubergines left, but fortunately found one floating as I frantically swam for home. My trail streaked red and all I could think was *shark shark shark!* - NONE of the locals swam, they were all too frightened!

Takeo had breakfast waiting for us. After baguettes and fresh coconuts, I clambered on the cheval while the boys walked behind – my minions. The first obstacle of the day was passing the giant toro (bull) that blocked the road. I felt untouchable on the horse, but I could see Karl's

---

[56] Being a small island, the probability of genetic defects related to in-breeding were high.

303

suffering. Next came "scary horse corner" where we lost Karl while he found the courage to pass. We paused at the dock to wash the horse and allow it to coat itself in its own faeces. Success! Continuing, we wound around the village collecting the "sweetest mangoes" from this person and the "best guavas" from that... a plethora of avocados, bunches of bananas, grenadines, limes, sour sap, rambutans, coconuts, sugar cane... too much! We dropped in on people all over the place and never really knew who we were visiting or why; but there were always friendly attempts to make conversation and more food to bestow upon us. They were either genuinely overly-hospitable or trying to fatten us up for something.

With the horse tied up and coated in a well-packed plethora of fruit (and the remnants of its faeces), we went for a walk. Takeo pointed to the island's land-locked boat and motioned to Karl. The captain had died and they needed a new one. He wanted me to stay too, to come and live with him. *Did he want me to be his wife?*

We tried to work out how to get all the bags of fruit back to the boat. We could swim them over or... Karl went and grabbed the dinghy. Takeo and I stood on the rocks poised and ready. Karl would ride the unruly waves over to the rocks and we'd throw in whatever we could in the second he hovered before he paddled away for dear life. I have no idea how he didn't crash up on the jagged rocks. Especially the last time when, without warning, Takeo jumped in. I smiled seeing it unfold. And then smiled even more as I remembered [and I quote] Karl is "not the kind of guy that goes around gathering fruit."

I swam back and had a friendly encounter with a massive blacktip shark.

In a whole day of toilsome labour, we accomplished very little apart from sinking Karl's favourite tool and screwdriver. It was almost 16:00 by the time we were ready to pull up the anchor. It took both of us to do it with the mainsail up because even though the engine lights came on, it would not start and sparks were flying off the batteries. When far enough offshore, we ventured forward to do the two-man job of raising the jib. It wouldn't budge, the halyard was stuck. We had a cup of coffee while we debated what to do: Continue with just the mainsail? Or turn back and reconnect everything all over again?

We may have anchored a little too close to the rocky shore, but we weren't doing it again. It was flipping dark, the current was strikingly powerful and the anchorage deep! We spoiled ourselves with pizza and sat in the cockpit watching the Chartplotter. The sea was so rough and the rocks so close that it really was Reality TV at its best [or worst].

Being a Sunday, Karl reckoned I should go to church before we departed. (Mostly, this gave him the excuse to splurge and buy tobacco.) I made him a water-proof peanut butter jar wallet and tidied up the cockpit first. Unfortunately, I threw our only bowl overboard with the mango skins. I was about to dive in and get it, but there were jellyfish everywhere and they looked like see-through tampons with an ominous eye. Others were bright orange and seemed to pulse electricity through their bodies. I bid the bowl farewell.

Twenty minutes later though, we gave up waiting for the jellies to pass. We dove in and swam our way through them. They stung, but it wasn't nearly as painful as anticipated. The next challenge was the rocks, followed by the toro, then an angry dog and finally scary horse corner. We were late.

We knew nothing about Pacific customs and we probably shouldn't have gone into the chapel dripping wet in shorts and t-shirts. Still, it was good to hear the beautiful songs and the strange sermon in a language we could barely comprehend.

Six of us walked back and put up an army for the horses, dog and toro to reckon with. We purchased some "juice" that wasn't pleasant to the pallet, but definitely had some other pleasing sensory effects. We sampled all the fruity flavours as Lily strummed away on her guitar and the other girls sang while the BBQ was prepared.

As the meat perfected and the grog finished, we were herded into the Isuzu. Takeo threw his cock in before he, myself and Karl clung to the back of the car and the very drunk, stoned driver sped his way along the bumpy path back to the village. The cock fell out thrice and I'm really surprised it survived the adventure. And then, without warning or goodbyes, everyone went home, leaving four of us to devour an army's rations.

Karl still wanted tobacco, so we walked back. We were on the far side of the village when I turned to Takeo and enquired about his cock. He'd forgotten it in a tree. Why he brought it with him in the first place I'll never know. Life on the island was an enigma. We wished we could speak French.

Karl tried to hold the bird, but it didn't like him one bit. I found myself with the pheasant as the captain clung to the giant chunk of fresh bloody toro the driver had gifted us. We'd thought it was a joke [seeing as we had to swim back through shark-infested waters in the dark], but no, it was a real gift; and we didn't want to be rude.

We stopped at one house to buy Bison tobacco, and another for rolling papers before finally returning to the "juice" house for some "goya grog". The toro was even scarier when we passed it carrying its dead kin (which Karl made me carry, with the cock, for that stretch). This time it even ran at us. It began to rain, so we took shelter at Takeo's. We smoked and drank while we watched the crazy sea swirl below us. The waters were rough! The friendly local offered us shelter for the night, but we couldn't leave *Yoldia* unattended in those conditions, especially when she was so close to the rocks.

I handed Takeo his cock and bid him au revoir. Karl still clutched the chunk of bloody toro. There was no moon and we couldn't see a thing. He went in first. I followed and as soon as I cleared the break I yelled "Karl?" He yelled back. He too had survived the plunge. I made a dash for *Yoldia* and swam for my life through branches, coconuts and logs. Who knows what else it was ricocheting off my limbs. I made it. "Oh shit!" I heard Karl yell. I called out to see if he was okay. There was no reply. I called again. No answer. Louder. The sea was so wild that I couldn't even hear his splashing. I yelled again, even louder. Nothing. I paced the cockpit an anxious wreck as I fumbled for the spotlight. In the foreboding darkness, the whitewash sea that thrust in every direction looked like rock breaks. Eventually, the captain pulled himself on board and we embraced one another. "I thought you were dead!" we said simultaneously.

Spring tide. Driftwood and coconuts strewed everywhere. The blue anchorage now brown. The seas still flared their fury. We freed the halyard and reattached the stay, but after a steaky breakfast break, we found it loose again. We did it again. And again. By sunset we had it all reconnected and somehow managed a surprisingly good sleep as a storm raged outside. We rocked and rolled far too close to the shore because we still hadn't re-anchored.

The knot survived the night, but the furler was still too long and bent. It was trying, frustrating work that had our muscles aching and bodies blued with bruises. We left the rocky anchorage to further test the rigging while we braved the jellies and dark waters to swim ashore. Karl had lost his "wallet" in the "death swim" and wanted (he calls it "needed") tobacco.

Takeo was very happy to see us and show us the "legumes" he had rambled on about. We walked into town and braved all the elements en route, stopping to peck at the fallen mangoes that lined our path. We returned triumphantly and sat down to a final coconut with our friend and the last gawk at his legumes (still unsure what exactly we were looking at). A final embrace and we swam home. This time Karl made it back with his Tobacco inside a zip-lock bag, which was inside an Ikea box inside another zip-lock "wallet". He was almost ready to be responsible for his own cash again, something he hadn't done since Trinidad.

The stays were still tight. After coffee and a cigarette, we rebuilt the furler, played around with the new auto-helm (sadly no luck), tightened the tiller, somehow started the engine, and bid the Marquesas au revoir!

ON THE ROAD AGAIN

It's Saturday already and, instead of trying to recall the days passed, I'll mention the most important things. Firstly, as I'm writing this long after departure, you would probably assume that we didn't hit those rocks by Hannah Tafau, and you'd be right. Secondly, and this is ridiculously amazing, we still have a forestay and it's holding a jib. In fact, even though the forestay is still crazy crooked and the furler has dropped a foot, we are currently sailing downwind under a jib alone. Thirdly, we have yet to run out of propane and we are living like kings. Fourthly, we have somehow managed to run out of mangoes and we are already a whole bunch of bananas down – that's impressive by anyone's standards! The sea is flipping wild and the waves are far bigger than the boat. Despite being able to tie up the tiller from time to time, we are both exceedingly exhausted. Yoldia is a bit like being in a washing machine, flung around wet all the time. Everything is wet. Everything is dirty. But the sea is still amazingly beautiful and we are making good speed (5-7 knots) as we head towards our next destination: The Tuamotus.

Life is such a smorgasbord of emotions at the moment. It's so good to be out at sea again and to be heading on to new lands. It's exciting too that my time on the little Swedish vessel is coming to an end and that new adventures lie ahead. But I should not have read up on the Tuamotus, because they are curdling my blood! They're supposedly some of the scariest sailing waters in the world and should only be attempted with good sails, a functional engine and radar... They're so low-lying that you can only see them from a few miles out, depending on the height of their tallest palm tree. The currents are something outrageous... I suppose I wanted adventure, and that's exactly what I'm getting! I'm also terrified about what comes next. And the real thing plaguing me: How will I say goodbye to Yoldia*? And more importantly, Karl? We haven't been apart for more than 24 hours in over six months. How will I adjust to civilisation? To clothes? To routine? To work? To whatever lies ahead? I suppose for today I better stop fretting and just make the most of where we are and try to steer a decent course. We have three islands to dodge before arriving. 161 miles remain.*

Sunday came with refreshment. Sunday came with joy. Sunday morning I sat "ashill on the till" listening to music and marvelling at the ocean when my tranquil world was disrupted by a loud bang. It took me a while to work out what it was, but sure enough, our make-shift masthead had snapped. Fortunately, thanks to us being a bit lazy, the former halyard was well and truly wrapped around the stay, keeping it levitated. This was the first reason I decided to awaken the captain. The second was that I desperately needed to wee!

After relieving me so that I could relieve myself, Karl scraped together the final tobacco shreds to roll the last cigarette while I put the coffee on. Then the battle began braving the tempestuous swell and gargantuan waves. We found creative solutions and although it was a few hour-long fight, we came out triumphant and didn't destroy the sails [or ourselves] in the process. We sat down to another cup of coffee before raising the main. It was just like the not-so-good old days: sailing as close to downwind as possible, trying not to gybe. At least this time we had only 90ish miles remaining and we were still making five knots.

As the low-lying island got closer, coconut trees filled the horizon and the white sandy beaches suggested that we'd teleported into a postcard. I'd been terrified of the nine knots of current in the passage for so long that I must have worn it out of my system because when it came, I was just excited! A mile out, we prepped the anchor and tested the engine. Half a mile out, we remembered to find clothes. We had no tidal charts and although we radioed through to ask, there was no reply. We peeked through the binoculars and went for it.

Karl tried to hand me the tiller, but with about thirty knots of wind, I thought I would let him do the honours. We cleared the passage and rounded the coral island in the middle of it. I stood as the lookout on the bow for rouge coral heads. I'm not sure I did too good a job at it though – Karl had to point out the giant whale that swam over to welcome us. Two masts loomed in the distance, so we headed for them through the bluest waters yet.

The engine started, then suddenly sputtered and died as the furious wind ensued. Karl ordered me to re-raise the main as he dropped the anchor simultaneously. We had no idea how deep the waters were. While the sail jammed, the anchor held. I dove in to inspect it, and found that we were deceivingly deep in those clear waters. We sat down to another cup of coffee and waved hello to *Ruby Rocks*. After 139 hours and 57 minutes, we'd arrived! And we had done it our style: we could survive gale force winds, crazy currents, and a sail through a treacherous passage; but we couldn't dock. We were an alternative breed of sure-footed sailors!

MAKEMO

We tidied up the boat and had a much-needed sea-shower before we swam ashore with Karl's newest wallet, a Nutella jar. We stopped by to greet Liam and Ruby before continuing to the shops. They only opened again at three so we had two hours to kill before Karl could get his cigarettes and we could have a very long-overdue, well-deserved beer. The dusty town was almost deserted in the midday heat. An incongruity of ruins, dreary new constructions and colourful shacks. Stray mangy dogs lay in whatever shade they could find. We strolled past the church and the lighthouse while we stared out at the madness that ensued outside the ring reef; glad to be nestled in the calm safe beauty of the atoll.

At the first shop we found no beer, but we did find popcorn. At the second one we found beer but no tobacco, so we kept walking. We returned to the first shop who sent us to a third, who then sent us to a fourth that was next to a shop that actually sold Bison. Karl needed to get less complicated addictions. We returned to the second shop, bought beers and sat on the dock overlooking the anchorage. Our afternoon beer turned into a sundowner by the time we savoured it, but that was also the time when the friendly villagers came out to play.

I got quite a shock waking up to the unearthly turquoise luminescence of the sunrise. It was one of those days that you just knew was going to be a good one. Surreally good. Banana pancakes were the first order of the day. Next, came an attempt to wash, dry and fix everything we'd broken. The day culminated with sundowners on *Ruby Rocks* where good company, awesome conversation, gin, baguettes and brie were bestowed upon us. They were one of the few couples who took a chance and purchased a joint asset (the boat) when they were still just getting to know each other. They made it work. They'd met at a place called Ruby Rocks. The boat name had two meanings, but we think Liam chose it for the more obvious one. We paddled away watching the couple throw Pamplemousse to unsuspecting passerby. Being a reef atoll, the Tuamotus didn't bear much fruit.

We sat by the stream, munching a baguetty breakfast as fish attacked our crumbs. They were vicious critters, we had to mind our toes. The island had the freshest baguettes yet, beautiful salty brooks and phenomenal snorkelling with a plethora of insane sea life. Whales played just a brick's throw away, and sunsets and sunrises were all perfect.

We watched the Canadians sail off and took their advice to try some local food. With takeaways in hand, we sat on the shore staring out at the beautiful night sky watching the waves ripple around us. The seas had calmed considerably since our arrival. We'd allegedly sailed in on their roughest waters in five years.

After dinner, we sat and watched *Yoldia*'s departure video. What a different boat she was. She'd once been clean, shiny and functional. It was awesome to see how far both she and Karl had come, but it suddenly petrified Karl. Jonas was not expecting to find *Yoldia* on her last legs.

We went to bed after two, but I was still up long before the 06:00 alarm commanded a long hard-working day. The rain was bucketing down with "big wind" (as the Marquesans say). I tried to catch as much water in pots, pans and buckets as I could and took the opportunity for a freshwater "shower."

After coffee and crackers, we sped into action getting things in order. Restoring and stacking the remnants of our Panamanian provisions amazed us at how much we still had left! I cleared space for the newbies and tried to get my belongings in order. I'd be leaving *Yoldia* soon. Karl had just decided he wanted to do the same.

18.

A BOTTLE A DAY KEEPS THE BIRD FLU AWAY

S*ATURDAY, 13 September. Paradise is chilled as distant ukulele tunes float over from the dock. It's a bluebird day and the whispering breeze makes life onboard bearable. The coffee is made, but I haven't awoken the captain yet. I want to take it all in. This might just be the day our new crew arrives. A scary notion seeing that the crew is about to double. It has been just Karl and I for so long that we don't even need to talk anymore. We always know what the other is thinking. It is probably time for a change, and it will probably be fun. But three Swedes? One is crazy enough!*

Breakfast was no laughing matter: coconut banana pancakes with chocolate pudding on top. As we feasted, we discussed the prospect of covering the whole boat in flowers because there was no way we could possibly fix all the broken entities in time! We worked long and hard getting everything in order and then spent our last local currency on a couple of beers to amplify the beauty of the sunset. We had no idea how Jonas was getting there, or when for that matter. We kept a watchful eye all day and night; and the next morning, we carried on carrying on. Every boat, every bicycle, every big sea creature and car – we kept joking that it was "The Swedes." We put our guard down for a second and suddenly, there they were. We were four.

Jonas and Mooberry were not what I was expecting. Karl neither for that matter. But what delightful additions to the crew. We went for a little *turn around* in the town and returned to *Yoldia* for a "real drink," they'd brought vodka. With instruments playing, stars twinkling, bad Swedish jokes being translated and vodka being the only constant, it was a most excellent night. Even the captain ended up feeding the fish off the bow before I followed suit.

After an amazing few days chilling, snorkelling, fixing things, drinking, filling tanks, chilling some more and drinking *karsks* (vodka coffee), it was time to get going. And with our newly designed masthead, we were ready. I excused myself and lay on the deck (my new bed) staring at the stars. With so many new Swedish idioms going around in my head, it hurt (but that could also have been from the alcohol).

"Ingen ko på isen" – *"There's no cow on the ice"* – *"No worries."*
"Skägget i brevlådan" – *Caught with your beard in the mailbox*
– *"Surprised in a guilty pants down kind of posture."*
"På kanelen" – *"On the cinnamon"* – *"Wasted."*
"Ge tillbaka för gammal ost" – *"To Give back for old cheese"*
– *"To seek revenge."*

We were up before seven eating leftover French fries and veggie patties.

We raised the jib on our new rigging and then the anchor. A little way out of the shallows, I raised the main and we were making a comfortable 3.5 knots on the calm flat waters of ultraviolet blueness. We rotated through as look-outs and helmsman while munching on yesterday's baguettes. It was a beautiful day of computer-game-like coral head dodging. With the sun descending in front of us, it was becoming increasingly difficult to see. We still had ten miles left to go, so we decided to find somewhere to shelter for the night. This came in the form of a small picturesque, most perfect, crazy beautiful gorgeous beachy paradise oasis of palm trees (that may be a few too many adjectives for one sentence, but I don't think it nearly gives credence to the scene).

I jumped in to check the anchor while the boys tidied up the sails. We all swam ashore. The sandy beach turned out to be coral. The coconuts were all eaten out by rats and giant hermit crabs, but it was still pretty. We lay on the beach, smiling at the setting sun while I made hermit crabs a garden in the shade (I couldn't find an octopus). We watched a couple of blacktip sharks pace the waters immediately in front of us, patiently scrutinising their dinner. We had to brave the waters regardless, there was no other way home. I'm pleased to say that we all survived: the sharks and dinner too. Mooberry had never cooked before and it was long past his turn in the galley.

With the first alcohol-free night on the vessel, we all called in early in our designated sleep spots. The Marquesan style "big wind" made the deck a little harder to drift off on; but the shooting stars lit up the sky like fireworks. With Karl snuggled up next to me, there was nowhere else in the world that I would have rather been.

After a very slow morning [and lunch], we set off again. Our charts were terrible and we failed to find the atoll's exit passage so, in the remnants of the afternoon, we gave up and settled in a cosy bay. I jumped in to check the anchor and was quite glad that it was correctly orientated because there was no way I was diving to those depths! I did a loop to scrutinise the surrounding coral heads and saw a black tip circling beneath me. It was getting higher and higher, closer and closer. I weed myself a little bit (always better to do in the sea) as I did a casual pretend-to-not-be-afraid swim [for my life] back to *Yoldia*, trying to minimize splash and limit curiosity.

We packed up the sails and ventured ashore. Jonas and Mooberry got in the dinghy; and because I didn't want to look like a coward, I dove in and swam after Karl. I think it might have been a mistake though because a massive shark (far bigger than me) came to greet me. It circled me twice and then moved away. When I reached Karl, he was chilling with another one. Parrotfish abounded and some of the coral shone peculiar purple and orange-ish hues I'd never seen. By the time we reached the shore, I had counted 17 sharks. As we took a stroll down the long soft sandy beach, the number drastically increased. They got smaller and smaller, and stranger too; we appeared to be in some sort of breeding ground. Apart from the overabundance of sharks, the shore excursion was sensational: beautiful shells, picturesque pools and edible coconuts. I'd already decided that there was no way that I'd be swimming back. After seeing the biggest and strangest shark yet, Karl decided he wasn't either. The newbies wouldn't even dream of it. All four of us piled into the dinghy so we were dangerously close to the waterline. Karl and I took it in turns bailing buckets of water out while Mooberry rowed for our lives, swearing like a seasoned sailor while the sharks circled.

It rained twice thar night, but the showers were so short-lived that we didn't even have time to get the sun shelter up for protection. I drifted off into some bizarre dream where I was volunteering at a special needs school. A girl asked me to tie up her hair and when I did, it turned into a tumour. I visited some of the other patient's rooms and went with them to assist at group therapy where I was given the very difficult task of monitoring a young boy who had turned into a hamster. He managed to sneak off twice, but I managed to catch him both times and bring him back.

The third time though, I accidentally squashed him.

Karl and Moob teamed up to raise the anchor while I worked the sails. Jonas steered us clear of all the haphazard coral God had strewn about. This time we found the exit channel, but it was less than perfect timing. Four knots slowed to two, then one as the sea shot raging ripples of current in every direction. We inched forwards and then backwards, and then forwards and then sideways. The short passage took almost forever. Eventually, we shot out the other side and said goodbye to the calm waters of Makemo. We were back in the Pacific we had come to know so well (and not well enough). Almost immediately, the shallows disappeared and we were floating in thousands of feet of purple-blue water. Destination: **Tahiti.**

ʕ

00:56, Thursday 25 September
17.24.182S, 149.23.508W
12.7 Miles to Tahiti
Course: 227
Obviously, we now have absolutely no wind, that's why the sails are down. Instead of a tiller, I hold a pen. They aren't as different as you may think. Both have great power in steering lives in whichever direction you choose.
I'm sitting alone in the cockpit listening to the still night. After seven months onboard, I'm so used to the clinking of loose wiring in the mast that it doesn't sound at all. The swooshing waves only get noticed when they stop. Tahiti looms in the distance and as we inch nearer, my fear grows. I don't think I could sleep now even if I tried.
Yesterday marked my one year of unemployment – and what a crazy year it has been! Nereid *across the Atlantic,* Pirates, Fiddler *in the* Caribbean, *heart-breaks, and then* Yoldia. *Through Panama's*

bureaucracy and hospitals, through hand-steering and lost-rigging and propane-less days. Yes, it's been good, but a bit too extreme. Ahead, looms yet another big chapter, possibly the biggest yet, who knows?

In a few hours, we will sail into Papeete where Yoldia*'s future will be decided. Will she go up on the hard for some time? Will we discover holes in her and a failing rudder? Will she rest there for the hurricane season? Or will they simply decide to stuff it and sail a limping vessel onward across the Pacific to New Zealand or Australia?*

We plan to jump ship, but are there even any ships to jump on to? Where are they going? Who is the crew? If this little guy is sailing on, would I? Should I? I've done a lot of it this year, but I'm sitting here awaiting forecast (and 02:30, so I can relinquish the helm).

TAHITI

Well, we made it. We aimed for the city docks, but the wind died and there was a spur of the moment sudden change of plans. The captain ordered us to turn and head for the beach. Dolphins swarmed to greet us and before we knew it, we were dropping anchor in what looked like someone's back garden. Karl inflated his tiny red dinghy that I thought I would never get the pleasure of seeing. Because he'd lost the paddles, we tied the two boats together and rowed ashore dragging Mooberry and Jonas behind us.

The black volcanic sand was the softest we'd touched in a long time. We ventured further inland and, after licking land hello, we found beer. Despite the incredible heat, life was most brilliant. The canal streams teemed with eels. Apart from that, there was no animal life, not even a stray dog, in sight.

In Papeete, we sat down to enjoy a small over-priced beer. We contemplated civilisation before scouting the City Docks and seeking out friends. Further exploration led us to a supermarket where we gawked at the extensive selection available [at exorbitant costs].

Karl and I got into trouble with the police for drinking on the streets. When the next supermarket arrived, we did it again anyway. I cooked dinner and we celebrated life with box wine and vodka. It was a great night, even if it didn't last very long.

Instead of embracing the hang-over, the morning began with the remnants of the former night's party. We played Swedish card games and had the first big discussion of the day: what we would do when we finished the alcohol?

With our primary concern dealt with, another crew meeting was summoned. The announcement was made: "*Yoldia* is going to New Zealand this year and anyone who wants to, can join." I opted in. So did the Moob. The owners were definitely in, which left only one thing to do. We raised our glasses and cheered: "To New Zealand!"

❦

Too much has happened since I last wrote, so I shall skip ahead to Tahiti, day ten. It's almost noon and we are about to have a two-day old baguette for breakfast, deliciously fried in garlic and sweet chilli. We're trying to combat the hangover the toxic blue vodka gave us. We're still anchored at Arue Beach but maybe, just maybe we will move today. We almost have the engine working again and everything.

It had been a bit of a frustrating week. We had successfully found every marine shop in Tahiti, but hadn't found a single thing that we needed. We spent more money that week than in the previous four months combined. Life had developed a horrible routine: we accomplished nothing all day and then got drunk in the evenings so we could do the same the following day. My biggest achievement that week was building a paddle for the inflatable dinghy from a scooter handle and wooden crate. It doesn't sound like much, but it improved our transportation issues tenfold.

A few days earlier I had taken a break from the Swedish ways and snuck ashore early, while the boys were still sleeping. I was more hungover than ever, so I bought a coke and a baguette in an attempt to avoid throwing up on the bus. I had the whole day perfectly planned and sat patiently awaiting transport to Marina Tahina. One hour later there was still no bus (and fortunately no vomit either). A friendly Polynesian offered me a ride and as we dodged traffic, he detoured the beautiful rural middle of the island. He told me how his wife had died from a brain tumour and how he had had to give his son to his sister so that he could come to Tahiti and find a job. His smile was so big that I would never have expected a story so sad!

It was a long walk from the airport, where he had dropped me, but I had needed to sober up. I met so many friendly locals on the way that it suddenly felt more like the Polynesia I loved. I finally arrived and sat down for an ice-cold coke with lime. You wouldn't believe it, but the first person I bumped into was Mauricio! He hadn't changed one bit and was wondering whether he should turn around and head back to Panama or push through to New Zealand. I asked him how his rudder was doing, just to hear him say it one more time: "Nooo pro-ba-lem!" He had also avoided further run-ins with mythical sea creatures and angry fishermen.

I met some friendly Mexicans on their way to Panama and hung out with the *Nes-puck* cream cheese lady. On the way back, I bumped into Dutch Henk who we had met in Hiva Oa. He had managed to snap two more shrouds on the crossing and was competing with us to see who could have the most rigging issues.

Karl gave the go-ahead, it was moving time. I took the helm while Mooberry and Karl worked the anchor, leaving Jonas on engine duty. We dodged canoeists left, right and centre as we chugged out of the sheltered, dolphin-filled bay. The waves got bigger and it soon became apparent that towing the dinghies was a very bad move. A wave poured over the fibreglass dinghy, and just like the old days, she began to sink. Karl and I both almost fell overboard during the rescue mission. By the end of it, the only thing we lost was his left shoe. Inside the break-wall, we radioed Port Control to ask permission to pass the first airport runway, then the second. Finally we made it to Marina Tahina where we dropped anchor between a blue ketch and a catamaran.

By five we were paddling in with Tobias (Two-Beers), a zany Germany who had conveniently arrived to welcome us just as Karl was trying on my bra and skirt. Henk swung by and threw us a line and we formed a four-dinghy chain as his two-year-old daughter jumped up and down singing "Happy hour, happy hour, happy hour!"

We ducked into the laundry on the way back to investigate the book exchange. There wasn't much, but there was a notice board. Two boats were looking for crew: a Canadian Jerry and a Kiwi Stu.

It was a day of laundry and freshwater washing before the guitars came out. We had our first proper jam session in far too long. The music sounded lovely, even if all the lyrics were about *bajs*[57] porn. That day was the first time we all actually worked together on something. *Maybe, my morning attempt at a motivational team talk had done some good? Maybe we could actually do the four-person sailing thing?* Karl was still sceptical and I was still considering jumping ship. It was hard work living in such close confines. And harder still as we all seemed to have very different agendas we couldn't quite communicate.

---

[57] Poop.

❦

Jerry kept us very entertained as we sipped on cold well-earned [for a change] beers. His tender-hearted soul had so many crazy stories and even more dreams. He planned to open a hostel, hike the Amazon and become mayor and... It was a little bit like looking into my future (although I hope that in twenty years, I'm still female). His former Mexican crew member got drunk one night and confessed to murdering a mother and child. Jerry reported him and was in all sorts of trouble with the authorities who wanted him to pay for the Mexican to be sent back. Jerry wanted to escape Tahiti but needed crew to do it. The best thing he had on offer was a psychic that sometimes blacked out under the presence of spirits.

I paddled next door to Jerry's ketch first thing in the morning. What was he looking for in crew? How did he feel about crew that were broke? Would he be willing to take more than one of us? Could he delay his departure? - No! The Frenchies were kicking him out that Friday so he couldn't wait. But he would be so happy to have us. Both of us. Broke or not. He wasn't sure about destinations, but he wanted adventure. I went home in a bit of a buzz. I knew we had to do it. I just needed to get Karl by himself to tell him.

❦

We weren't particularly good at writing a pro's and con's list, as Bill and Laura had suggested we do. We floated home confused. The day continued with even more confusion. A cyclist got run over... Mooberry got home smashed, took one look at the boat and decided to go on another turn around. He fell out of the dinghy twice on the way. We took the opportunity to have a real conversation with Jonas, but couldn't bring ourselves to be completely honest. What were we even trying to say? What did we need? What did we want? Jerry kept asking what we were doing.

He wanted to check out first thing in the morning.

Whatever happened, someone was going to get hurt.

We helped Jerry raise his anchor and hugged him goodbye as he sailed off alone to new lands, wondering if we had made the right decision.

That night during happy hour, we met Stu. Two-Beers invited us all for dinner aboard his beautiful boat. Stu sponsored a ceviche starter and tequila. Mooberry sponsored beers. Two-Beers sponsored Cuban cigars. And we sponsored some food that assembled itself into an exceptionally tasty curry. Tobias had had several of the *Sea-Stars* on board, but he'd kicked them all off because he needed some space. Hippies were nice, but he needed a bit more mental stimulation. He'd been in the Pacific before on other people's boats, and had spent months in Vanuatu being amazed by women's libido's and their willingness to serve him. Eventually, he ran away because he couldn't take their energy any more. He'd jumped on a fishing boat and started to learn the language and the culture. He was quite smitten with the lifestyle. He was on his way back with his own boat which he hoped to earn a living from, transporting mahi-mahi heads. Stu was on his way back to New Zealand and he was going straight. He wanted crew and needed less alcohol[58]. Somehow sensing we had been looking at jumping ship, he used the latter to try and win us over. We said we would think about it.

ʕ

Alone time! We desperately needed it. Karl and I took the opportunity to have the proper picnic we'd been fantasising about since about day 23 adrift on the Pacific. Brie, baguettes, olives, REAL wine, salami and pate.

---

[58] Strict Kiwi rules about how much each individual can bring into the country.

We needed the break. We needed time off the boat. We needed to pull ourselves together so that we could pull the crew together.

Things eventually started to get done. We got good at hitchhiking to where we needed to go. We got creative with problem-solving. We built yet another masthead, stitched another sail, filled the tanks, scrubbed the hull and caught up with many friends. We met some Fins and while they were fun to hang out with, they reminded me why I needed to stop drinking. So, I did. Mostly. And you'd be surprised how much faster things happened. Instead of box wine, we afforded to cook a late Swedish Midsummer meal. Instead of happy hour, we had a Sunday roast. I was even more decisive. When I bumped into Stu at the supermarket, I gave him a definite "no!" I had more energy than ever and I used it to snorkel, walk, run and socialise. Finally, even though we hated Tahiti, it didn't feel that bad anymore.

"One last Happy Hour drink!" Our Finnish friends must have been spying on us for they arrived at exactly the same time as we did. And then came *Ruby Rocks*, Two-Beers, *Sunrise, Nes-puck*, and Henk… and 18:00: the time we had told the authorities we'd be leaving by[59].

Friday, 17 October, 15:49. I'd stowed everything away. Karl had checked the rigging, Jonas had the engine running. We pulled up the anchor and chugged into the wind. A few minutes later the engine sputtered and died and we were forced to sail out the perilous passage past the treacherous surf break.

I feel anything but ready for this, but it's time to go. Tahiti has held us captive for far too long. We are finally on our way again;

---

[59] But it also disappeared… and allowed the night to transform into a wicked party. It was Jonas' birthday after all!

destination: Niue, 1153 miles away.

I took the 20:00 - 00:00 shift. While I was exhausted, I needed it. I needed to clear my head, get my thoughts straight and breathe again. Tahiti was one of those places (like Panama) that made us crazy, sceptical and turned us into drunken sailors. It made me question everything, including myself.

I think that's what this next leg will be: A quest to find myself again!

19.

SPIT IN THE WIND

IT'S so good to be out in the ocean again. Land has almost vanished and our world is nothing but blue (and a small lump of an island lurking distantly in our wake.)

The winds shifted west, and all we could do was sail North or South. As we sped along in the wrong direction, the water crashing over the bow led us to find two new leaking screws in the front berth, which Karl and I had just reorganised and transformed into our bed. Our mattresses were soaked!

Turtles. Dolphins. Good vibes! But by the third day, with the Westerly wind still prevailing, our noon reading showed that we'd moved ten miles further away from Niue. We were wondering if we should duck in and give Bora Bora a visit after all?

Forget Westerlies, we had no wind! And while it was frustrating, it was the perfect opportunity to Sikaflex screw leaks and dry mattresses. We were moving so slowly that swimming loops around the boat weren't even a worry (apart from the morning shark sightings).

When the winds did return, they did so with vengeance. We clung on for dear life until eventually they shifted and we were soaring comfortably downwind. With four of us on board, we only had to do four-hour shifts before having a full twelve hours off. I had so much free time on my hands. I read, I wrote, I drew and I even had time for Sudoku. Nobody has time for Sudoku!

I may have passed Spain, but I've now sailed halfway around the world [from South Africa] and instead of getting further away, I'm inching closer to familiar shores!

By Saturday, we'd settled into the watery way of life and permitted ourselves a couple of karsks. The day was chilled because that is what Swedes do best: they chill (although they continue to pronounce it "shill"). We saw our first ship and whale and managed to avoid colliding with either.

We carried on to be spoiled with the best night sky of the leg. I was struggling to stay awake on night watch, even with all the phosphorescence. The wind was dying and it was hard work keeping alert. I had just handed Jonas the tiller and gone inside when I heard a *Zwoooop* followed shortly by "Adeena?! I think the genoa fell down." Which it had. I raised the main and then dropped to sleep.

Sunday began with both an early start and an early shit. The wind had died and we were swimming again. Mooberry was finally brave enough to give it a try. He paused before leaping to inquire, "Is it deep here?"

There was still no wind on the tenth day out. Great smells were arising from the kitchen though. The captain, who could not decide between noodles and mash, was making a strange combination of the two. I thought I saw signs of civilisation and yelled to the others, but it turned out to be just an empty corn can that Karl had thrown overboard.

A small drizzle cloud moves in closer, which is a welcome relief from the heat. Maybe it will bring with it some wind so we can start moving again. Maybe, we will even move fast enough to fish? Maybe we can even catch one! Wait! I think I am getting a carried away here. I'm over-excited. Right now, the sea is glass and it is hard to imagine that we will ever move again, let alone make it to Niue.
Do they really have cyclones in these parts?

THE COOK ISLANDS

There stood the agricultural man. After welcoming us, he inquired about our mango and banana status. Those two questions cost us twenty dollars. He bid us farewell and sent us through to customs and immigration. Then came a vital next step: a beer. Every new country had to begin with a beer. We found one at a supermarket with a bar-like balcony and sat down to enjoy it before trying the other variants. After sampling all of them, we bought a six-pack of our favourite and returned to our watery home.

The following morning, the health man made us stand on a rock and performed a small friendship ceremony. He then asked for another twenty dollars. We weren't sure how we felt about this friendship. We bid him farewell and went on a quest for bread and eggs.

We found fresh bread at the morning market, but the eggs were a little more challenging. The search for them led us on quite an adventure as we got drawn into the mysticism of the island. **Aitutaki** was beautifully strange. Wild, green and lush. Scattered with "No Sunday Flights!" signs here, there and in all the most bizarre locations. A former king had his son devoured by dogs. Since that day, there had never been another on the island. Karl was rather excited about that. Four-legged beasts still terrified him.

The bureaucracy of the four-day stay cost us $86 each, not to mention all the damages to our livers. We probably should have continued straight on to Niue. But Aitutaki was full of fascinating humans like Joe, who desired to lavish us with breadfruit. "The preacher," who laughed like a duck, spent an evening debating the rising and falling moon with us before filling our boat with pumpkins (and gifting us a hangover). Tamatona, the local policeman, told the boys that they HAD TO be at a festival otherwise he would arrest them. The festival came with free food and beautiful women dancing [they were warned not to masturbate while they watched]. There was no prison on the island. When he arrested people, he took them back to his home but made sure that they knew they were not allowed to sleep with his daughters.

It wasn't quite the kind of festival we had envisaged, but we had to attend [otherwise, we would be arrested.] It was a flipping long walk, but a pretty one. Eventually, after miles and miles, we heard the music and started to believe that maybe we weren't on a pointless mission. Vaipac School was celebrating 50 years of education and was having a jubilation to mark the occasion. The speeches were boring and we'd missed all the dancing; but the officer certainly wasn't joking about the free food.

One person descended upon the feast, then ten. Suddenly, there was a feeding frenzy as everyone dived in. People grabbed whatever was closest to them - a pack of ravens vandalising a dustbin in desperation for the last source of protein. With the food gone, everyone left.

ʄ

With the current working with us for a change, we flew through the pass and got spat back into the Pacific. We raised the main and were making seven knots with Karl then myself taking the helm. The seas were fierce and my stomach even fiercer. I abandoned my ingenious attempt to stop the many new leaking bolts with sanitary towels and ran for the deck to puke my brains out. It was the first time I'd been sick on Yoldia.

The following day started with mashed pigeon peas for breakfast. I'm not going to say who cooked it, but we weren't his biggest fan! Fortunately, the day improved. For lunch, we had a fresh dorado (with sushi starters). Dinner was creamy steaks. With life restored to our beings, we smoked a cigar to celebrate. I stood up and danced while I butt-steered to quite a melody of marvellous music on my midnight watch. In the last 15 minutes, a shark circled the full-moon-lit boat to keep me company. I just hoped he didn't think we were sinking.

By the seventh day, there was land everywhere. Rocky reef that leapt out of the ocean depths. The wind shifted so we dropped the sails, fired up the engine and motored in. We grabbed a mooring line, tied on and radioed Port Control before settling down to a bowl of breakfast.

NIUE

So, there we were again, land! I even remembered to lick it straight away. That was easy enough, the landing not so much. It was hard not to. We walked up the wharf and into town in search of customs and immigration, but found the Tourist Information Centre and beer first.

"Are you off the yacht?"

"Yes."

"Have you spoken to anyone?"

"Yes, the Tourist Information Centre."

"What?! You're going to get fined $200, you have to go back to your boat now!"

The tourism lady was new and recommended that we follow Ryan's orders. We later discovered that he ran the yacht club.

We grabbed a sneaky roti before returning to our rocky mooring. We tried the radio again and again. At 15:00, we gave up and ventured back in to see if we could find Port Control; or at least speak to the yacht club.

Just outside the wharf sat a customs officer. He had been waiting for us to call him, but now he was off duty.

"If you go any further, I am going to have to fine you."

"Well, can we clear in?"

"No, it's too late now, there's a cruise ship coming in tomorrow at 06:30, you can do it then."

"Well, can we walk around?"

"No."

"Can we just go to the supermarket?"

"No."

"Can we..."

"You can, but if you don't go back to your boat right now, I'm going to have to fine you $200."

We started back to *Yoldia* planning to sail straight on to Tonga when the officer drove up behind us with a change of heart. "Look, if you give me your last port clearance, I'll do the rest tomorrow and I'll let the others know about the problem with your radio."

We wandered off to find beer and discovered that we got an allotment of duty-free alcohol on arrival. We walked away with a case [or few] of Steinlager each. We sat at a table overlooking the bay and dug deep into our supplies before we returned to the docks, launched the dinghies and loaded them up with the precious cargo. Karl and I soon discovered our little inflatable was punctured, we were sinking fast. My first instinct was to save the boat papers. Karl's was to save the beers. Between us, we did okay chasing and flinging the prized consignment into the other dinghy before treading water, waiting to be rescued.

I was up long before dawn and saw the *Caledonian Sun* approaching on the horizon. As the sun arrived, the docks filled with vehicles. By the time their anchor was dropped, the wharf was a teeming mass of customs, immigration and tour guides. They launched five of their nine tenders and began frantically ferrying geriatrics ashore. We got ready and patiently awaited a gap in traffic. We needn't have hurried, the first chance came just before eight. We rowed in and weren't surprised to find that no one was waiting for us.

Despite the "no swimming on a Sunday" policy and the strict bathing attire rules, Karl and I skinny-dipped in beautiful cave pools and chasms. When hunger overcame us, we hitched back to find *Yoldia* filled with delicious fika delicacies and good wine. The Swedish chef from the cruise ship just happened to be from their hometown.

The island abounded with natural beauty. After an excellent day spent exploring, the seas had turned furious. One look at the angry anchorage told us that there was no paddling back in those conditions. We decided to wait it out by having a drink at an Italian restaurant. When that closed, we checked the conditions again - still crazy. Everything was shut, so we napped on the marketplace tables while we waited for calm.

It was 03:15 when an eccentric lady in a green t-shirt turned on the lights and started preparing for the morning bizarre. We sheepishly wandered off and checked the dock again. The sea seemed to have quieted, so we piled in and started rowing. We were a fair way out when a wave crashed over and sunk us. We swam the dinghy back to relaunch. There was no way we were all going to make it home that night. We let the boys return and Karl and I went on a journey.

"Soaked and cold, shivering in the hours of dawn. Naked from the waist up due to lack of cover. The bench is hard, but a warmth strikes me from the surrounding crowd. Unable to speak and unable to focus

my eyes in any direction other than the non-existent far horizon. Terrified that someone will notice my appearance as scared to bits. The setting is friendly and welcoming, but still my soul shivers. Old ladies with an odd set of toes, serving the most disgusting porridge around. I gathered strength and left." - Karl

We went for a walk to dry off and warm up, but mostly so that Karl could shake the old-lady fear. For such a valiant young soul, he bore some strange trepidations. We stumbled upon the deportee-American's boat. The skipper had kidnapped his own son in San Francisco and spent eighty-something days at sea. His first port of call was Niue, an island he had visited years before. He was expecting to rock up with no questions asked and begin a new life. Instead, he found himself arrested on arrival. His poor nine-year-old son was taken away, screaming for his daddy.

We found two balls and a club at mini-golf, and our morning was filled with excitement. We met friendly tourists, explored the beaches, snorkelled and even treated ourselves to sushi. And then, because it was still early, we hitched out to the chasm.

In the icy waters of the fresh-water pool, I met my third South African in as many days. She, and her fifth husband, recommended we visit the Lima pools too. So, we hitched on and found them even more beautiful in the calm of the sunset.

We took the boys to see the chasm. We'd planned a BBQ, but they already had an evening BBQ invitation. Karl and I packed a liquid lunch while the others suffered terrible hangovers and opted to go alcohol-free. We hitched out with the friendliest, most generous people in the world (after my mother, of course), who gifted us bananas and wished upon us good luck. It worked, an excellent day of swimming, snorkelling, and jumping off cliffs ensued.

Already inebriated, we were excited that the bottle store was still open. Their BBQ date never arrived and instead we all sat at the table overlooking the bay sipping tasty bourbons, wondering what to do next. "Our answer lies in that car," Karl prophesied. He was right. Parked up, they started chatting to us, finding out who we were and why we were there. "Is that your boyfriend?" I was asked while I heard the other man asking Karl a similar question on the far side of the table. "Yes," we replied in almost unison, shooting each other cautious glances. Apparently, we weren't in denial any more. "Would you like to come drink with us at the primary school?" Asked Chase. We had nothing better to do.

Jeremy and Chase were far too friendly and hospitable. And for teachers, they were surprisingly colourful. They convinced us that Clayton's Bar was boring and so, instead of staying for one drink, we continued to sit with them sipping beer and talking nonsense. They brought out the kava; Fijian kava. They soaked the cloth-full of the powdered root into a giant mixing bowl and blended it up until the water was sufficiently muddied. The coconut shell was dipped time and again as the murky liquid was passed around. While it was anything but pleasant on the pallet, we were curious to see what effects it would have. Three bowls in, we were all dancing.

"Adeena Adeena Adeena," cried Mooberry, pulling me aside, "what do I do?"

Chase had started pulling the moves on him. It wasn't subtle, he'd offered to suck his cock.

"Well," I replied, trying not to giggle, "do you want him to suck your cock?"

"No!"

"Then just say no."

The poor guy was so far out of his comfort zone that it was both painful and hilarious to watch. Jeremy tried it on him too. Again, I got dragged aside to glean wisdom off. The haze of an evening culminated in a delicious lamb stew.

Hearing a car, Ryan had woken up and taken the liberty of pouring himself a drink.

"Make yourselves at home," he said.

"Hey," Karl slurred, when Ryan was almost out of sight, "do you think I can buy a beer?"

"I think you may have already had enough," replied Ryan, who poured us both a glass of water instead. The others rowed home while Karl and I cuddled up on a couch under my newly gifted Fijian sarong, drifting off into some sort of deep coma.

I woke up clutching on for dear life. The yacht club was spinning like a Ferris wheel. I was scared to stand up, but I had to, the remnants of the previous night were stirring inside of me. I finally conquered the public toilets, staggered back and lay down again just before Ryan entered in his towel and grabbed his morning beverage. His wife was out of town, he was making the most of it. Simply the sight of the liquid made me ill. The day blurred in a daze of recovery before we crashed at the yacht club again, too spent to swim home. I swore I'd never drink again, or at least not until Tonga, and I meant it.

Feeling ever so slightly more alive, we dunked crackers in a guacamole dip as we plunged into deep and meaningful conversations. Both Karl and I were stressed about finances and the uncertainty of what was happening next. It was driving us crazy. We headed back to the cave to clear our heads. The same friendly locals picked us up, stopped off to introduce us to their family, gave us ice-creams and then drove us out. Just as it had before, the cave worked wonders.

Two overly-friendly hitchhikes later, we found ourselves in Avatele and opted for a quick snorkel. "Be careful out there, the sea is dangerous," a tourist warned us in a patronising voice. I held myself back from replying that we were "sea people," and we could handle it.

The further I ventured in, the more beautiful the coral became. Feeling a current, I played it safe and stayed inside the breakwall while Karl pushed deeper. I was a little ashamed of being a wuss. When I saw him again, he was standing on a rock way out in the middle of nowhere. *Man, is he brave!* "You okay?" I asked and he gave the thumbs up. But when I looked again, he was even further out in the depths. He swam towards the reefy rock again, pulled himself up and then got washed off by a wave and swept straight back out to sea. He repeated the whole roundabout process and was anything but okay.

It was a terrible thing to watch. I felt so helpless. Do I swim out and try to rescue him? Or go ashore and find help? I gazed away for an instant and found it was too late, I was caught in the same rip. I tried in vain to swim back, but it was no use. The current was far too strong. I would inch forward only to be washed back out again. Eventually, the current seemed to ease and I made it onto some reef where I battled the shallow currents and stumbled towards the shore. I was hit by a wave and washed back into the rip. I tried again. The third time out in the deep ocean, exhausted and gasping for air, I looked around for alternative landings; it was all cliff face. I spluttered out the water in my mouth and was relieved to see that Karl had made it ashore. A crowd of people had gathered with him on the beach and they all looked to be in a bit of a panic. I fought myself back to the reef and this time I tried to surf the wave as it came to wash me off... I returned to the rip. I was losing strength so quickly that I knew if I didn't do it that time, I would probably not make it. I swam for the reef and pulled myself up. Then I walked sideways as far as I could get, digging my heels into whatever coral heads I could find before turning towards the shore. A Samoan boy stood knee-deep in the water yelling at me to come to him. I needed a goal, a destination. If I could make it to him, I knew I'd be okay. I could barely breathe as I lurched and took his hand before he helped me stumble to the shore where I collapsed in a bloody pile on the beach. Karl had swallowed so much water he was ill. He swore he would never snorkel again.

ſ

We had to be ashore by 09:00 to check out. After doing the dishes, hanging up wet clothes, choosing books to swap and cleaning the cockpit, we skipped breakfast and wandered in. I was the only swimmer and had to brave the striped sea snakes alone.

Ryan called immigration, who told us we would have to wait till Monday. We burst out laughing. They'd told us that Friday was their day off and that we had to check out on Saturday morning. They reconsidered and agreed to meet us at the yacht club at 11:45. We were re-rescheduled to 14:30, at which time the friendly officer actually arrived, charged us $34 and sent us on our merry way.

We squared up with Ryan, who kindly charged us for six instead of seven nights. What a lovely and strange man he was; and an even stranger yacht club. It's the only one in the world that didn't have any of its own boats.

The saved cash sponsored chips, coke and a crew meeting. After much debate, it was decided that we would head for Vav'au instead of Nuku'alofa. I took a deep breath and announced that Tonga would be my last stop onboard *Yoldia*. Karl echoed it.

TAHITI TO TONGA – A GYPSY'S TALE

Alofi, Niue. 15 November 2014

By looking back at pictures from the past few months, I think I'm starting
to realise why so many people have mistaken us for hippies.
But in fact, we're gypsies - there is a difference!
(I shave my legs sometimes).

While we've learned to overcome far too many adversities, the ocean
keeps luring us on to new adventures.

You'd imagine that there is a limit to the number of beautiful places a person can visit in their lifetime, but each island group of the Pacific has proved that wrong.

Tahiti was the exception, but at least there were other things to get us through:
It was full of good people, good food and there was good beer (albeit crazy expensive).
No, Tahiti was not nearly as nice as the rest of the Pacific, but it was an important stop.

Like so many others who have completed the 3600+ mile landless ocean crossing, it's a bit of a shock coming to actual civilisation. For those who have had troubles along the way either with the boat or with the crew, it's the first place you can dump either.
And I'm not going to pretend like we weren't thinking of leaving *Yoldia* behind...

But the more we spoke to other yachties, the more we believed we could and should carry on.
And so, the lot of us continued into the unknown:
To the dog-free turquoise coastlines of the Cook Islands where the primary belief was the wrongness of Sunday flights.
And then, several spews later, we were on to Niue where caves, chasms and murderous rip tides consumed us.
We were even fortunate enough to have all our rigging, propane, and four helmsmen!

We're still in awe. Still wanderlusting.
But, with the hurricane season upon us, we've just had yet another serious crew meeting.

The boat needs a rest, some paint work, some waterproofing and lots of
serious TLC.
The crew are all tired of being mistaken as hippies.
They need showers, clean clothes and a psychiatrist.

It has just been decided that Tonga will be *Yoldia*'s final destination for
this year.
It's with sadness that we're about to set the sails one last time and
complete the final leg (for now).
But it's exciting too, it's almost time for new adventures!

❦

Up at six, Karl was on cockpit and coffee duty while I repacked the bow
and prepped for sail. By 06:54, we were on our way. While the lee of the
island was calm, we soon found the wind. Too much of it. We were flying
between 8 and 11.8 knots which was way too fast for little *Yoldia*. It took
all four of us to reduce the sail so that we could breathe again.

*It's been a pretty chilled trip: nothing breaking, no arguments and we
even almost caught a fish. I had two full days without any sleep and
crazy hallucinations (both visual and audible) on my night watches.
I've maintained alcohol-freeness for almost a week and that's
probably the root of my problems. We didn't quite cross the
international dateline; but with Tonga breaking the rules in its own
choice of time-zone allocation, we sailed into tomorrow and missed a
full 24 hours of our lives.*

*Tonga looms quite freakishly on the not-too-distant horizon on this
dark dark moonless night. I guess it's a perfect setting for my life right
now. In Tonga I will get some answers:*

Where am I going next?

How will I get there?

What will my next job be?

Where will I turn 30?

What's life like in your thirties?

Should I be having a crisis?

TONGA

I steered us closer and closer with instructions to awaken the captain in an hour. I tried and failed, so I heaved to and went in to shake him. He was fully out. I decided to make the most of the opportunity and made a cup of coffee before watching the second most beautiful sunrise of my life. The blood-red exploded into the deep black over the hundred-odd islands that littered the water in every direction. At 06:40 I tried again and instead got Jonas. The wind wasn't behaving and we needed to start the engine.

Finally, we cleared the last bend of the lee-shore and could see **Neiafu** and its many boats. Quarantine boarded first (25.30TOP and a box of cigarettes) then health (100TOP and a few cigarettes) followed by immigration and customs (just cigarettes). In no time at all, we'd effortlessly exhausted our cigarette supply, cleared in, moored and were celebrating with cold beers and pancakes. Happily sated, we all ventured ashore to explore the jubilant town. There was an abundance of good people and colourful bars.

It took only one beer to land Jonas a job at a vanilla plantation.

It took two beers to get the run-down of the island from Maggie:

- That night was the ladyboy fashion show at the hotel across the way.
- Marina Wine Bar had a free movie every Sunday at 16:00.
- Aquarium was the only bar with draft beers. It was South

African owned and they were well worth getting to know.

❦ And the most important thing to understand about Vava'u was the *WooHoo's*: crazy people who swarm to Tonga purely to swim with the whales. One of these [alternative breeds of humans] had recently bought a whale carving. After an evening prayer meeting, she had had to return it because the spirits told her the whale had been murdered.

We explored the streets and checked out the ladyboy show, but we needed an early night; and we took it. Jonas had life, success and excitement pulsing through his veins, so he went all-out for an evening turn around.

We chose a bad night to sleep on the deck. It was Friday and the music was pumping. When it finally stopped, I started dozing off. There were voices, and the voices were getting louder. Louder and closer. Jonas was returning with some company. *Great.* From the pitch of the voices, I thought they must have been ladyboys.

"Mooberry Mooberry, wake up, I brought you someone." The conversation turned to Swedish. Both of them were about to get lucky. I smiled, but still had my doubts about them having the right holes as both "girls" stood and peed off the deck (I later discovered that it was actually them both peeing straight onto the deck). It was getting light already when the boat stopped rocking. Jonas was all smiles as he rowed Karl and I ashore to find breakfast.

He was no longer loving his life when we found him again. His "woman" had become attached and was making it all too clear that he was now off the market. Even Maggie had seen him do the dinghy of shame. We ventured off to follow leads on boats out of Tonga, while Jonas went to the village to meet his future in-laws.

I almost burst out laughing when I found "the couple" squashed into the starboard mattress. When they finally did awake, I had to admire Jonas' enthusiasm about having her hanged.

The boys created an "urgent boat meeting," and ventured ashore to find her a taxi. There weren't any. It was Sunday. Fortunately, Glen from a nearby restaurant understood the urgency of the dilemma. He'd made the same mistake years before and had ended up married to her cousin.

An Australian boat sailed in and moored next to us. We rowed over to say hi and I was about to introduce ourselves but was cut short: "Adeena?!" I'd met the skipper all the way back in Dominica, almost a year earlier. Matt had been the first to offer me a Pacific crossing. Sadly, they too were stopping in Tonga for the cyclone season, but joined us for the evening movie at the Wine Bar. Halfway through *ShawShank Redemption*, the "girlfriend" rocked up. Jonas thought he finally got rid of her. He told her he didn't have any money.

❦

Decision day: New Zealand or Australia?
It's a tough one: New Zealand is so beautiful and adventure-laden, but Australia has so many more jobs…

I thought long and hard and did much needed soul-searching (or, "spleening," as Karl would say). I even reattempted pro's and con's lists. Eventually, I spun the decision-making spinning top James had gifted me. It circled and spun and carried on flashing green and purple until finally, it tumbled down.

I like the outcome! I already have a Tax File Number, a bank account and I know how it works (a little bit at least). I can either return to an old job or start where I ended travelling, in Queensland. Karl is going to Australia too…

343

I began emailing the farms I'd worked at so that I could prove I had completed the 88 days of rural farm work that qualified me for a second working visa. It took four days to get the application through. I hoped I had it in on time. I was only two days away from 30.

༄

You have no idea how much stuff you have, until you try and squeeze it into a bag that it never really fitted into in the first place. We were still hungover from the previous night's farewell party, so packing was especially difficult. After a week in Vav'au, we realised that everyone around was parking-up for the cyclone season and our only hope was to head through to the nation's capital and try there.

Karl signed over his captaincy to Jonas and we plastered the Swedes with hugs. We reminded Mooberry to be wary of the Chase's of the world, and Jonas to *knull* wisely. Matt gave us a lift ashore as we watched *Yoldia* shrink into our past. She really had been so good to us:

8023.6 Nautical miles (14923.9 km)

252 Days

127 Sailing days

7 Countries

6 Colourful crew members

1 Captain Karl-Oskar

LAND PEOPLE

We claimed our spots on the floor of the ferry and I'm glad we got there early. Every centimetre had been transformed into somebody's bed. Land vanished behind us and soon we could feel the familiar swell of the open ocean. It was a rough night's sleep, but we'd had worse. I lay awake staring out at the water wondering what Nuku'alofa would be like. Where would we sleep? How long would we be there for? How would we get to Australia? I suddenly wondered if our visas would even be approved.

We were in Ha'apai by sunrise and a beautiful archipelago surrounded us. I was pretty sure that it was Jonas' "girlfriend" sitting across from us sending us evil glances, but I was too scared to ask.

It wasn't surprising that the Tongans held little bags that they ever so politely kept throwing up in, as they played cards, chatted and tried to nap. It was however very unexpected watching Karl get seasick for the first time since I'd known him. I don't think I was doing much better though. Karl said that when he looked at me sleeping that morning, I looked more 30 than ever.

It was evening when we walked down the gangplank. We dumped our big bags in the little cabin under the mango tree. There was a problem with the communal bathroom, so we were pointed to the Master Suite. After eight months of sea swims and rain washes, we finally had our first shower. It was amazing. It was incredible. We'd never felt so clean! But the feeling only lasted five minutes. With all the salt washed off of our bodies (or most of it at least, for it had seeped deep into our veins), we found ourselves feeling sweaty for the first time in months. Reintroducing them to real beds was the next step.

Life is all about the contrasts. One minute you're eating breadcrumbs for breakfast, the next you're at a guest house where they serve you fruit, cereal and a full English breakfast with fruit juice and real coffee.

We rolled across the road to the gargantuan second-hand market. In preparation for Australia, Karl walked away with a pair of smart shoes, two pairs of long trousers and a t-shirt for 17 TOP (about $9US). I bought four dresses, three t-shirts and a scarf for the same price. We found the internet and Australian Immigration informed us that we needed chest X-rays before our visa applications could be considered. More money. More time. More bureaucracy. It was too late on a Saturday to do anything about it. Besides, Jerry was in town.

"Hello!" We yelled. All the yachties popped their heads out simultaneously. We were just in time to slack the lines for two boats who'd already cleared out and were headed for New Zealand. Two remained: Jerry's and yet another Australian Matt's. Both were headed for Vava'u.

Jerry had sailed alone to Rarotonga where he had taken on a Swedish crew member, his worst yet. He finally agreed that it was better to sail alone than to endure bad crew.

Tim, a German-Canadian doctor and marine-pathologist had moved on board. He had been stationed on a remote volcanic island for months with only his dog, Pip, for company. One day while on top of the volcano, he watched a catamaran pull in and steal all his belongings including his solar panels, sat phone, food and credit cards. He had arranged a pick up for November but had no way to contact his boat to come earlier. For a full two months, he lived only on coconuts and spent hours every day scraping muscles off the rocks for Pip. By chance our French friends on *Djerpie*, had pulled in and rescued him. They brought him to Nuku'alofa where he met and took up residency with Jerry.

We looked at the time. It had just gone happy hour. We followed Tim to Bill Fish.

ʄ

They say you wake up 30 and you suddenly know who you are and exactly what to do with your life. I woke up even more confused.

Teddy turned three. I know I would make a bad parent because I forgot to give him a gift, let alone a shower! I, on the other hand, not only had the luxury of a shower; but I was lavished with gifts. We enjoyed our luxurious breakfast with champagne. Strangers gifted morning beers. The guest house owner cooked me a birthday lunch. After a drink on Jerry's boat, we all wandered over to the only place open on a Sunday: The Fishing Club. They wouldn't let us in (members only), but birthday girls always get what they want. One beer turned to an afternoon, evening and night of celebrations. It's not quite the way I pictured celebrating my thirtieth: broke, unemployed, and practically homeless. But it was awesome!

With a killer hangover, we headed off to Viola ("Tobacco Tree") Hospital to get our medicals done by the only doctor in Tonga the Aussies deemed qualified. We waited and waited and waited some more, until she eventually wandered over barefoot and carefree. We followed her to her office where she had a long phone call with her son before attending to us.

To get an X-ray in Tonga you need the following:

- Your Passport
- A copy of your Passport
- An ID Photo
- Form 160

We left downtrodden. But, as the captain always says: "tomorrow is another day also."

We started towards the Tobacco Tree with all our documentation in hand. A little down the road someone stopped to offer us a ride and we got delivered to the doorstep. It was looking like things were finally flowing in our favour [for a change]. The receptionist sent us on the mission of paying. It was hard, but nothing compared to the fiasco we had been through in Panama! We showed our sketchy receipt and were told to wait. So, we did. For more than an hour. I returned to ask her how much longer it would take... She'd forgotten about us.

It was a quick and simple job apart from the radiologist trying to be too polite in asking me to take my bra off. My biggest fear was that the previous week's alcohol would somehow show up in my lungs. A long wait for the doctor later, we went in. Her son called again. We waited again. We handed over the paperwork only to discover we had the wrong form.

We hitched back to town, found the visa office (where half of Tonga sat trying to get to Australia) and stumbled back to the hospital just before they closed. "Now it is my project," said the doctor.

We went to bed happy. But it was short-lived. Karl woke up in agony in the middle of the night, his feet hurt. I blew it off, but by morning his feet were swollen bigger than his head. He looked like a freak, but I told him he was beautiful anyway (because he was)!

Doctor Tim pretended like he wasn't enjoying it, but the smile on his face suggested otherwise. Cigarette in mouth, he pierced the skin and forced the infested puss free as Pip ran around lapping it up. When Karl's feet finally stopped jetting out gushes of goo, he filled up a syringe and pumped disinfectant in; and the squirting resumed. It was utterly disgusting, but in a mesmerising kind of way. Tim prescribed antibiotics plus soaking his feet in wild ginger and potato water twice a day.

It actually worked. He got better and better, and a couple of days later he even managed to dance at the Bill Fish (after one happy hour drink turned to ten and tequila).

We followed up with the hospital and were assured that our X-rays had been passed on. Being a land of bureaucracy, they had to be collected by the visa company who would deliver them to the Australian Embassy in Fiji. It would then be sent on to Australia, where our results would be carefully scrutinised and our fate would be decided. We found the visa company and tried to push to get things moving, but it was a dismal situation that we could do nothing to accelerate.

We attempted to find cheaper accommodation, but not even the local backpackers came close to the deal I had wangled at the guest house. We visited the blowholes and enjoyed watching the waves pulse up, break and shoot great jets of water in the air. We explored the markets, walked and hitched to the far reaches of the island. But we were quite ready to leave Tongatapu. After much deliberation, we booked one-way flights to Auckland. The cheapest way to Australia was via New Zealand.

It was our last day in Tonga and we wanted to enjoy it, so we forget about our worries and spent a day on Pangalau. The island that normally buzzed with sailors and tourists alike was virtually dead. Big Mama welcomed us with open arms, as we basked in the cyclone-damaged tropical paradise. Reluctantly we ferried back, and just so happened to coincide our arrival with happy hour. We treated ourselves to margaritas. When they arrived, the waiter brought great tidings: it was the annual Christmas party and all regular customers got free drinks until 21:00. Being a regular for two weeks didn't quite cut it, so we were debating whether to try again or call it a night when a local friend walked in... The night vanished in a blur of dancing and we had to speed off to the airport. By "speed," I meant we were flying. The taxi got pulled over by the police, but fortunately, our driver was related to one of them and managed to talk herself out of a ticket.

We hoped we had the right day. We hoped that our luggage was not too heavy. We wondered about the many shells and cultural artefacts we'd collected on our adventures across the Atlantic and the Pacific. Would New Zealand accept them? The most stressful part of the morning however, was checking in.

We handed over our passports and smiled at the attendant across from us. "And your exit tickets please." We'd prayed we didn't need them. Not knowing when [or if] our Australian visas would be approved, we'd used

Microsoft Paint to carefully craft fake ones. If inspected closely, you could clearly see the font changes. I handed them over reluctantly and we both held our breath as she entered all our data into the system. She squinted and grimaced and eventually, after what felt like hours, looked up. We were handed our boarding passes. We could finally exhale. Suddenly, a kid rammed a trolley into the back of Karl's wounded feet and blood started squirting everywhere.

I had been dreading flying, but takeoff went rather smoothly. I found the seats surprisingly comfortable. We sat back and watched The Hobbit and didn't have to check the course or the wind, the pilot did that for us while the air hostesses served us hot food and tasty beverages. In fact, flying was amazing. We did in three hours what would have Yoldia *three weeks!*

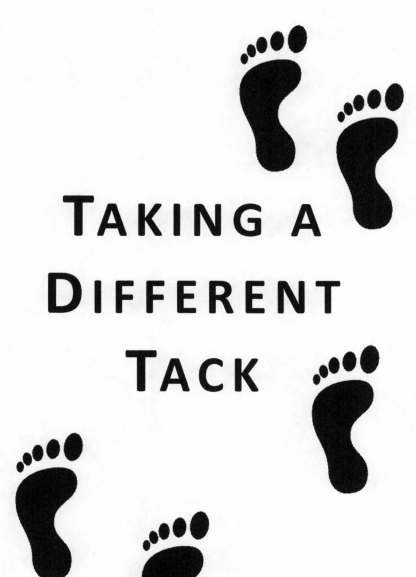

TAKING A DIFFERENT TACK

20.

S **UNDAY,** *21 December 2014.*
Our bags are packed. The sun is shining. Everything is ready,
except for us. We are terrified. Karl and I are about to step
out onto the road, stick out our thumbs and begin another
journey of trying to stay alive.

We stepped out of the airport and quickly pulled on every warm(ish) item
of clothing we owned. New Zealand was freezing, even if it was meant to
be the height of summer. We conveniently found ourselves both outside
Burger King and hungry, so we ventured in. We sat on their free Wi-Fi,
hunting for hostels. We probably should have done that before we'd left
Tonga, but we weren't really planners. When you make plans, life tends to
take those carefully calculated schemes, toy with them, chew them up,

swallow them, regurgitate them, do some more chewing, do a half swallow and then spit you out on a totally different path anyway. The sun only set after nine in **Auckland** so we had no idea it was so late when we gave up and started the foot pilgrimage to find shelter. Full. Full. Full. Everything was full. It was a terribly frustrating exercise roaming the streets with all our life belongings in the freezing cold, while still hungover, tired and feeling a little desperate. We eventually found a room. But at $84 for a bed we couldn't, we shouldn't...

We slept well, but there was no way we could afford that again. We made sure we were packed, showered and checked out before they billed us for more. We left our belongings in the storage area and wandered the streets wondering what we were to do, apart from finding breakfast. So many beggars, charity collectors and religious mind washers attempted to accost us that I suppose we didn't look quite as poor and broken as we were. An old man approached us and stopped us in our tracks. *Here we go again.* "It's so nice to see young people holding hands. My wife and I have been married for 63 years and we still do it!" His smile lit up with a glimmering twinkle.

We failed to find alternative accommodation so we gave up on hostels and walked the docks instead, hoping to find a familiar face or hull. Auckland has more boats per capita than anywhere else in the world.

However, we did find Helena, my Czech shipwreck compatriot. I more than approved of her significant other. They drowned us in beers before breaking their lease agreement and harbouring us like refugees in their campervan.

ſ

There's something about being broke that leads you on strange costly adventures that you should not be affording yourself. Maybe it's the pleasure of reaching rock bottom and knowing that there's no way

down from there? Or maybe it's a way of quailing your worries into
believing that you're not broke? It may also just be stupidity. Either
way, we went to the zoo.

We'd decided to escape Auckland, but I couldn't get out of bed, let alone the city. For two full days I lay motionless, sweating and willing myself better. By the third, I actually managed to venture outdoors. We hitched across the bridge with the garbage collectors and tried to plead with the Australian visa office. They only helped people who had applied in person, in New Zealand.

Karl's feet were aching again and the pharmacist suggested that we both saw a doctor. Second opinions confirmed it. We knew we couldn't afford it so we took a stroll, bought $1 coffees and sat silently staring at the docks. We didn't need to speak. We even knew when it was time to stand up again and carry on walking. Our minds had synced.

We took two steps and braced our ears for the "Kurwa!" Martin Doleček beamed in our path. Trust him to make an appearance when we were at an all-time low! "I just looked on the internet to find you," he said. The "Kurwas" continued as we traded tales of all the idiocy that we'd respectively ensued. "Okay my friends, I need bed," said Martin. We took him on a tour of the nicer options we had scouted in the city. The fifth establishment took him in, and Martin checked into his first-ever hostel. He loved it. He was surrounded by young beautiful women and some of them even shared his room. After helping him select the right cheese, olives, bread, gherkins, toothpicks and box wine to win anybody's heart, we returned to Rosie's with restored souls. There were 17 of us staying in her tiny house. To our amazement, there was no problem with sharing the little bathroom or the kitchen.

꙳

Feeling almost completely recovered and being on the brink of bankruptcy, we stowed most of our belongings in Rosie's garage and prepared to head off into the unknown. She warned us how expensive it would be up North. With empty bank accounts and $13.70 (in coins) between us, Auckland wasn't an option either.

People passed in drips and drabs until finally, a man in a red Mazda doubled back for us. He'd wrecked his back working an IT job in London and had had to return home to New Zealand. This was further evidence that real-life jobs (i.e. office) are bad for you! We were dropped off at the BP service station just outside Orewa where we sat munching dry bread. A car drove up and the driver felt so bad for going in the wrong direction that, despite our declining, she gave us ten dollars.

A doctor on her way to an early Christmas in Kiri Kiri picked us up. She'd actually planned to find hitchhikers for the company. Cindy enjoyed working the festive season, mostly due to the large array of ham and turkey injuries. She suggested **Whangarei** as a good spot to look for jobs. Before dropping us off, she phoned around to see if any of her acquaintances were looking for volunteers. Sadly, nobody was accepting the week before Christmas. We tried the backpackers and scouted the Town Basin Marina in the hope of picking up some boat work or a place to crash. The only familiar hull was *Trepidation*, and they still scared us.

Three car rides later, soaked, tired and dying of thirst (for we really sucked at swallowing rainwater) we thrust out our thumbs with our last fleckles of hope. The sun was rapidly descending. I said a little prayer and a small miracle happened. A couple pulled up, told us to hop in, gave us water, fed us pizza and drove us all the way through to **Ngawha.**

Hazel came out to meet us and showed us to the room she'd prepared for us after a caring driver had called through and told her we were coming. She asked if $10 for the night would be okay. "And it's only $5 each if you want to use the hot pools," she added. We thanked her and declined. It wasn't quite what we had been looking for, but at least we wouldn't be homeless for the night. "Just let us know if you need help with anything," I said as she walked away. She spun around and came back. "You mean you're not in a hurry to leave?"

NGAWHA

It was a bright and early start because we had responsibilities. After a morning meeting, Karl and Hazel disappeared on a shopping spree while I started cleaning the toilets, change rooms and camp kitchen - they were long overdue for scrubbing! Karl accidentally forgot his wallet (the proper one we bought him to prepare him for the real world). He swore he really did forget... It worked in our favour though, all our food needs were now being met too.

Cleaning turned to gardening and lawn mowing. While I was happy to be doing something productive again, I was really glad when Hazel called us in for beer o'clock. After dinner, we wandered down to the hot pools to soak. I'm not sure that I believed all the health benefits listed on the different mud baths, but the pungent smells suggested that they must have been good for us.

After a couple more days of toilsome labour, we asked permission to go through to Opua for Christmas. Hazel was hesitant but obliged on condition that we could still get some hours in on either day. As we strolled towards the road to begin the hitchhike, she threw us her car keys.

It was good to be back in the driver's seat. I didn't quite trust Karl's navigation, but after a lot of sheepy fields and paddocks (and a quick stop to spend our last money on box wine and some crisps), we eventually arrived in **Opua.** We found the Marina, parked and began looking for Martin.

We should have known that there would be too many boats. We spotted *Alya II* docked in the quarantine zone and Henk's boat in the anchorage, but we couldn't get to either. Perplexed, we scavenged some cardboard cups and returned to the car to crack open the wine. There's nothing quite like a car bar. Loaded with Dutch courage, we decided to try a different approach. We stepped out of the car and straight into Martin. The "Kurwas" flew. We embraced. Laughed. Caught up. And then discovered we were a day early for the Christmas party he'd invited us to! He was celebrating European Christmas[60] at a private party on a Polish boat. We didn't know what to do. A whole lot more "Kurwas" flew.

After a beer, a game of darts and the winning of a raffle we never even entered, Martin [as always] devised a plan. We would skip dinner and the gift-giving. Then, when the older ["boring"] people had gone to bed, he would sneak us in.

In the hours we sat cramped in the front seats of the little Mazda, Karl and I had one of the best conversations we'd ever had. We were actually surprised when Martin knocked on the window just after 23:00.

We joined the friendly drunken crew feeling like we had known them for years. We danced, played the guitar and drank wine by the boxful. Eventually, as the sun was rising, we bid farewell to the crazy group and Martin rowed us ashore. Upon returning to the car, Karl and I's relationship went to a whole new level as he stuck his finger down my throat to make me puke.

We were just driving into Ngawha [after stopping several times to involuntarily discharge more fluids] when I felt a strange stinging in my hand. By the time we greeted Hazel, my hand had swollen to twice the size and was growing still.

We moved our belongings to the top house (a promotion for our hard work as well as an extra room for Hazel to rent out with the post-Christmas

---

[60] December 24th.

rush). My promise to never drink again was short-lived as we helped with a few chores and then sat down to celebrate. Hazel had cooked us a scrumptious pork roast with veggies. While we feasted (and continued to consume more wine), my hand swelled to the point that I couldn't bend my fingers to hold the knife.

The neighbour stopped by to inform Hazel about some politics at the bus stop. He took one look at my arm and told me to go straight to the hospital. When I refused, he proposed a long list of alternative treatments.

Hazel disappeared to check out the "political situation" while we tried to reduce the size of my limb. She returned and told us to meet her in dark clothing at midnight. She needed bodyguards. I quickly sent off "Merry Christmas" messages and checked my mail. I checked Karl's too and there was a shocker. His Australian visa had been approved! I checked mine again in hope – nothing. I checked my immigration account - nothing. Before I wept in front of Hazel with my aching hand, hungover head and breaking heart, I crept away to the top house. "See you in twenty!" she called behind me.

It was the last thing either of us felt like doing. We didn't want to be accomplices in anything "political," but what could we do? We followed Boss Lady up the street and sat quietly in the decrepit bus shelter as she nullified the issue. We were scared about how the neighbours would retaliate but hoped that we would be long gone by then. After both the weirdest and worst Christmas of my life, we finally went to bed.

I'd woken up several times in the night struggling to breathe. If I could have afforded it, I would have gone to the hospital. By morning my hand had swollen up to my neck and the throbbing was excruciating. I transformed a sarong into a sling to elevate it and stop the blood pulsing through it. Hazel offered to pick up some more antihistamine. I didn't feel at all bad about that after consulting the morning task allocation.

At least days go quickly when you are busy. Only it was going to take forever, I had to do it all single-handed. By sunset, all my chores were done and we successfully opened up two new rooms of the dilapidated "hotel" to be let out. When we had first arrived, she had only three rooms. Now, she had seven. We really enjoyed the pools that night!

Hazel started breaking down regular morning schedules and Karl interrupted. "Before you get too excited, we have some news," he paused for effect, "...our visas have come through and we will be leaving soon." We decided to make that our official last day, right then and there. I was a people pleaser and an overly-committed hard worker. Karl was dragging me away for my own good.

We worked hard all morning and when all the main chores were done, I asked Hazel what I could give her a hand with. "Well, what are you drinking tonight?" She handed me twenty bucks and sent me to the bottle store. She may have been a workaholic alcoholic with anxiety issues, but she had a beautiful heart! While we sat drinking a bottle with her, Karl [in the hopes that my visa might still come through] asked if we could stay the following night too, but have the entire day off. She was drunk, it was a good time to ask.

ſ

"Where ya heading?" We didn't recognise Nancy (one of the "spa" customers) at first, but when she rolled down the windows and lifted her glasses, we were all smiles.

Nancy had planned a scenic drive and asked if we would mind doing a few detours. We joined her on a beautiful coastal tour, where we stopped to swim in picturesque beaches, hike and gawk at waterfalls. A few hours later, she dropped us right at Rosie's door. Hitching just doesn't get any better than that!

We were a little afraid that there would be no room at the inn. We emailed

Rosie from her kitchen, and twenty minutes later she welcomed us home. This time we weren't lucky enough to have our own room and shared with a French girl and three young Germans. At least we had beds. I cooked us dinner while Karl sorted his life out, looking at flights and talking to his parents. When the confirmation email arrived, we both stopped dead. Our hearts flatlined. The tears tore straight through our hearts, doubling us over in pain.

This was going to be the hardest goodbye of our lives.

❦

Wine for breakfast. It was Karl's last day and we needed it to be a good one. We lugged our belongings to Westhaven Marina and hugged *Djerpie* hello. "Do you know the Finnish guys?" they asked. "*Homeless*?" "And the Dutch guy?" "Jean-Michel?" We were in for more of a reunion than we had hoped.

The same people we had hung out with nine months earlier all sat reunited in the little cockpit! Homebrew came out and drinks were passed around with stories.

Everyone disappeared to Jean-Michel's for one last drink, leaving Karl and I behind for our final goodbye. This was my best friend in the whole world that I was saying goodbye to. He knew every tiny detail about my life. He knew me better than I knew myself. After ten months spent within eight meters of each other, we were now going to be world's (well, time-zones) apart. He apologised time and time again for leaving me behind, but we both knew it was the right thing for him to do.

ALONE AGAIN

I wasn't quite sure what to do with myself when I woke up, half of me was missing. So, I did what anyone in my position would do: I lay frozen on the couch and tried to turn off my emotions. When the *Djerpie* boys started stirring, I forced myself to get up, plastered on a fake smile and joined them for coffee and breakfast. We were all a little tender from the previous night.

Physically I was all set for the new year. I lugged my potato salad and alcoholic remnants over to Jean-Michel's boat and met the masses. There were a plethora of other yachties and boat hitchhikers whose legacies had preceded them. Jean-Michel had invited a harem of Couch Surfing women along too. When *Homeless* and the Norwegians eventually rocked up, it was quite the party. We were all broke, so the assortment of homebrews and box wines were fantastic. By eleven, people were throwing up all over the place. The neighbours [slightly perturbed] had rocked up with fancy cheese platters and even fancier beverages. I felt like a complete stray. I made conversation and sipped at drinks, but I was a vacant vessel on the overcrowded boat. The countdown began 5....4...3...2...1... Happy 2015! We were the first people in the world to see it. Everyone hugged and cheered as the city exploded into colourful fireworks. I exploded into tears.

❢

With a full tummy, a giant backpack and an air of goodness, I started the long walk to town. I was just about there when a man pulled up to offer me a ride. He had simply been off to grab a cup of coffee, but was nice enough to drive me to the highway and show me the perfect hitching spot. It was so perfect that there were other hitchers already waiting. I chatted to them for a little while but didn't want to steal their spot. "Woa!" they cried as I strolled ahead, "Those spots are already taken!" I turned and retreated down the street.

Ten minutes later I waved at them all as I passed with a Sri-Lankan man. He was nice at first, telling me all about his wife and kid and how they were home for the holidays. But then he started getting creepy nice.

"Do you just want to stay with us?"

"No thank you, it's still early I..."

"How about just a beer before you go?" He asked, taking my hand.

"No thank you, I really want to get a move on."

"Or we could just have something...you know... I'll even pay you if you like..."

I was quite relieved to get out of the car and even more relieved that it was a whole Fijian family that picked me up next. They dropped me at a fuel station and wished me luck. It worked! Marty and Sam found me there. The father-son duo was rather awesome, super chilled and down to earth. They ran student accommodation. Seeing as all the students were away, they invited me to stay with them, use the internet and make life plans. In fact, I was not permitted to leave until I had life plans. Apparently, you can't just hitch aimlessly about.

21.

PRISON.

WELL, *it's quite a start to the year! Prison. Cell 24, in the women's wing. It isn't exactly what I'd been anticipating when I left Auckland, or Hamilton either for that matter... but life is full of surprises, and at least I have a roof over my head!*

Four walls, a bunk bed, a very high mesh barred window and a door. It perfectly matches my reality: I'm trapped in New Zealand against my will.

ƒ

My volunteer application had been accepted, only they hadn't told me when to come… But I had a plan, and Marty wouldn't let me leave without one. He drove me to the Napier highway and wished me luck.

Minutes later a green pick-up pulled up. While the driver looked a bit suspect, I had a good feeling about him and hopped in. The former All Blacks star and I sat comparing travel notes. He had travelled all over the world for rugby, staying in fancy hotels and being pampered, fine-dined and waited on. I educated him on the other side of the spectrum.

I walked across a colossal bridge and just reached the other side, when a gigantic ball of a friendly Maori offered me a ride. Bear had the biggest grin imaginable. His wife had died two years earlier and he was just about ready to restart his life as a carver in a caravan. He gave me a tour of Napier's vineyards, orchards and blueberry fields before we crossed the bridge into town. He drove me all along Marine Parade and up a hill to my destination. If I were his daughter, he'd have wanted someone like him picking me up.

I thanked Bear and grabbed my belongings. I was nervous, I still didn't know when they wanted me. I checked the address and walked up the stairs of the ominous building. I rang the bell with some hesitation and a smiley face slid the tiny window on the iron door open. The gate was opened to me. I ventured in and met Canadian Rachel briefly before she ran off to find someone who knew what was going on. I was the second person to randomly rock up that day.

After making my bed, I wandered over to meet my fellow inmates: two Canadians, two Sri-Lankans, two Germans and the Dutch guy who had arrived only a few hours before me.

Everyone sat on their computers as a Christmas movie played on the TV. One by one, people dropped off to bed and eventually, I did too. I crept through the dark hallways and found my chamber. I was the only person in the Women's Wing, and everyone pulled quite a face when they found out which cell I'd been assigned. I preferred to be left in the dark on the incidents that had happened in my supposedly ghost-infected cell. The general tales of suicides and murders on the grounds were disturbing enough; and to make it worse, the most sinful were buried standing up so that their souls could never rest.

I was put on door duty, and every time the bell rang, I followed the script: "Hello, welcome to Napier prison. Can I interest you in a self-guided audio tour?" When visitors entered, they'd select their tour and we would program the code for "Historic," "Ghost" or "Kids" onto their audio device. All available in a plethora of languages that had similar codes and tons of room for mistakes. We'd lead them to the starting point and tell them that "The prison only closed in 1993. It was the only building to survive the 1931 earthquake, New Zealand's biggest, with the most fatalities." We then taught them how to use their devices and sent them on their merry way. I was bored after an hour. I had no idea how so many of the others had been there for so long.

It was a routine of door duty and audio tour scriptwriting (for cities we'd never visited) followed by evenings spent staring at laptop screens while B-grade movies played in the background, before somewhat sleepless nights in the somewhat haunted cells.

Without a phone, Rachel was my alarm clock. She always woke me up far too early. Showers formed part of the tour and had to be taken before the prison opened. If you slept in, you would normally end up bolted into your cell by a curious tourist.

Two cruise ships pulled into Napier and the prison was packed. I was off duty and decided to find a quiet spot far away from the masses. Napier turned out to be a remarkable little city. Avoiding the crowds led me to all sorts of hidden gems and eventually landed me in the marina. I returned in time for the Monday tradition of pub quizzing at the Irish Bar. I couldn't afford a drink, so I was glad to be on a team with some very intelligent people because we won a $30 bar tab. While we were debating what to do with it, the table behind us donated us their winnings too. It afforded us two jugs of beer and a whole lot of smiles.

We were just getting up to leave when I recognised a familiar face. "Weren't you hitchhiking out of Auckland the other day?" Greg jumped up and hugged me. "It's you!" He cried "I was just telling these guys how you stole my ride!" All the other hitchhikers had failed to find a ride out of Auckland and had clubbed together to rent a van.

Work. Explore. Hang out at the marina to try and make boat friends and find cash jobs. Work. Explore. Watch bad movies. Work. Explore. Follow up on visas. Work. Explore. Skype. The nights were mostly sleepless and I'd started seeing and hearing things making my cell the last place I wanted to be. The days were filled with far too much activity in a trivial attempt to exhaust myself into sleep.

I finally had a day off, and it aligned perfectly with the yacht club's race day. It was great to be out on the water again, even if racing was not quite my thing. While everyone else packed away, I wasn't quite sure what to do; and for a moment, I just stood there. It was the first time I'd allowed myself to stand still since Auckland, and I suddenly missed Karl enormously. I snuck off silently to have a spleen and some much-needed God time.

After cooking up a tawdry dinner, I opened up my computer. My visa was approved. I reread the message again just in case I'd misunderstood. MY VISA WAS APPROVED! There were no complications. Nothing else needed. I was free to go to Australia when I pleased! I'd almost forgotten why I was in New Zealand in the first place and I suddenly didn't know what to do. *Where was I going? When?*

By Monday I had life plans sorted. That same night we won first place at the pub quiz and celebrated our victory with a bowl of chips and a jug of beer! It's the small victories that make life worthwhile.

Evening plans had been made and the goal was to get Rachel drunk. We did a team walk to the supermarket and all invested in various cheap beverages at the Pak & Save. The kitchen buzzed as we prepared our evening meals before sitting down at the table to feast together. It was the first time we all had dinner and drinks together. It was the first time everyone forgot about the free Wi-Fi and the TV. It was the first really good night. Because I had a very early start, others offered to get drunk on my behalf; but they needn't have bothered, I did a very good job of it myself!

Rachel agreed to wake me up at 05:00 and I hadn't taken into account that I had been getting my alarm clock drunk... At 02:45 I started saying goodbyes and tried to pack all my freshly washed belongings away. For the first time since arriving at the prison, I fell asleep straight away!

It was light when I awoke, so I knew something was wrong. I ran out of my room and discovered it was 08:40. The music video I was assisting on had started at 07:30 and I had told them I would be late, but that was ridiculous! Two lifeless souls sat at reception, but otherwise the prison was a hungover cemetery.

It didn't take long to get a ride. I was only expecting a lift to the edge of town, but Conrad was going all the way to Auckland. He was in such a good mood after a very successful job interview that he offered to swing by Tauranga to drop me off. He was a maniac driver and flew through the unearthly beautiful mountains. At that speed, we would be there in no time!

Taupo was only meant to be an hour and a half away, so I am not sure how we ended up stopping there for lunch. After an awkward silence, he asked if he could kiss me. Despite the feelings I still had for Karl, he really wasn't my type.

The world got more beautiful as we followed the coastline, but the hangover got worse. It didn't help that he was smoking in the car and the passenger window didn't open. At the next traffic circle [brace yourself because this next part is really disgusting] I opened the door, leaned out and puked my guts out, much to the horror of all the nearby cars. Conrad still maintained that I was sexy.

"The hitch-hiker!" cheered the coordinator with a big grin on her face as I followed her to the shoot. Minutes later they called, "That's a rap," but I was in time for the behind the scenes stuff and the interviews. I finished my undeserved camera time and ran for the bathroom and spewed again.

ᶜ

I thought I had my directions right, but the thirteenth-ish car stopped simply to tell me that I was hitching in the wrong direction. My first ride had a tradie drop me just outside of town. The second was a lovely mum and child who dropped me in Bethlehem. A mother of three, whose husband was in prison, was next. Then, a man took me as far as the intersection where yet another tradie picked me up – he was going right through to Auckland.

The nice man stopped and bought a coffee. I opted for bananas because they are the only food that tastes the same on the way in and out. After the previous day's performance, I thought they were the safest option. I was just about to jump back in the car when he looked at the fruit and yelled, "Don't even think about it!" He was anaphylactic to them. We stopped in Bombay Hills to do a quote on a kitchen, and then the marvellous man dropped me off at Westhaven Marina.

Djerpie was deserted. It seemed Erwan had been redecorating, so I vacated a tiny floor spot to stow my belongings in. I went for a wander to see if anyone else was still around and walked straight into a drunken Miko. "Adeena!" he said hugging me, "You will come with me to supermarket?" Miko talked me into buying a bottle of red instead of a sarmie.

We drank Miko's bottle on the way back, before Johanna found him and dragged him back. Their parents were around and she needed support. While the other two Frenchmen were away, Erwan had found work on a 110-foot racing catamaran and was living the actual high life. He whisked me away to a colleagues' fancy apartment for dinner. I was glad I had the wine, even if it was cheap! The dining turned into dancing.

It was a late start waking up in the apartment lounge. Beer for breakfast: the hair of the dog... Only we weren't hungover, we were all still drunk. One beer turned to two, three, four, wine, a swim, wine, more wine, beer. It was just before 21:00 when we said our goodbyes and returned to *Djerpie*. Not even bothering to change, I picked up my stuff, hugged Erwan goodbye and started towards the bus stop.

"Adeena!!" I spun around on the bridge to find Colin busking with his guitar and harmonica. He'd arrived just four days earlier, flown in straight from Tahiti. If I ever needed a reminder to keep living my best life, Colin was it. After a long catch-up, I wished him all the best and continued, smiling.

My lovely bus driver was nice enough to let me know that I smelt like crap and probably wouldn't be allowed on the plane. Which is why my first destination at the airport was the bathroom to brush my teeth, change, and try to make myself presentable. And then to find somewhere to sleep. The viewing lounge was perfect, but it was too quiet and I would never wake up without an alarm or a Rachel. The kids-corner was second best, apart from a game that sang out every 5 minutes: "Plane 243 has arrived. Plane 462 has been cancelled," in a silly American accent. I found a comfy corner and befriended some friendly Germans who promised to wake me up. As a backup, I made a sign asking to be awoken at 03:55 [with artsy arrows] which I placed on a table above my head. I fell into a deep sleep for about 4 minutes before the silly machine spoke again.

22.

TAMING A BARBARIAN AND GIVING HER SHOES

AFTER clearing customs and immigration [and having a wee], I took the plunge and became a functional member of society again. I bought a phone.

I boarded the train exhausted, scared and really smelly. I found a beaming Lucy waiting for me at **Newcastle** station and jumped in the Astra staff car. It was just like the old days – except then we were both new, inexperienced, clueless youths and now she was a head-honcho. It was only when we'd almost arrived that I discovered that induction had already started and I was late. I'd been given the wrong dates.

We pulled into camp just before dinner where a flock of familiar faces welcomed me back. I passed the smelly hugs around and then wandered over to meet my peers. After more than three years away from the job, I was starting from scratch again. I too was a "newbie!"

I forced the [Lost Property] shoes off my feet and crawled into bed. It had taken me almost five years to come full circle. I was back where I'd started. Although it was as if I was there for the first time.

I might not have made it to Spain, but what an adventure it has been. Life is a beautiful journey of finding, losing, and rediscovering yourself.

THE REAL WORLD IS GOOD FOR YOU

Port Stephens, Australia. 15 March 2015

Thirty.
Broke.
Unemployed.
Single.
…It's not quite what I had planned... but man was I loving life!

It was a big step, but after years of flightlessly travelling towards Spain, I decided to take a break by jumping on a plane heading back to where I'd begun, back to Australia
(with only a large smelly bear to my name.)

While almost the whole staff and the uniform had changed, it was good to return to life as an outdoor instructor (even if they were a bit of a bizarre bunch.)

I became the proud owner of my own bedroom for the first time in years.

(Back in the luxury confines of my half of a shipping container)
I even saved up enough money to buy sheets and pillows.

Having a home base, I got to make friends who I'd know for more than
just a few days...
Friends who didn't mind going camping or spending a night in a cave.

And friends are important too:
You need people to laugh with and cry with.
You need people to motivate and inspire you.
And sometimes you need people around to slap you across the face to
stop you from making bad life decisions.

It gets better too.
In the real world, there are life jackets.
And if you do get shipwrecked at sea, you don't have to swim for your
life or drift for 50 days.
There are rescue boats.

The real world has paved roads,
And beautiful walkways.
And when you have a home, your friends of old can come to visit you for
a change.
(Even if you do force them to stay in a tent outside the front gate,
because we work with children and strangers aren't allowed on the
property. Or you take them free camping without a toilet)
The real world has toilets.

And while it's an adjustment staying in one place, having to be in places
at set times and having responsibilities... it's good to get out of your
comfort zone.

It's good to be challenged to find new exciting local things to lick.

It's good to have to find new ways to challenge yourself.

It's good to be able to find your most favourite local hangouts and return to them.

You can still find trees to hang your hammock in.

You can still watch the sun rise and set.

You can still lick, live, and be awesome.

No, even with all its routines, the real world can be exciting too.

In fact, it might even be good for you!

THE END.

Who am I kidding?

I couldn't bear wearing shoes!

My feet had an unscratchable itch!

And while I was surrounded by a multitude of inspirational people and awesome friends, life without Karl sucked.

Like that mahi-mahi trapped to follow the smell of his wife's blood, I could not shake the scent. The ocean's blood stained my hands, my nostrils and my soul.

And while I tried to fight it, adventure beckoned. I needed to heed its call....

"I really don't know why it is that all of us are so committed to the sea,
except I think it's because in addition to the fact that the sea changes,
and the light changes,
and ships change,
it's because we all came from the sea.
And it is an interesting biological fact that all of us have in our veins
the exact same percentage of salt in our blood that exists in the ocean.
Therefore, we have salt in our blood, in our sweat, in our tears.
We are tied to the ocean.
And when we go back to the sea
- whether it is to sail or to watch it –
we are going back from whence we came.

—John F. Kennedy

Appendix

INSIGHTS, DIAGRAMS AND ANSWERS TO SOME BIG QUESTIONS

What is the difference between a Gypsy and a Hippy?

HIPPY /ˈhɪpi/ *Noun*
A person of unconventional appearance, typically having long hair, associated with a subculture involving a rejection of conventional values and the taking of hallucinogenic drugs.
Similar: *Flower Child, Bohemian, Free Spirit, Nonconformist*

GYPSY /ˈdʒɪpsi/ *Noun*
A nomadic or free-spirited person.
Similar: *Traveller, Nomad, Migrant, Rover,* ***Roamer****, Wanderer, Wayfarer, Bedouin, Bohemian.*

Many people tend to use these words interchangeably but as you may have noticed in the *Oxford English Dictionary* definitions above, there are a few MAJOR differences!

Hippies tend to accept the world the way it is and live in peace and harmony with it, often removing themselves from the aspects of civilisation that they don't like (like civilisation itself). While Gypsies thrive on freedom and do whatever they need to do to survive.

The Odyssey Online differentiates the two by saying that free-spirited *Hippies* work with the hand they are dealt while free-souled *gypsies* work against that hand until it is the hand they want.

(They also say that meeting a hippy leaves you feeling warm and fuzzy while interactions with gypsies leave you more confused than ever.)

Not all hippies smoke pot. Not all gypsies are out to steal souls and empty your pockets!

Why did the Netherlands not win the 2010 Soccer World Cup?

Life is full of surprises. Some things just don't make sense. In fact, even things that were seemingly predestined sometimes fall apart without any explanation! It's not always the best team that wins.

Perhaps it was just not where I was meant to be heading.

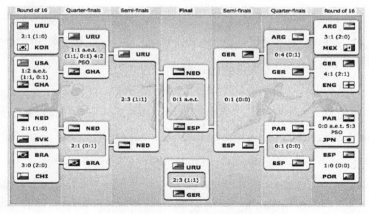

Image source http://worldcup--southafrica.blogspot.com/2010/07/2010-world-cup-brackets-and-knockout.html

When is the right time to start your adventure?

YESTERDAY! (But today is another day also!)

Do you have plans to see the world? Dreams of epic voyages to distant lands? A secret desire to learn Yupik? Or lick the Dali Lama? But you're not sure how or when?

You'll never be ready! The truth is that if you wait for all your geese to line up, you'll never get gosling! (Sorry for the terrible pun).

There will always be something that you "need" to do first. You will always get the things that you "have to" done. But you have to make time to do the things you really want to do (I keep learning this the hard way).

You will possibly never have the budget you want. But travelling the world doesn't have to cost the Earth. There are many options for affordable and even free travel. Get a bicycle. Get a tent. Stick out your thumb. You can go anywhere! You can do anything! You might have to get a little bit creative and lower your comfort levels, but the planet is yours for the exploring!

Even after years on the road, every time I start a new chapter, I get petrified. Every time I stop for more than three days, I get moving-on-anxiety and itchy feet (strange dichotomies really). It's normal. Humans are designed to be afraid of the unknown. That's why we have comfort zones. Some wise person once said that life starts at the end of your comfort zone.

Forget about finding the perfect travel partner. If you already have a travel buddy, great! If you don't, even better!

You will meet the right tribe along the way.

Unfortunately, while getting permission to include characters in this book, I discovered that some of them no longer share this beautiful planet. And while it saddens me that I'll never have the opportunity to cross paths, sip coffee or conquer mountains [and beers] with them again, I know that they made their life an adventure, had no/minimal regrets and lived their legacies.

You don't know how many tomorrows you have.

Life is short. GO ADVENTURE!

How do you cycle tour ("Bikepack")?

Do you have a bicycle?

No? Then get one!

(Make sure that it has air in the tyres, that it is properly assembled and that it has not jammed up from the rust accumulated in the years it has spent decorating your back garden).

Now, work out where you want to go (The next town? City? Country? Continent?)

Work out what you might need to get there (Food? Water? Shelter? Clothing? Money? Maybe some spares? A completely unnecessary giant teddy bear?)

Calculate how to get all the "necessities" onto your bike in a manner where you can still pedal without causing any major harm to yourself or others.

START PEDALING.

People get carried away by the fanciness of their equipment, determining the best route and working out all the logistics of the journey. These things should be contemplated, but the truth of the matter is that cycle touring is as easy as riding a bike. (Oh, I forgot to mention, you should probably also know how to ride a bicycle...)

How do you hitchhike?

Decide where you want to go and work out in which direction it is. Then, find a spot, stick out your thumb/ make a sign/ wave down a vehicle heading that way.

Simple! And if you don't know where you want to go, it's even simpler!

And you can make it simpler still. Glean my gypsy wisdom:

Placement! – Find a spot on the outskirts of town where enough traffic is passing in the right direction. Make sure that there is somewhere SAFE and easy for vehicles to pull over. Fuel stations are often good options.

Patience! – Sometimes cars pull over straight away. Other times you may have to wait hours or even days. But remember that you only need one good ride. That is normally worth the wait alone! DO NOT jump into a car you have a bad feeling about just because you think it is the only shot you have. THE RIGHT RIDE will come around sooner or later (and from experience, I might add that it is normally later).

Appearance. - If you look like you might be a serial killer, you probably won't get a ride! Show, by whatever means you can, that you are a traveller, not simply a derelict or a freeloader. Smile (even if it hurts). Wave your thumb or sign like you believe vehicles are actually going to stop for you!

When cars do pull over, ask where they are heading to buy yourself time to do the three-point check:

Do the hairs on your neck stand up when speaking to them? If yes, make an excuse and wave them on. Use your gut instincts. Sometimes for no apparent reason you "just know" something is either wrong or right.

Are they drunk or high? If yes, gage how likely they are to crash the vehicle or be arrested. If the risk is too high or you're not comfortable, wave them on.

Do a quick visual car sweep. If there's a baby seat, they are likely a care-giver and possibly trustworthy. A mass of empty beer cans suggests they may be less responsible. Firearms, human arms (or other limbs) and tied up passengers may suggest that you should probably find another ride.

(Of course, these are just guidelines… I've been pleasantly and unpleasantly surprised on many occasions.)

If you need to move in a specific direction or to a fixed destination, choose your ride wisely. Even if the nicest person does offer you a ride, make sure that where they are taking you is better than where you are right now. Sometimes, a few hundred meters might work brilliantly in your favour. Other times, a hundred-mile journey may leave you stranded in a place you'll struggle to leave.

And when you do finally get that good ride, BE YOU! Remember that someone else has welcomed you into their space. Make conversation. Be courteous. The kind of people who pick up hitchhikers are generally warm and open-hearted. Sometimes it's people with problems who need to talk to a friendly stranger. Sometimes it's just simple caring citizens who are trying to save you from psycho killers... Whoever it is, I'm sure they have an interesting story! Sit back, make yourself comfortable and enjoy the ride!

How do you hitchhike on a sailing boat?

It is a lot easier than it sounds! But make sure that you do it in the right seasons (ask a friendly yachtie or read up on when the winds are favourable for the routes you want to take). Also, know what you are looking for!

If you have never stepped foot on a sailing boat before, go down to your local (closest) marina and make some friends. Ask them to show you the ropes and maybe take you out on a day sail adventure. Experience isn't everything, but when it comes to choosing crew, a lit bit of know-how (and often a sense of humour and some personal hygiene) can make all the difference between a captain picking you or the other guy.

As we all know, the **Internet** is full of some useful information and there are a lot of crew-seeker sites and social media pages designed specially to help you find a ride. Personally, I have never had much luck with it, I prefer a more personal approach and I like to know who I am sailing with. Similarly to hitchhiking on land, I like to see and speak face to face with my captain and crew to gage the things email and phone calls can't.

Yacht clubs and marinas are great places to meet sailors. Make friends with everyone, even if they don't ever intend to move their boat. Sailors (and cruisers even more so) are a small community. They might just be able to hook you up with a vessel and crew that would fit your purposes perfectly!

Both yacht clubs and marinas generally have a notice board where you can either place a classy advert (if there are lots of other prospective crew, be creative!) or possibly find vessels who are looking for crew.

The Bar has generally been my best bet. Obviously, there are a lot of bars in this world, so you need to know where sailors go to rehydrate. Salty sea dogs tend to mingle and loiter together. Take the plunge and make a couple of friends, and before you know it, you will meet a whole community!

Make sure you feel safe getting aboard the vessel! I worry a lot more about who I am sailing with as opposed to the state of the vessel!

When you hitchhike on land, you can still get out and escape. In the middle of an ocean, it is a VERY long swim!

Things will break and go wrong, so make sure that you are with someone who won't panic! Ensure you sail with someone (or a crew) you can live in small proximity with. Even the biggest vessels can feel tiny when you're with the wrong crowd.

Seasickness is a part of life. Not everyone suffers from it, but for those who do, it has a way of removing all aspirations, hope and strength from your being. 99% of the time you get over it within the first three days [those days could feel like years]. While it may seem impossible, it is totally worth it! There is no feeling as great as being adrift in the great vortex of blue with the wind in your hair, the salt on your skin and an infinite abyss of stars smiling down on you!

What happened next?

Did I ever step foot on another boat?

Did Karl and I ever see each other again?

Did I ever actually complete the overland (and sea) mission to Spain?

Well, it's a very long story. And not necessarily a happy one. If our paths happen to cross, I'll be happy to fill you in on all the missing details. Otherwise, you'll just have to wait long enough for me to write the sequel.

Answers to the Africa Day Questionnaire: (Page 86)

1) How many wives is a South African president allowed to have?

How many times has Donald Trump offended people?

2) What is the basic objective of *Bok Drol Spoeg*?

To see how far you can spit a ball of buck poop.

3) What is the South African name for a traffic light?

A robot *– of course!*

4) Which of the following is not a South African national dish?

a) Hoendervleis *(This actually means goosebumps – directly translated "chicken skin." We may be third-world, but we don't eat anything off a human in South Africa).*

b) Pap en sous

c) Bunnychow

d) Bobotie

6) Correctly pronounce the word "khaki."

"Car-kee." Not! "ka-ki."

7) Which African animal translates directly from Afrikaans as "lazy horse"?

The leopard, or "luiperd."

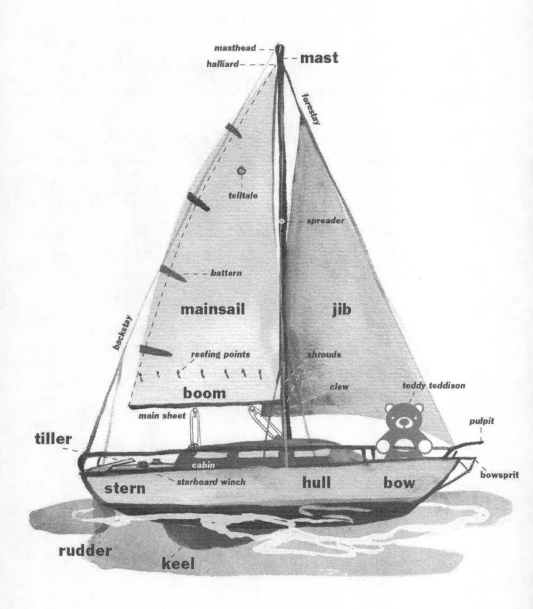

masthead
halliard
mast

forestay

telltale

spreader

battern

mainsail

jib

backstay

reefing points

shrouds

boom

clew

teddy teddison

main sheet

pulpit

tiller

cabin

bowsprit

stern

starboard winch

hull

bow

rudder

keel

Glossary

Please note that these are ~~useful~~ personalised definitions rather than those of the dictionary.

SOUTH AFRICANISMS:

Boerie Roll A delicious fire-grilled African sausage stuffed into a hotdog bun smothered with too many caramelized onions and your pick of tantalizing sauces.

Braai An excuse to have all your friends over to drink beer, watch sport and hang out while copious amounts of culinary goodness barbeque on a fire.

Kiff Anything that is exceptionally awesome!

Kak Something that really sucks.

Lekker What you say when you enjoy a thing or idea. You can use the word in almost any context. It can even form a sentence by itself.

Mampoer A raw, often home-made brandy that is designed to burn its way down your oesophagus.

Ouma The affectionate name for a [super/exceptional/inspirational] grandmother.

Packet A plastic shopping bag.

Robot A traffic light.

Wuss A weak coward with no sense of adventure. A "wimp".

AUSTRALIANISMS:

Bogan Those who dwell in the lowest class of unsophisticated society.

Dunny A toilet

Fair-Dinkum Confirmation of the truth of something.

Goon Box wine. One of the favourite consumables of *bogans*.

Sunnies Sun glasses. The Aussies have a habit of shortening everything.

Swag A tent and sleeping bag built into one.

Tradie A tradesman or skilled worker.

Ute A utility vehicle ("bakkie" for the Saffas, "pickup" for the Yanks)

Wife-Beater A singlet. It's almost uniform amongst both *tradies* and *bogans*.

Wolf Creek The 2005 thrilling horror film based on backpackers who ended up brutally murdered in the Australian outback.

SWEDISH-ISMS:

Fika The quintessential Swedish custom of making time for loved ones whilst sharing a cup of coffee or tea and a snack.

Knull To fornicate. It generally results in *Knullrufs* which is a hairstyle that can only be attributed to a wild romp.

Karsk Coffee "watered" down with alcohol.

Lagom Just about enough.

Shill The Swedish word for "chill".

Spleen To do a bit of soul searching and thinking. But this is more of a Karl-ism really.

Turn Around An evening of "rolling hats," drinking, bar-hopping, or seeing what sort of trouble one might be able to get themselves into.

SAILING TERMS

(They really aren't as complicated as they sound!)

AIS A very well programmed Automatic Identification System that shows other boats where you are and how you are moving in relation to them.

Anchor Alarm A really loud and annoying noise that shows that your boat has drifted too far away from where it was meant to stay put.

Autopilot A most appreciated invention. It holds your boat on course so that you can busy yourself with other more important things like chilling out and being mesmerized.

Bearings The direction between one object (for example your boat) and another object (the land you want to eventually reach).

Beat Trying to sail directly into the wind. It is not comfortable and results in a lot of zig-zagging as you try and force your way (often unsuccessfully) forward.

Bilge The inside of the *hull*. It's the coolest part of the boat and a great place to cool beers or keep chocolate from melting (assuming your boat is not leaking).

Boom The pole that extends at 90 degrees from the mast to hold the *mainsail*. It makes a very loud "boom" upon connecting with your head.

Bow The front of the boat (Normally the pointy side).

Bowsprit An extension of the *bow*. It makes an excellent toilet when the seas aren't too rough.

Bunk Your bed on a boat. When seas are rough it forms your "bunker".

Buoys Floating warning signals that show you where you really ought [not] to be.

Chart A map that helps you navigate to avoid colliding with land, rocks and other haphazard extremities that find themselves in your path.

Chartplotter The nautical version of Google Maps. It uses a GPS to show you where you are in relation to everything else and often gives you speed and depth information as well.

Cleat A device for securing ropes.

Clew The lower corner of the sail to which the *sheet* is attached. It tends to rip and cause havoc at inopportune moments.

Cockpit The control centre of the vessel where you'd find the *tiller* or the *helm*. It is also a great place for intoxicating guests and marvelling at sunrises and sets.

Companionway The steps leading from a ship's deck down to a cabin or lower deck.

Dinghy The little row or motorboat that gets you ashore without you having to swim. Although sometimes they sink and you end up having to swim regardless.

Doldrums The windless belt that hugs the equator. Seeing as sailors need the wind to move, it's a particularly frustrating stretch of water.

Dyneema Super strong and absorbent "miracle" rope that shouldn't ever break.

Epoxy The glue that fixes everything on a boat.

EPIRB Emergency Position Indicating Radio Beacon. It is designed to send out distress signals to search and rescue services when all hell breaks loose at sea.

Fender The inflatable "bumpers" that stop you from crashing up against walls, jetties or other vessels.

Furl To roll up the sail so that you can either make it smaller or completely stow it away.

Furler The fancy contraption on the *bow* that [should] neatly roll away your *jib* or *genoa* [sail].

Galley The culinary heart of a vessel known in layman's terms as "a kitchen."

Genoa A type of *jib* [sail] that reaches further aft than the mast.

Gimbal Stove A fancy contraption that minimises *galley* swearing by keeping your stove still while the ocean tosses your vessel about on the waves.

Gybe When the wind suddenly jumps from one side of the *mainsail* to the other. This is usually an accidental shift that results in sails breaking and ripping whilst the crew are thrown from their *bunks*.

Gybe Preventer A rope that tries to hold the boom in place to minimise the risk of an unplanned *gybe.*

Halliards/Halyards The ropes that hoist the sail.

Head The toilet or *dunny* on a boat.

Heave-to turning the sails "inside-out" to balance the *helm* and the wind to slow (almost stop) the vessels down.

Helm The steering wheel of a ship.

Heel The tilt of the boat that allows the rudder to bite and the boat to sail on its lines.

Hull The bottom of the boat. The side you want to keep in the water.

Jib The triangular sail that you should find on the *bow.*

Keel The backbone of a boat. It runs along the bottom of the *hull.*

Keel-hauling Punishment that constitutes dragging an unruly crew member over the barnacles (and other extremities) that protrude from the *keel.*

Ketch A two-masted sailing boat where the forward mast is taller than the aft one. If the aft mast is taller, you have yourself a *schooner.*

Lazarette The nifty storage lockers you find in the *cockpit.*

Lee The side away from the direction from which the wind blows. The side of the boat you should pee or puke off.

Lee Cloth The nifty cloth, plank or rope that stops you from rolling/flying out of bed when the boat tilts at uncomfortable angles.

Line Any rope on a boat.

Lock A device designed to lower or raise boats between stretches of water that are at different levels.

Main/ Mainsail The sail that is connected to the main mast. It tends to be the sail you spend the most time stitching up and repairing.

Masthead The top of the mast. When it breaks, your front *stays* (forestays) go tumbling into the water and you often lose the use of the pulleys that would have previously held useful *halliards.*

Mooring Tying a boat up to a fixed structure, generally a mooring *buoy.*

Nautical Mile 1852 meters. It translates directly as one minute of latitude along any line of longitude so that along the equator there are exactly 360 degrees and each degree is sixty minutes.

Pilothouse The deckhouse for a helmsman, and a nice place to navigate from when storms hit. It makes a good *bunk* when crippled by seasickness.

Port The left-hand side of the boat if you are standing aboard and facing the *bow*. It is marked by red *running lights*. It's easy to remember because there is never any *PORT* left.

Q-Flag The "Quarantaine" flag. You hoist it when entering port to show that the crew are healthy and that your boat meets the health regulations of the country you are arriving at.

Radar A nifty device that sends out radio signals to detect boats, landmasses and weather systems in the vicinity of your vessel.

Reef It is a great thing to snorkel and dive on. But in boating, to "reef" is to reduce the size of your sail.

Running Lights The navigation lights that show that a boat is underway.

Sail Cars Little sliders that run up and down the mast to allow your *mainsail* to be hoist up or dropped down.

Saloon The living and dining room on a boat.

Sand blasting The uber-powerful method of abrasively blasting unwanted organisms and old paint off the *hull*.

Sea / Drift Anchor A device that drags behind the boat in an attempt to slow and stabilise a vessel in heavy weather.

Shackle A connecting link that normally consists of a metallic U-shape bend and a locking pin. The pins sink very quickly.

Sheet The *lines* that control the movable corner (*clew*) of a sail to pull them either over to *port* or to *starboard*.

Shroud The rigging that holds the sides of the mast up.

Sonar/Fish-Finder A system that detects things lurking under the *hull*. It emits sound pulses through the water and returns a depiction of coral/fish/wales/mermen/sunken containers that lie beneath.

Starboard The right-hand side of the boat if you are standing aboard and facing the *bow*. It is marked by green *running lights*.

Stay The rigging that supports the weight of the mast and make it "stay" put. The forestays normally hold the *jib* and *genoa*. The *backstay* holds you if you are using the *stern* as a toilet.

Staysail A triangular fore-and-aft sail that is attached onto a stay.

Stern The backside of the boat.

Sloop A sailing boat with a single mast.

Spinnaker A very colourful light wind sail that tends to be more complicated than it is useful.

Tack Turning the *bow* of the boat through the wind so that the wind changes from one side to the other.

Tender A *dinghy*.

The Hard The dry land one places their boat on [normally in a boatyard] where boat work that cannot be done in the water is carried out.

The Trades/ Trade Winds The steady winds that define regular sailing routes and make journeys far more comfortable.

Tiller The stick that functions as a steering wheel on a boat.

Travel-Lift This vehicle picks boats up, carries them to the water and then puts them back where they belong.

VHF Very High-Frequency radio.

Wake The water that is disturbed by a boat moving through it. This has nothing to do with the Irish vigil of bidding farewell to the deceased.

Watch The hours spent keeping yourself entertained while trying to make sure that the boat maintains its course and avoids colliding with anything.

Water Maker A magical device that transforms seawater into drinking water.

Waypoint The points you steer towards on your journey to keep you progressing in the right direction whilst avoiding running aground or colliding with rocks.

Wind Vane An *autopilot* that uses the wind to correct your course and doesn't require any electricity. You should ensure that this is firmly attached before embarking on ocean crossings.

Acknowledgments

There is no shorter way to say it than: I'm blessed! THANK YOU!

Too many extraordinary humans have lined my paths, and while I'm trying to save the trees by not listing them all here, please know that you are appreciated! It is because of the likes of you that I have kept moving forward. Even the most beautiful places in the world are nothing if you have nobody to share them with!

To all the people who played an integral part in helping me shape and tell this story, THANK YOU! Lynn and Kirk, thank you for diving in and battling my grammar [while building my self-worth]. Karina, thank you for editing this book. Jess and Mary-an, thank you for enduring the early edition and urging me to keep at it. Elizabeth, Sophie, Judith, Chloe, and the rest of my beta readers and launch team– thank you for your insight. Mary-An, this book would have been incomplete without your cover and images! (Thank you for putting up with my neurotics and being my voice of moral reason over so many years. I promise I'll be on the phone again soon with more life drama.)

To the many people I have crewed with over the years! Thank you for having me aboard and enduring my chili-loaded dishes! Kirk and James, if you hadn't taken me aboard, I don't know if I would have found the passion for sailing that still consumes me (I would however probably have actually made it to Spain years earlier). Thank you David for welcoming me aboard and cementing my ocean love, even when things got sketchy! Memo, Di, Si, Ewa, Katrin, Jonas, Mooberry, and the Bulgarians – I'm so glad to have been drifting through the ocean depths with all of you!

Karl. I don't know how to thank you for keeping me alive, but I would have never survived the Pacific without you! You inspired me to fully embrace everything life throws and accept that *lagom* is also a way of life.

Rohan, thank you for your patience and inspiration to not only start cycle touring, but to embrace it as a passion.

To all those I have travelled, hitchhiked, beer-ed, dined, danced, sang, sank, stowed-away, run, chilled, beached, swum, and made out with; thank you for brightening up my journey and my life!

To the many sailors and shining souls who donated time, meals, and equipment throughout my [mis]adventures; I hope to somehow pay your kindness forward.

And to the many many drivers who have stopped to pick me up along the road, I'm so glad I had those moments where our lives could overlap (also, thank you for not killing me)!

To all those who employed me and worked with me, thank you for literally teaching me the ropes! (And lining my pockets.) Loz and Steph, it's thanks to you I can now master knots [and shoelaces].

To all the people that have housed me for a night or month, thank you! Especially those who have provided the shelter and electricity necessary for me to tell this tale (Van Der Wals, Renate, Papillon, Mortlocks, Mats, Nuno, Hendrick...)

Thank you to all of you who have prayed me through horrific

circumstances and near-death experiences! I am glad that my time has not yet come and hope to keep making the most of all the days I have left.

To my family and teachers (both formal and informal), thank you for preparing me to take on the world!

Matthew, thank you for saving me from technical nightmares and salvaging my many corrupted hard drives.

Jeandré and Brendon (and Daisy and AJ) thank you for being amazing brothers. And thank you for so many awesome adventures, may life throw us many more!

Ouma, thank you for all the time you have spent on your knees!

Mom. I'm sorry that this is how you had to find out the finer details of my former epics. Thank you for trying to talk me out of them. And thank you for praying me through them when I have failed to take your advice.

God, there is no way I could have endured any of this without you.

About the Author

SURVIVING volcanoes, sharks, pirates, dragons, a shipwreck, motorbike crashes, and the 2012 predicted world end... Adeena Gerding, (A.K.A. the "Bearfoot Gypsy") has expended at least 14 of her 9 lives. At twenty-two, the thaasophobic South African stepped out of her front door and found herself perfectly lost in the world. After years spent studying and preparing to adult, she found travel to be a far better teacher and growing up to be over-rated.

In more than a decade of unprecedented adventures, Adeena has accidently sailed across oceans and cycled across continents. She is living proof that hitchhiking does not always kill you.

The vagabond wanderluster has taken breaks from adventures to manage bands and companies, teach rock climbing and survival skills, write for newspapers and create some TV shows, amongst many other things that sound far less exciting. When not feeding her anorexic bank account, she has also paused to help communities in need and lend her grubby hands to worthy projects. Her biggest accomplishments to date are once fixing an engine with a clove of garlic and making death blink.

While Adeena doesn't own wives, children, or a husband, she does have an oversized Teddy Bear to care for.

You can find out more about Adeena's [mis]adventures and life at

www.bearfootgypsy.com

Images pertaining to this tale can be found on the afore-mentioned blog. (You can also delve deeper into these adventures through the Facebook or Instagram pages for First We Ate Your Wife and Bearfoot Gypsy).

Thanks for reading my story! Please add a short review on Amazon and let me know what you thought!